Obituary

Dr MARTIN LLOYD JONES

DR MARTIN LLOYD JONES, who has died aged 81, was associate minister and then minister of Westminster Chapel, Buckingham Gate, one of the foremost Free Church appointments, from 1938-70.

He was a doctor who left medicine for the ministry on the eve of a promising career.

His decision in 1927 to leave medicine for the Presbyterian ministry was an answer to a call which had been with him since his boyhood in the Cardiganshire village of Llangeitho, where the celebrated Welsh preacher, Daniel Rowland, ministered for 50 years.

Lloyd Jones was born in Cardiff in 1899, but the Llangeitho atmosphere was with him all his life. He was never happier than when preaching in Welsh to great audiences in his native land. He was educated at St Marylebone Grammar School and St Bartholomew's Hospital, where he qualified as M R C S, L R C P and M B B S with distinction in medicine in 1921. Two years later he became M D (London).

Under Lord Horder's direction he was a chief clinical assistant to the hospital medical unit and a research worker on endocarditis. He also began practising as a consultant physician. But the call to preach was insistent, and at weekends "the young doctor," as Welsh audiences called him, was found in many of the famous Welsh preaching centres.

Persuasive preacher

In 1927 he decided to enter the regular ministry at Sandfield Church, Port Talbot, where he ministered for 11 years. In 1938 Westminster Chapel invited him to be associate minister with Dr Campbell Morgan, and he assumed the sole pastorate in 1943.

Possessed of the Welsh gifts of speech and presentation of the spoken word Martin Lloyd Jones added to them his scientific approach which gave him a persuasive, argumentative manner in the pulpit. He relied little on oratory as such, but always moved his audience more by reasoned statement. He was specially gifted in expository preaching, and for one not trained specifically in theology his grasp of biblical fundamentals was remarkable.

He drew large audiences of Bible students and was widely popular in evangelical circles and among university students in his special campaigns. In 1927 he married Bethan Phillips. Their daughter, Elizabeth, married Sir Fred Catherwood, Euro-MP for Cambridgeshire and Wellingborough and director-general of the National Economic Development Council, 1966-71.

GOD THE HOLY SPIRIT

OTHER CROSSWAY BOOKS
BY D. MARTYN LLOYD-JONES

The Cross

The Heart of the Gospel

The Kingdom of God

Out of the Depths

Revival

Truth Unchanged, Unchanging

Why Does God Allow Suffering?

GREAT DOCTRINES OF THE BIBLE SERIES:

God the Father, God the Son

God the Holy Spirit

JOHN 17 SERIES:

Saved in Eternity

Safe in the World

Sanctified Through the Truth

Growing in the Spirit

STUDIES IN 1 JOHN SERIES:

Fellowship with God

Walking with God

Children of God

The Love of God

Life in God

GOD THE HOLY SPIRIT

VOLUME II
GREAT DOCTRINES OF THE BIBLE

D. MARTYN LLOYD-JONES

CROSSWAY BOOKS • WHEATON, ILLINOIS
A DIVISION OF GOOD NEWS PUBLISHERS

God the Holy Spirit

Copyright © 1997 by Elizabeth Catherwood and Ann Desmond

Published by Crossway Books
a division of Good News Publishers
1300 Crescent Street
Wheaton, Illinois 60187

First published in England by Hodder and Stoughton Ltd. 1997.

Cover design: Cindy Kiple

First printing, 1997

Printed in the United States of America

Library of Congress Cataloging-in-Publication Data

Lloyd-Jones, David Martyn.
   God the Holy Spirit / D. Martyn Lloyd-Jones.
      p.   cm. — (Great doctrines of the Bible ; v. 2)
   Includes bibliographical references.
   ISBN 0-89107-959-9
   1. Bible—Theology.   I. Title.   II. Series : Great doctrines of the
   Bible (Crossway Books) ; v. 2.
   BT121.2.L59   1997
   231'.3—dc21   97-25586

08	07	06	05	04	03	02	01	00	99	98	97
15	14	13	12	11	10	9	8	7	6	5	4	3	2	1

Contents

Preface

On Friday evenings after the war, Dr Lloyd-Jones held discussion meetings in one of the halls in Westminster Chapel in London. The subjects of these discussions were practical issues in the Christian life and the meetings were attended by many people. The questions which arose demanded a knowledge of biblical teaching of all kinds; often, too, a matter of doctrine would arise which the Doctor would deal with, usually in his summing up at the end of the discussion. It was partly as a result of this, partly, too, because the numbers were becoming too large for the hall, and, perhaps even more, because so many people were asking him about the biblical doctrines, that he felt it right to move the 'Friday night meeting' into the Chapel itself and to give a series of lectures on those great subjects. He did this from 1952 to 1955 and after that he began his magisterial series on the epistle to the Romans which continued until his retirement in 1968. The doctrine lectures were very much appreciated by the large congregations who heard them and, over the years, many have borne testimony to the way in which their Christian lives have been strengthened by them.

Later, the Doctor himself felt happier about preaching doctrines as a part of regular exposition – 'If people want to know about a particular doctrine, they can find it in the doctrine text books,' he once said. But the great strength of his doctrinal studies is that they are not arid text-book lectures. He was, above all, a preacher and this shines through in all of them. He was also a pastor and wanted men and women to share his sense of wonder and his gratitude to God for the mighty facts of the gospel; so his language is clear and not encumbered by complex academic phraseology. Like Tyndale, he wanted the truth to be in words 'understanded of the people'. Also he did not want the teaching to remain in the head only, so there is an application in each lecture to make sure that the heart and will are touched also. The glory of God was his greatest motive in giving these lectures.

Those who know the preaching and the books of Dr Lloyd-Jones will realise, on reading the lectures, that his views on a few subjects developed over the years and that his emphases may not always have been the same. But this is all part of the richness of his ministry as it has been of the ministry of many of the great preachers of the past. However on the essential, fundamental truths of the Word of God, there is no change and his trumpet does not give an uncertain sound.

We have had one difficulty in preparing these lectures for publication. They were delivered in the early days of tape recording so that in a few places the words have been difficult to decipher and a few tapes are missing. Also, only a very few of the lectures were taken down in shorthand so in one or two cases we have neither a tape nor a manuscript. Fortunately, however, the Doctor kept his very full notes on all the lectures so we have used them, though, of course, it means that these chapters are not as full as the others.

The Doctor's tapes are distributed by the Martyn Lloyd-Jones Recordings Trust and, of all his tapes, by far the largest number of requests is for these doctrine lectures. The lack of knowledge of the vital truths of the Christian faith is greater now than ever before – certainly greater than it was in the 1950s – so it is our prayer that God would use and bless these lectures again to our strengthening and to His glory.

The Editors

Introduction

We began our lectures by saying that we find ourselves, as men and women in a confused and difficult world, aware of principalities and powers which we cannot understand and which we cannot explain. The spirit of man, therefore, searches for something which it cannot find, and having shown that no human learning or teaching could ever solve that problem, we came to the conclusion that there is no hope for men and women save that they submit to the revelation that God has been pleased to give of Himself. He has given that revelation in nature. He has given it in history. He has given it by sending His only begotten Son into this world and, in a very special way, He has given it in and through the book which we call the Bible. We, therefore, are to spend some time in examining our authority. We have no authority apart from this book, and we either take it as it is or else we must of necessity be in the position in which we say that we are superior to it, and we can pick and choose, and select and reject. There is only one logical, reasonable attitude. Either we do accept the Bible as God's word and God's revelation and submit ourselves to it whether we understand it or not, or else – I repeat – we assert that our understanding is the supreme authority.

So, coming to the Bible in that way, as little children, confessing our ignorance and our inability, we listen to its message, and it starts with a message about God Himself. So we spent our time at the beginning on the doctrine of God – His character, His nature, His attributes, then His works in creation and especially in the creation of man. Also, we considered the being of God – the three Persons in the Godhead, the Father and the Son and the Holy Spirit. And then, having looked at those mighty doctrines with fear and trembling, we came to the biblical teaching about man, because, in a sense, that is our starting point from the experiential standpoint. Why is man as he is? Why is the world as it is? Well, the Bible has its answer. It is all due to what it calls *sin*. So, having looked at man as he was made by God, we saw sin coming in at the suggestion of the devil, and that was the doctrine of the Fall with all its consequences in Adam himself and in all his posterity. We considered the biblical teaching with regard to all that. And we summed it up by saying that as we consider men and women we can use the analogy made by an old Puritan. Sometimes you see an old ruin in the country, an old castle or hall, and there is a notice saying that 'So and so once lived here.' And the old Puritan said that that kind of notice can be put up over human beings: 'God once dwelt here.'

But then comes the glorious doctrine of salvation. So we went on to consider the person of the Lord Jesus Christ. The teaching of the Bible with regard to His person is that there are two natures in one person. We did not claim to understand all this but we said that it is vital and essential biblical teaching.

Then, having looked at the person and at various heresies which had arisen even in New Testament times, and which still are current with regard to His person, we went on to consider His work. And that brought us face to face with the great central doctrine of the atonement as it is expounded in the Scriptures. And there we saw that He made a perfect provision. He became a substitute for us. Our sins were punished in His body and He has reconciled men and women to God in that way.

1

The Person of the Holy Spirit

In our consideration of these biblical doctrines, our method has been to follow the order and the plan of salvation, so we come now, by a logical sequence, to the great doctrine of the Holy Spirit. Now I cannot begin to talk about this doctrine without pausing for a moment to express again my sense of wonder and amazement at the plan of salvation. I believe that people who are not interested in the plan of salvation as such, are robbing themselves of a great deal. When you try to stand back and look at it as a whole, you must at once be impressed by its glory, its greatness, its perfection in every part; each doctrine leads to the next until there it is, the complete whole.

It is a very good thing in the Christian life to stand back periodically and look at this great plan. That is why I think it is important to observe Christmas Day and Good Friday and Easter Sunday, and to preach on those days. They are convenient occasions for reminding ourselves of the whole plan of salvation. Look at it as a whole, look at the separate parts; but always remember that the parts must be kept in their relationship to the whole.

So it is very important that we should be studying the Bible in this particular way. I would always recommend that you read the Bible chapter by chapter, that you go steadily through it – that is also good. But in addition I do suggest that it is of vital importance to take out the great doctrines that are taught there, and look at them according to the plan or the scheme of salvation. The Church has done this from the very beginning, and it is a tragedy that it is done so infrequently at this present time because if you are content only with reading through the Scriptures, there is a danger of missing the wood for the trees. As you read through, you become so immersed in the details, getting the

right translation, and so on, that you tend to forget the big, outstanding doctrines. So the reason for taking a series like this is to remind
ourselves that the purpose of the Bible is to tell us God's plan for the
salvation of this world.

Another thing which I must emphasise is this: I know nothing
which is such a wonderful proof of the unique, divine inspiration of
the Scriptures as the study of Christian doctrine because we see then
that this book is one, that it has one message though it was written at
different times by different men in different circumstances. There is
great unity in the message, one theme running from the beginning to
the end. From the moment mankind fell, God began to put the plan of
salvation into operation, and we can follow the steps and the stages
right through the Bible. And so as we come to consider the doctrine of
the Holy Spirit, we are reminded that here again is a doctrine that
appears both in the Old and the New Testaments. We find a reference
to the Holy Spirit in the second verse of the Bible, and the teaching
goes right the way through. This amazing unity, I repeat, is proof of
the unique, divine inspiration and infallibility of the Scriptures.

So, then, we find that in this great plan the Holy Spirit is the applier
of salvation. It is His work to bring to us, and to make actual in us, in
an experiential manner, that great salvation which we have been considering together and which the Son of God came into the world in
order to work out. In the Godhead, the Holy Spirit is the executive,
the executor. I shall have to come back to this again when we deal
particularly and specifically with His work, but that is His great function in the plan.

Now it is a remarkable and an astonishing thing that this doctrine
of the Holy Spirit, His person and His work, has been so frequently
neglected in the Church – yet that is an actual fact of history. It is
quite clear that the first Christians believed the doctrine, they almost
took it for granted. Then you come to the early centuries of the Christian era and you find very little reference, comparatively speaking, to
this doctrine. That is not surprising, in fact it was more or less inevitable, because the Church was constantly engaged, in those first centuries, in defending the doctrine concerning the Son. The Son of God
had become incarnate: He had been here in this world. Jesus was
preached, Jesus as the Christ, and, of course, the enemy was constantly attacking the person of Christ. This was the linchpin in the
whole of the gospel and if it could be discredited, the whole scheme
would collapse. So the attack was upon the person of the Son and the

Church had to give herself in defence of that doctrine in order to establish it.

Tragically, the result was that the doctrine of the Holy Spirit was comparatively neglected, until the time of the Protestant Reformation. Now it is our custom to say that the Protestant Reformation is primarily the epoch in the history of the Church in which the great doctrine of justification by faith only was rediscovered in the Bible, and that is perfectly true. But let us never forget that it is equally true that the doctrine of the Holy Spirit was also rediscovered in a most amazing manner, and the great Dr B. B. Warfield is surely right when he says that John Calvin was the great theologian of the Holy Spirit. With the whole Roman system the Holy Spirit was ignored; the priesthood, the priests, the Church, Mary and the saints were put into the position of the Holy Spirit.

So the Protestant Reformation rediscovered this mighty doctrine; and let us, in Britain, take partial credit for that. The doctrine of the Holy Spirit was, beyond any question whatsoever, worked out most thoroughly of all by a Puritan divine who lived in this country in the seventeenth century. There is still no greater work on the doctrine of the Holy Spirit than the two volumes by the mighty Dr John Owen, who preached in London and who was also at one time, during the period of Cromwell, the Vice Chancellor of the University of Oxford. And not only John Owen. Thomas Goodwin and other Puritans also worked out the doctrine of the Holy Spirit. It has never been done so thoroughly since, and certainly had never been done before.

Now generally speaking, the position today is that the doctrine of the Holy Spirit is either neglected or it tends to be emphasised and exaggerated in a false manner. And I have no doubt at all that the second is partly the cause of the first. The doctrine of the Holy Spirit is neglected because people are so afraid of the spurious, the false and the exaggerated that they avoid it altogether. No doubt this is why many people also neglect the doctrine of prophecy, the last things and the second coming. 'The moment you start on that,' they say, 'you get into these extravagances and these disputes.' So they leave the whole thing alone and the doctrine is entirely neglected.

So it is with the doctrine of the Holy Spirit. Because of certain exaggerations, excesses and freak manifestations, and the crossing of the border line from the spiritual to the scientific, the political and the merely emotional, there are many people who are afraid of the doctrine of the Holy Spirit, afraid of being too subjective. So they neglect it altogether. I would also suggest that others have neglected the doctrine because they have false ideas with regard to the actual teaching concerning the person of the Holy Spirit.

In view of all this, therefore, it is obviously essential that we should consider this great doctrine very carefully. If we had no other reason for doing so, this is more than enough – that it is a part of the great doctrine of the blessed Holy Trinity. Let me put it very plainly like this: you would all agree that to neglect or to ignore the doctrine about the Father would be a terrible thing. We would all agree that it is also a terrible thing to neglect the doctrine and the truth concerning the blessed eternal Son. Do we always realise that it is equally sinful to ignore or neglect the doctrine of the blessed Holy Spirit? If the doctrine of the Trinity is true – and it is true – then we are most culpable if in our thinking and in our doctrine we do not pay the same devotion and attention to the Holy Spirit as we do to the Son and to the Father. So whether we feel inclined to do so or not, it is our duty as biblical people, who believe the Scripture to be the divinely inspired word of God, to know what the Scripture teaches about the Spirit. And, furthermore, as it is the teaching of the Scripture that the Holy Spirit is the one who applied salvation, it is of the utmost practical importance that we should know the truth concerning Him. I am very ready to agree with those who say that the low spiritual life of the Church, today or at any time, is largely due to the fact that so many fail to realise the truth concerning the person and the work of the Holy Spirit.

One other thing under this heading. I wonder whether you have ever noticed, those of you who are interested in hymns and in hymnology, that in most hymnbooks no section is so weak as the section devoted to the Holy Spirit? Here the hymns are generally weak, sentimental and subjective. For that reason, I have always found myself in great difficulties on Whit Sunday. We are lacking in great doctrinal hymns concerning the Holy Spirit and His work. Indeed, there are those who would say (and I am prepared to agree with them) that in many hymnbooks a vast majority of the hymns under the section of the Holy Spirit – these hymns that beseech Him to come into the Church and to come upon us, and to do this and that – are thoroughly unscriptural. That is another way of showing you again that this great doctrine has been neglected, that people have fought shy of it, and there is confusion concerning it.

The best way to approach the doctrine of the Holy Spirit is to start by noticing the names or the descriptive titles that are given to this blessed person. First of all, there are the many names that relate Him to the Father; let me enumerate some of them: the *Spirit of God* (Gen. 1:2); the *Spirit of the Lord* (Luke 4:18); the *Spirit of our God* (1 Cor. 6:11). Then another is, the *Spirit of the Lord God*, which is in Isaiah 61:1. Our Lord speaks, in Matthew 10:20, of the *Spirit of your Father*, while Paul refers to the *Spirit of the living God* (2 Cor. 3:3). *My Spirit*, says God, in Genesis 6:3, and the psalmist asks, 'Whither shall I go from thy Spirit?' (Ps. 139:7). He is referred to as *his Spirit* – God's Spirit – in Numbers 11:29; and Paul, in Romans 8:11, uses the phrase *the Spirit of him* [God the Father] *that raised up Jesus from the dead*. All these are descriptive titles referring to the Holy Spirit in terms of His relationship to the Father.

In the second group are the titles that relate the Holy Spirit to the Son. First, 'If any man have not the *Spirit of Christ* he is none of his' (Rom. 8:9), which is a most important phrase. The word 'Spirit' here refers to the Holy Spirit.[1] In Philippians 1:19, Paul speaks about the *Spirit of Jesus Christ*, and in Galatians 4:6 he says, 'God hath sent forth the *Spirit of his Son*'. Finally He is referred to as the *Spirit of the Lord* (Acts 5:9).

Finally, the third group comprises the direct or personal titles, and first and foremost here, of course, is the name *Holy Spirit* or *Holy Ghost*. Some people are confused by these two terms but they mean exactly the same thing. The English language is a hybrid which has borrowed from other languages, and 'Ghost' is an old Anglo-Saxon word while 'Spirit' is derived from the Latin *spiritus*.

A second title in this group is the *Spirit of holiness*. Romans 1:4 reads, 'Declared to be the Son of God with power, according to the spirit of holiness, by the resurrection from the dead.' A further title is the *Holy One*: 'But ye have an unction from the *Holy One*' (1 John 2:20). In Hebrews 9:14 He is referred to as the *eternal Spirit* and Paul says in Romans 8:2, 'For the law of the *Spirit of life* in Christ Jesus hath made me free from the law of sin and death.' In John 14:17 He is called the *Spirit of truth*, and in chapters 14, 15 and 16 of John's Gospel, He is referred to as the *Comforter*.

Those, then, are the main names, or descriptive titles, that are applied to Him. But have you ever thought of asking why He is called

1. See the translation in the New International Version and the references in various commentaries. (*Ed.*)

the *Holy Spirit*? Now if you put that question to people, I think you will find that they will answer, 'He is described like that because He is holy.' But that cannot be the true explanation because the purpose of a name is to differentiate someone from others, but God the Father is holy and God the Son is equally holy.

Why, then, is He called holy? Surely, the explanation is that it is His special work to produce holiness and order in all that He does in the application of Christ's work of salvation. His objective is to produce holiness and He does that in nature and creation, as well as in human beings. But His ultimate work is to make us a holy people, holy as the children of God. It is also probable that He is described as the Holy Spirit in order to differentiate Him from the other spirits – the evil spirits. That is why we are told to test the spirits and to prove them, and to know whether they are of God or not (1 John 4:1).

Then the next great question is the personality or the person of the Spirit. Now this is vital because it is essential that I should put it like this. The person of the Holy Spirit is not only forgotten by those whom we describe as liberals or modernists in their theology (that is always true of them), but we ourselves are often guilty of precisely the same thing. I have heard most orthodox people referring to the Holy Spirit and His work as 'it' and 'its' influence and so on, as if the Holy Spirit were nothing but an influence or a power. And hymns, too, frequently make the same mistake. There is a confusion about the Holy Spirit and I am sure there is a sense in which many of us find it a little more difficult to conceive of the third person in the blessed Holy Trinity than to conceive of the Father or the Son. Now why is that? Why is there this tendency to think of Him as a force, or an influence, or an emanation?

There are a number of answers to that question. They are not good reasons, but we must consider them. The first is that His work seems to be impersonal, because it is a kind of mystical and secret work. He produced graces and fruits; He gives us gifts and He gives us various powers. And because of that, we tend to think of Him as if He were some influence. I am sure that this is a great part of the explanation.

But, furthermore, the very name and title tends to produce this idea. What does *Spirit* mean? It means breath or wind or power – it is the same word – and because of that, I think, we tend, almost inevitably and very naturally, unless we safeguard ourselves, to think of Him as just an influence rather than a person.

Then a third reason is that the very symbols that are used in speaking of Him and in describing Him tend to encourage us in that direction. He descended upon our Lord, as John baptised Him in the Jordan, in the semblance of a dove (Matt. 3:16). And again, the symbols that are used to describe Him and His work are oil and water and fire. In particular, there is the phrase in the prophecy of Joel, which was quoted by Peter in Jerusalem, on the Day of Pentecost, about the Spirit being poured out (Acts 2:17). That makes us think of liquid, something like water, something that can be handled – certainly not a person. So unless we are very careful and remember that we are dealing with the symbols only, the symbolic language of the Scripture tends to make us think of Him impersonally.

Another reason why it is that we are frequently in difficulties about the personality of the Holy Spirit is that very often, in the preliminary salutations to the various New Testament epistles, reference is made to the Father and the Son, and the Holy Spirit is not mentioned. Our Lord in the great high priestly prayer says, 'And this is life eternal, that they might know thee, the only true God, and Jesus Christ, whom thou hast sent' (John 17:3) – He makes no specific reference to the Holy Spirit. And then John says the same thing in his first epistle: 'And truly our fellowship is with the Father, and with His Son Jesus Christ' (1 John 1:3). He does not mention the Spirit specifically at that point.

Then also, the word *Spirit* in the Greek language is a neuter word, and, therefore, we tend to think of Him and of His work in this impersonal, neutral sense. And for that reason, the King James Version, I am sorry to say, undoubtedly fell into the trap at this point. In Romans 8:16 we have that great statement which reads, 'The Spirit itself beareth witness with our Spirit, that we are the children of God.' You notice the word 'itself', not 'Himself'. Again in the same chapter we read, 'Likewise the Spirit also helpeth our infirmities: for we know not what we should pray for as we ought; but the Spirit *itself* maketh intercession for us' (Rom. 8:26). At this point the Revised Version is altogether superior since in both instances it gives the correct translation: 'Himself', even though in the Greek the pronoun, as well as the noun, is in the neuter.

And thus we have, it seems to me, these main reasons why people have found it difficult to realise that the Holy Spirit is a person. People have argued – many theologians would argue – that the Scripture itself says the 'Spirit of Christ'. The Holy Spirit, they say, is not a distinct person; He is the Spirit of Christ, the Spirit of the Son, or of the

Father, and thus they deny His personality.

How, then, do we answer all this? What is the scriptural reply to these reasons that are often adduced? Well, first of all, the personal pronoun *is* used of Him. Take John 16:7–8 and 13–15 where the masculine pronoun 'He' is used twelve times with reference to the Holy Spirit. Now that is a very striking thing. Jesus says, 'Howbeit when he, the Spirit of truth, is come, he will guide you into all truth' (v. 13) – and so on. And this, of course, is of particular importance when we remember that the noun itself is a neuter noun, so the pronoun attached to it should be in the neuter. Now this is not always the case but it is in the vast majority of instances. It is most interesting and it shows how important it is to realise that the inspiration of Scripture goes down even to words like pronouns! So that is the first argument, and those who do not believe in the person of the Spirit will have to explain why almost the whole Scripture uses the masculine pronoun.

The second reply to those who query the personality of the Spirit is that the Holy Spirit is identified with the Father and the Son in such a way as to indicate personality.

There are two great arguments here; the first is the baptismal formula: 'baptizing them in the name of the Father, and of the Son, and of the Holy Ghost' (Matt. 28:19). Here He is associated with the Father and the Son in a way that of necessity points to His personality. And notice, incidentally, that this baptismal formula does not say, 'baptizing them in the *names*' but 'in the *name*'. It uses the unity of the three Persons – the Three in One – one name, one God, but still Father, Son and Holy Spirit. And so if you do not believe in the person and personality of the Holy Spirit, and think that He is just a power or a breath, you would have to say, 'Baptizing them in the name of the Father, and of the Son, and of the breath' or of 'the power'. And at once it becomes impossible. The second argument is based on the apostolic benediction in 2 Corinthians 13:14: 'The grace of the Lord Jesus Christ, and the love of God, and the communion of the Holy Ghost . . .' – obviously the Holy Spirit is a person in line with the person of the Father and of the Son.

The third reply is that in a most interesting way we can prove the personality of the Spirit by showing that He is identified with us, with Christians, in a way that indicates that He is a person. In Acts 15:28 we read, 'For it seemed good to the Holy Ghost, and to us, to lay upon you no greater burden than these necessary things.' This was a decision arrived at by members of the early Church, and as they were persons, so He must be a person. You cannot say, 'It seemed good to a power and to us,' because the power would be working in us. But here is someone outside us – 'It seemed good to *him* and to *us*'.

The fourth reply is that personal qualities are ascribed to Him in the Scriptures. He is said, for example, to have knowledge. Paul argues, 'For what man knoweth the things of a man, save the spirit of man which is in him? even so the things of God knoweth no man, but the Spirit of God' (1 Cor. 2:11).

But – and this is very important – He has a will also, a sovereign will. Read carefully 1 Corinthians 12 where Paul is writing about spiritual gifts, and the diversity of the gifts. This is what we are told: 'But all these worketh that one and the selfsame Spirit, dividing to every man severally as he will' (v. 11). Now that is a very important statement in the light of all the interest in spiritual healing. People say, 'Why have we not got this gift in the Church, and why has every Christian not got it?' To which the simple answer is that this is not a gift that anybody should *claim*. It is the Spirit who gives and who dispenses these gifts, according to His own will. He is a sovereign Lord, and he decides to whom and when and where and how and how much to give His particular gifts.

Then the next point is that He clearly has a mind. In Romans 8:27 we read, 'And he that searcheth the hearts knoweth what is the mind of the Spirit' – this is in connection with prayer. He is also one who loves, because we read that 'the fruit of the Spirit is love' (Gal. 5:22); and it is His function to shed abroad the love of God in our hearts (Rom. 5:5). And, likewise, we know He is capable of grief, because in Ephesians 4:30, we are warned not to 'grieve' the Holy Spirit. The doctrine of the Holy Spirit, and especially this aspect of the doctrine which emphasises His personality, is of supreme importance. The ultimate doctrine about the Spirit, from the practical, experiential standpoint, is that my body is the temple of the Holy Spirit, so that whatever I do, wherever I go, the Holy Spirit is in me. I know nothing which so promotes sanctification and holiness as the realisation of that. If only we realised, always, in anything we do with our bodies, the Holy Spirit is involved! Remember, also, that Paul teaches that in the context of a warning against fornication. He writes, 'Know ye not that your body is the temple of the Holy Ghost which is in you . . . ?' (1 Cor. 6:19). That is why fornication should be unthinkable in a Christian. God is in us, in the Holy Spirit: not an influence, not a power, but a *person* whom we can grieve.

So we are going through all these details not out of an academic interest, nor because I may happen to have a theological type of mind. No, I am concerned about these things, as I am a man trying myself to live the Christian life, and as I am called of God to be a pastor of souls, and feel the responsibility for the souls and the conduct and behaviour of others. God forbid that anybody should regard this matter as remote and theoretical. It is vital, practical doctrine. Wherever you are, wherever you go, if you are a Christian, the Holy Spirit is in you and if you really want to enjoy the blessings of salvation, you do so by knowing that your body is His temple.

2

The Deity of the Holy Spirit

We are considering the reasons why we must regard the Holy Spirit as a person and so far we have seen, first, that personal pronouns are used with respect to Him and, secondly, that He is identified with the Father and the Son in such a way as to indicate personality. Thirdly, He is also linked with Christians in a way that indicates personality; and fourthly, certain personal qualities are ascribed to Him in the Scriptures, qualities such as knowledge, will and sovereignty, mind, love, and grief.

Our fifth reason for insisting upon the person and personality of the Spirit is that actions are ascribed to the Spirit which can only be performed by a person. For instance, in 1 Corinthians 2:10 we are told that 'the Spirit searcheth all things, yea, the deep things of God'. He *searches* – it is the action of a person. We are also told clearly that He *speaks*. In Revelation 2:7, we read, 'He that hath an ear, let him hear what the Spirit saith unto the churches.' Then He also *makes intercession* for us. 'We know not what we should pray for as we ought,' says Paul in Romans 8:26, 'but the Spirit itself maketh intercession for us with groanings which cannot be uttered.'

Then He also *bears testimony*. Our Lord said, 'He shall testify of me' (John 15:26). He bears testimony to the Lord: only a person can do that. Then we are told, again by our Lord, 'He will guide you into all truth' (John 16:13). Indeed, even in the Old Testament we are told that He teaches and instructs in the truth: 'Thou gavest also thy good spirit to instruct them' (Neh. 9:20) – the Spirit spelt with a capital 'S'.[1]

---

1. While this is not so in the King James (Authorised) Version, 'Spirit' is upper case in the Revised Version. Cf. also the New International Version. (*Ed.*)

Another personal action of His is found in Acts 16:6–7 where we are told, 'Now when they had gone throughout Phrygia and the regions of Galatia, and were forbidden of the Holy Ghost to preach the word in Asia, after they were come to Mysia they assayed to go into Bithynia: but the Spirit suffered them not.' Again, this is surely a very significant and relevant statement. All Paul's companions wanted to go and preach in Asia, but the Spirit prohibited them. Then they wanted to go into Bithynia, and again He would not allow them. That is a definite action by the Holy Spirit Himself, and it is proof positive that He is a person.

The sixth argument is His office, His assigned task – the very office to which He was appointed is personal. He is described as the *Comforter*, 'another Comforter', says our Lord in John 14:16 and a comforter is one who stands by our side and helps us. The same word is sometimes translated *advocate*, so our Lord was saying, in effect, 'As I have been with you during these three years; as I have taught you and guided you, and as I have sent you out on your missions, I will not leave you comfortless. I am going to send you another Comforter. You must not be troubled, you are not going to be left as orphans.' The Holy Spirit is one who takes the place of our Lord. He is within us to lead us and guide us, and that is why our Lord was even able to say, 'It is expedient for you that I go away: for if I go not away, the Comforter will not come unto you' (John 16:7). Obviously it is a personal office.

Then our last big proof, the seventh, of the personality of the Holy Spirit is that, according to the teaching of the Scriptures, the Holy Spirit is susceptible to personal treatment. In other words, we are told that we can do certain things to the Spirit, and that He reacts as only a person can react. First, we are told that the Holy Spirit can be *lied to*. In the terrible case of Ananias and Sapphira in Acts 5, notice what Peter said: 'Ananias, why hath Satan filled thine heart to lie to the Holy Ghost, and to keep back part of the price of the land?' (v. 3). Ananias and Sapphira had declared that they had given everything, but Peter charged them with having lied to the Holy Spirit. Not an influence therefore – not some vague power – but clearly a person.

Then we are told that we can *blaspheme* against the Holy Spirit. Our Lord says, 'All manner of sin and blasphemy shall be forgiven unto men: but the blasphemy against the Holy Ghost shall not be forgiven unto men . . . neither in this world, neither in the world to come' (Matt. 12:31–32).

Thirdly, we see that He can be *insulted*. Hebrews 10:29 refers to the man 'who hath trodden underfoot the Son of God, and hath counted the blood of the covenant, wherewith he was sanctified, an unholy thing, *and hath done despite unto the Spirit of grace.*'

And finally, as we have already seen, He can be *grieved*. Paul exhorts us in Ephesians 4:30, 'And grieve not the holy Spirit of God, whereby he are sealed unto the day of redemption.'

So, the Holy Spirit, we have seen, is a person. Yes, but we must demonstrate not only His personality but His *deity*. This is still a vital part of the doctrine of the Trinity, of course, and, indeed, we cannot emphasise too often that in many ways that doctrine is the first and the great doctrine of the Christian faith. It is only Christians who believe this doctrine; all other religions fail to do so, as do all errors and heresies. The Trinity is the key which unlocks all truth. So we must look at the evidence.

The first is that the Scripture itself specifically asserts the deity of the Spirit. I take you back again to that terrible incident with Ananias and Sapphira. After asking, 'Ananias, why hath Satan filled thine heart to lie to the Holy Ghost, and to keep back part of the price of the land?' Peter continued, '. . . not lied unto men, but unto God' (Acts 5:3–4). 'The terrible thing that you have done,' said Peter in effect, 'is that you have not only been lying to men; you thought that you were just lying to us, the apostles, and to the other Christians, but no, you have been lying to *God*.' And just previously he had said that Ananias had lied to the Holy Spirit. So clearly that is a specific statement that the Holy Spirit is God – God, the Holy Spirit.

But then we also find, as we have already shown, that the Spirit's name is coupled with the name of God, and this not only establishes His personality but His Deity, too. This is seen in the baptismal formula, in the Apostolic benediction, and also, of course, in 1 Corinthians 12, where Paul writes, 'Now there are diversities of gifts, but the same Spirit . . . And there are diversities of operations, but it is the same God which worketh all in all' (vv. 4, 6). At one point we are told it is the Spirit who does this, and the next moment we are told that it is God – the same God who works all and in all, and He is the Spirit. Therefore the Spirit is God – His deity is proved.

Then in the third place we find that certain definite attributes are ascribed to Him – and this is most important. We are told that He is eternal, and to be eternal is to be God, for God alone is eternal. In Hebrews 9:14, He is referred to as the 'eternal Spirit'. We are told that He is omnipresent; He is present everywhere. This again is only true of God. The psalmist in Psalm 139:7 cries out, 'Whither shall I go from thy spirit? or whither shall I flee from thy presence?' He is also omnipotent; there is no limit to His power, and again, this is an attribute of deity. When the archangel visited Mary and told her that she was to bear that 'holy thing', the Son of God, he told her, 'The Holy Ghost shall come upon thee, and the power of the Highest shall overshadow thee' (Luke 1:35). Our Lord was 'conceived of the Holy Spirit'. He was the power, this omnipotent power, the power of the Highest, that overshadowed her, and the Lord was born of Mary.

In the same way we are told that He is omniscient; He knows everything. Again we have an example of that in 1 Corinthians 2:10: 'The Spirit searcheth all things.' And not only that. We are told, 'Even so the things of God knoweth no man, but the Spirit of God' (v. 11). No man understands a man except the spirit of man that is in him. In the same way, no on understands the things of God, but the Spirit of God. But the Spirit does understand, and therefore His knowledge is equal to the knowledge of God. Or again, take those statements of our Lord about the Comforter: 'He shall teach you all things' (John 14:26) – He knows all things, and therefore He can so this. And furthermore, our Lord says, 'He will guide you into all truth' (John 15:13). There is no limit to His ability to teach us and lead us, because He knows all truth.

And then the fourth piece of evidence is that He does divine works. Certain things are done by the Spirit which we are told in the Scriptures can only be done by God. First of all, creation. In Genesis 1:2 we read, 'The Spirit of God moved upon the face of the waters.' There it is at the very beginning. Job says it also, 'The Spirit of God hath made me, and the breath of the Almighty hath given me life' (Job 33:4). This is the creative work of the Holy Spirit, again, a proof of His deity. And then, of course, we must remember that His is the special operation which we describe as regeneration; the third chapter of John's Gospel establishes that once and for ever: 'Ye must be born again' (v. 7). Yes, and, 'Except a man be born of water *and of the Spirit*' (v. 5). It is the action of the Spirit; He gives the rebirth. Original creation – the new creation; they are both the special work of the Spirit. 'It is the spirit that quickeneth' (John 6:63), says our Lord again.

Then we are also told very clearly that the work of inspiration is the work of the Spirit. 'No prophecy of the scripture is of any private interpretation,' says Peter; '. . . holy men of God spake as they were moved' – carried along, driven; it does not matter which translation you employ – 'by the Holy Ghost' (2 Pet. 1:20–21). All the Scriptures were written in that way: the Holy Spirit inspired and controlled the writers in an infallible manner. So we have our doctrine of the infallibility of the Scriptures, and it is proof positive to us that He is God. It is God alone who can give the truth and inspire men in their record of the truth.

And, lastly, the work of the resurrection is also attributed to Him. Very often people are surprised by this. But it is to be found quite clearly in Romans 8:11: 'But if the Spirit of him that raised up Jesus from the dead dwell in you, he that raised up Christ from the dead shall also quicken your mortal bodies by his Spirit that dwelleth in you.' And there is a hint of the same teaching in Romans 1:4 where Paul says that Christ was 'declared to be the Son of God with power, according to the Spirit of holiness, by the resurrection from the dead.'

So we have arrived at this – that the Holy Spirit is a person and that He is a divine person. Obviously, then, the next thing to consider must be this: What is His relationship to the other Persons of the Godhead? In Volume 1 we considered God the Father and God the Son and now here we are face to face with this great statement that the Holy Spirit is also one of these blessed Persons. We have also already considered the doctrine of the Trinity, so I must not go back to it in detail now. But this is what we have to say: the Scriptures tell us two great things, first that there is only one God. We must always assert that. But the Scriptures equally teach that there are three Persons in that Godhead – the Father, the Son and the Holy Spirit. God the Father is fully God. God the Son is fully God. God the Holy Spirit is fully God. Do not try to understand that; no one can; it baffles our understanding. We must simply come to the Scripture and bow before it, accepting its authority; but we cannot understand it. Do not be misled by the various illustrations and analogies that people use. None of them is adequate; none of them is complete. The essence of wisdom in this matter is just to confess the plain statements, and to say that there is only one God but there are three Persons in that blessed Godhead; and the three Persons are co-equal and co-eternal.

But let us try to enter, if we can, as far as the Scripture takes us into this question of the relationship of the three Persons. Now we notice at once that there is a difference in what we are told about the Son and the Spirit. We are told that the Son is 'begotten' (John 3:16, 18) of the Father but you never read that about the Holy Spirit. The term in the case of the Spirit is that He 'proceedeth from the Father'. We are told in John 15:26 (and this is an important verse), 'But when the Comforter is come, whom I will send unto you from the Father, even the Spirit of truth, which proceedeth from the Father, he shall testify of me.' Now that is obviously a very vital difference and one that should engage our attention.

Those of you who are interested in theology will know that the great theologians throughout the centuries have been trying to grapple with the difference between *generation* and *procession*. I shall not attempt to consider it; it seems to me that it should never have been attempted – it is entirely beyond us. The truth is so great and so transcendent that the human mind simply cannot get there, but we must recognise the terms – begetting, generation, procession.   The Spirit of truth, which proceedeth from the Father,' says our Lord, 'he shall testify of me.'

Then I must remind you of a further point: in John 15:26 our Lord says that 'the Spirit proceedeth *from the Father*,' and He does not say that the Spirit proceeds from Himself also. And yet what is believed and taught by the whole of western Christianity – and when I say western Christianity I mean both the Roman Catholic and the Protestant Churches – is that the Holy Spirit proceeds not only from the Father but also from the Son. Now this is a very interesting point in the history of the Church. The first great division in the Christian Church – I say the first great division, for there had been lesser divisions before that, and if you hear people saying that divisions only originated at the Protestant Reformation, tell them to go and read Church history. There were divisions, there were schisms, in the very earliest days of the Christian Church, but the first major division took place over this very question in the eleventh century.

There was a great discussion in the Church as to whether or not it should be taught that the Spirit proceeded from the Father only, or from the Father and the Son. The whole of western Christianity taught that you must say that He proceeds from the Father and from the Son. But the eastern section of the Church disagreed, so there was a division into what is called the Eastern Church and the Western Church.

Now it is very important that we should know this. You read references in the newspapers to the Greek Orthodox Church and the Russian Orthodox Church; they are representatives of the Eastern

Church which refuses to say 'and from the Son'. All that debate took place as far back as AD 589, just before the end of the sixth century; and, indeed, it is still one of the real points of difference between the Greek Orthodox and the Roman Catholic Church. Both Churches believe in the Virgin Mary in the same way, and even in the 'assumption', so-called, of Mary. The Orthodox Church does not believe in the infallibility of the Pope, of course, but it was this question of the Holy Spirit that caused the separation.

Why do we in the Western Church say that He proceeds from the Son as well as from the Father? Why does the Protestant Church at this point agree with the Roman Catholic Church? Well, this is the evidence: all the arguments that we have adduced for His deity force us to say that, as does the fact that He is called the 'Spirit of Christ' and the 'Spirit of the Son'. Indeed, in this very verse (John 15:26) our Lord says that it is He who is going to send the Spirit. He associates Himself with the Father, and He tells us that He Himself will operate through the Spirit, exactly as His Father does. Furthermore, the Scripture shows that wherever the Spirit is, the Father and the Son are there also. In John 14 our Lord says that He will 'send the Comforter', and, as the result of that, the Father and He will dwell within us. The three are always working together.

Indeed, it is very interesting to observe that, apart from that one statement in John 15:26, the Scriptures always apply exactly the same terms to the relationship between the Son and the Spirit as they do to that between the Father and the Spirit. That is why John 15:26 is so important from the standpoint of doctrine. I have drawn your attention to this because it does seem to me that anything which has caused such a dramatic incident in the history of the Church is one with which we should be familiar.

However, let me come on to something which is of still greater importance. The Scriptures teach that the Spirit is subordinate to the Father and to the Son. You remember that when we were studying the doctrine of the Son, we saw that the Son subordinates Himself to the Father. He said, 'The words that I speak unto you I speak not of myself: but the Father that dwelleth in me, he doeth the works' (John 14:10). The works that He did were not His own. The Father gave Him the works; the Father told Him what to do. Now here we are taught that the Spirit subordinates Himself to both the Father and the Son. That is what is meant in John 16:13. Our Lord says, 'He shall not speak of himself,' which means that He does not speak from Himself, just like the Son, He is given what to speak. And, indeed, His work, we are told, is to glorify Christ (John 16:14). The Spirit does not glorify Himself; He glorifies the Son.

Is this not wonderful? Here is the subordination. Here is the division of the work. The Son says that He has come to glorify the Father, and the Spirit's work is to glorify the Son. Each one reflects the glory of the other. Thus we look into the mystery of this amazing doctrine of the blessed Trinity: 'He shall glorify me: for he shall receive of mine, and shall shew it unto you' (John 16:14). This is, to me, one of the most amazing and remarkable things about the biblical doctrine of the Holy Spirit. The Holy Spirit seems to hide Himself and to conceal Himself. He is always, as it were, putting the focus on the Son, and that is why I believe, and I believe profoundly, that the best test of all as to whether we have received the Spirit is to ask ourselves, what do we think of, and what do we know about, the Son. Is the Son real to us? That is the work of the Spirit. He is glorified indirectly; He is always pointing us to the Son.

And so you see how easily we go astray and become heretical if we concentrate overmuch, and in an unscriptural manner, upon the Spirit Himself. Yes, we must realise that He dwells within us, but His work in dwelling within us is to glorify the Son, and to bring to us that blessed knowledge of the Son and of His wondrous love to us. It is He who strengthens us with might in the inner man (Eph. 3:16), that we may know this love, this love of Christ.

So let me end by putting it to you in this way: the Scripture teaches us that in this division of labour between Father, Son and Holy Spirit, in this subordination for the sake of our redemption, the Father is all the fulness of the Godhead invisible, without form, 'whom no man hath seen, nor can see' (1 Tim. 6:16); that is the Father. The Son is all the fulness of the Godhead manifested visibly, 'For in him dwelleth all the fulness of the Godhead bodily' (Col. 2:9); that is the Son. And what a tremendous statement that is! And the Spirit is all the fulness of the Godhead acting immediately upon the creature. You see the difference? The fulness of the Godhead – invisible; the fulness of the Godhead – visible; the fulness of the Godhead – acting immediately and directly upon us. So thus we can say that the Spirit by His power makes manifest the Father in the image of the Son.

That is the whole essence of this glorious doctrine. '[God] whom no man hath seen, nor can see' (1 Tim. 6:16). Well, is there any hope for me? Yes, in the Son. He has become visible, and through the Spirit the

Son is made real to me. So I go to the Father with confidence and with assurance. God the Son is the revealed God – God is known. God the Spirit is that divine Person who exercises His energy immediately upon me. Or, you can think of the Spirit as God the giver of life, the Lord.

So, when we face the season of Advent[1] and of Christmas and think about the birth of our Lord and the great gospel that comes out of that tremendous crucial event in history, we know that it will mean nothing to us, and can mean nothing to us, apart from this doctrine of the blessed Holy Spirit. Paul says, '. . . Which none of the princes of this world knew: for had they known it, they would not have crucified the Lord of glory' (1 Cor. 2:8). And yet the astounding thing is that you and I know that God – the eternal Son – was 'made flesh, and dwelt among us' (John 1:14). We know that this is true. We know that God did come, that the fulness of the Godhead was in Christ, that He died for our sins and blotted them out and bore their punishment, and that in Him we are just before God and clothed with His righteousness. How do I know this? I now it because the Holy Spirit, the third Person in the Holy Trinity, dwells within me, enlightens me, gives me understanding, unction and an anointing.

Let us not only think of what He does, let us realise who He is. What an act of humiliation and of humbling took place when the Son was born as a babe in Bethlehem! But it is an equal act of humiliation for this third Person in the blessed Trinity to come and to dwell in you and me. 'Know ye not that your body is the temple of the Holy Ghost?' (1 Cor. 6:19). He comes within us and we can grieve Him. Put that by the side of the incarnation and remember the humbling that takes place that you and I might be rescued, might be redeemed, might be raised, and might become the children of God. Blessed be God the Father, God the Son, and God the Holy Spirit! Amen.

---

1. This lecture was given on 11 December, 1953.

3

Creation and Common Grace

We come now to the *work* of the Holy Spirit although in a sense we have touched on it in dealing with His person. The main difficulty here is one of classification or arrangement – no two classifications agree. The best, though not perfect, one, it seems to me, is that which divides His work between *His work in general apart from the application of redemption* and then *His specific work in the application of redemption*.

Yet even before we come to deal with that, we must consider something which often perplexes people and which we can describe as the *dispensational aspect* of the teaching concerning the Holy Spirit. Pentecost clearly seems to be a turning point but in what respect? Now here there are two dangers – the danger of making too much of it and that of making too little of it.

What, then, are the facts? First, there is the Old Testament prophecy about Pentecost found in Joel 2:28 and following, which is quoted by Peter in Acts 2. But there are other prophecies also as, for example, Ezekiel 32:26–27.

Secondly, in the New Testament, we find John the Baptist speaking of the coming of the Holy Spirit, in Luke 3:16–17; and in John 7:39 we read, 'For the Holy Ghost was not yet given, because that Jesus was not yet glorified'; and there are many statements in John chapters 14–16. Then in Luke 24:49 our Lord, when speaking to His disciples, says, 'Behold, I send the promise of my Father upon you: but tarry in the city of Jerusalem, until ye be endued with power from on high.' And in the same way we read in Acts 1:4 that He 'commanded them that they should not step out from Jerusalem, but wait for the promise of the Father, which, saith he, ye have heard of me.' Finally, in Acts

1:8 He says, 'But ye shall receive power, after that the Holy Ghost is come upon you . . .'.

Then, thirdly, there are the facts of the Day of Pentecost itself of which we read in Acts 2.

Now all these statements seem to carry the implication that the Holy Spirit had not yet come, that the Holy Spirit would come, that the Holy Spirit was about to come and that the great day at last arrived when He did come. The statements became more and more urgent. The time seemed to be shorter and shorter until at last Peter got up and said, 'This is it, it has happened; this is that which was said by the prophet Joel. . .'. Now here is the problem. Here is the difficulty which has exercised the minds of people in the Church from the Day of Pentecost until now. Here are all these statements which seem to say that the Holy Spirit had not yet come and yet, on the other hand, there are many statements which describe to us the mighty activity of the Holy Spirit before the Day of Pentecost. So let us look at these also.

However, before we begin, let me interject a word about method. And if we do nothing else in these lectures, perhaps we may be of help to some by indicating the method of approach, the way to attack a problem. When you have a great problem like this, the one thing to do first of all is always collect your facts. Before you begin to theorise, before you begin to put up hypotheses and suppositions, gather together your details, get your facts together. We have done one side; we have seen all these statements pointing forward, so we are now going to put the facts on the other side. We are going to remind ourselves of what we are told in the Scriptures about the activity of the Holy Spirit before the Day of Pentecost.

First of all, we start at the very *creation of the world*. The second verse in the Bible, Genesis 1:2, says this: 'And the Spirit of God moved upon the face of the waters.' He was operative in the creation of the world. God the Father has made everything, through the Son, by the Holy Spirit. The blessed Trinity, as we have often reminded ourselves, is operative in the whole work, always, but the labour is divided up. And, of course, you will remember that the Holy Spirit is very specially involved in connection with the creation of man.

The second is the work of the Holy Spirit in *sustaining, in maintaining the creation*. Now there are many statements about this; I shall simply quote two. In Isaiah 40:7, we read, 'The grass withereth, the flower fadeth: because the spirit of the Lord bloweth upon it.' But, still more strikingly, in Psalm 104 you will find that magnificent description of creation, which is, perhaps, quite unsurpassed anywhere in the Bible. The psalmist makes the point that if the Lord withholds Himself or His power of His Spirit from creation, it all begins to droop and to wane, to perish and to die. He puts His Spirit back again and it all revives. It is the Holy Spirit that sustains creation. Now you will find statements in the Scripture which say that the Son does that and the answer is, of course, that the Son does it through the Holy Spirit. So the Holy Spirit has been active from the commencement in sustaining and maintaining the universe.

And now I come, in the third place, to a most important matter which is so often forgotten. It is the Holy Spirit who is responsible for what is called *common grace*. Let me give you some definitions of what this means. Common grace is the term applied to those general blessings which God imparts to all men and women indiscriminately as He pleases, not only to His own people, but to all men and women, according to His own will. Or, again, common grace means those general operations of the Holy Spirit in which, without renewing the heart, He exercises a moral influence whereby sin is restrained, order is maintained in social life, and civil righteousness is promoted. That is the general definition. The Holy Spirit has been operative in this world from the very beginning and He has had His influence and His effect upon men and women who are not saved and who have gone to perdition. While they were in this life and world they came under these general, non-saving operations of the Holy Spirit. That is what we mean by common grace.

Now, how does the Holy Spirit do this? Well, there are various answers to that question. You will remember that we are told in the prologue of John's Gospel about '*the true light which lighteth every man*' (John 1:9). It does not matter how you translate that verse – 'the light which lighteth every man that cometh into the world' says the Authorised Version; 'the Light that lighteth every man was coming into the world,' says another. We are not concerned about that. We are interested in the phrase 'the light which lighteth every man'. And there is such a light. It is a kind of natural light, as we call it, natural understanding. It is the light that is in *conscience* and there is that light of conscience in every person born into this world. Now that is one of the operations of the Holy Spirit in what is called common grace. It is a light that comes from Christ, because He is the Head of the human race, but it is the Holy Spirit who puts that light into everyone who is born.

Then this same general light also manifests itself in *governments*, and in *laws*, and in the various 'powers that be' as Paul calls them in Romans 13:1. You see, it is not man who decided to set up governments and states; 'the powers that be are ordained of God,' says Paul. God divided up the bounds of the nations. He decided that there must be rulers, governors and magistrates and that they should not bear the sword in vain (Rom. 13:4). This is God's work, and He has done all this and keeps it going by means of the Holy Spirit.

Now I think you see at once, without my emphasising it, that many Christian people are in grave error with regard to this matter. They seem to have the idea that God has nothing to do with the unsaved world. But that is not scriptural. Even those who are unsaved are under this influence of the Holy Spirit. It is not a saving influence, nor is it a redemptive influence, but it is a part of God's purpose.

Another way in which common grace manifests itself is by what may be called *public opinion*. There is such a thing as a general public opinion, a general consensus of opinion about moral subjects. People who are not Christian at all believe that certain things are wrong and should be prohibited, that other things are right and should be encouraged. There is a sense of right and wrong in humanity. Now that is nothing but a manifestation of common grace. If the Holy Spirit were not operative in men and women in this general way, human beings, as the result of the Fall and of sin, would have festered away into oblivion long ago.

Next to that is what is generally described as *culture*. By that I mean arts and science, an interest in the things of the mind, literature, architecture, sculpture, painting and music. Now, there can be no question at all but that cultivation of the arts is good. It is not redemptive, but it improves people, it makes them live better lives. Now, where do all these things come from? How do you explain men like Shakespeare or Michelangelo? The answer from the Scripture is that all these people had their gifts and were able to exercise them as the result of the operation of common grace, this general influence of the Holy Spirit.

So you see once more that not only sinners and those who do not believe in God deny common grace, but that often even those of us who are Christians do the same. People tend to glory in Shakespeare, as if he were responsible for his powers, but he was not. He had only what he had received. All these gifts that man and women have come from God. And that is why true Christians, as they look out, not only upon creation, but even at culture, discover a reason for glorifying and for praising God.

You see, what is wrong with culture is not the thing itself, it is rather that people give their worship, their praise and their adoration to those men and women who have produced the works rather than to the God who enabled them to do it. But if you look at these things under the heading of common grace, you will see that they all bring glory to God because it is through the Spirit that He dispenses these general gifts to humanity. We shall be reminded later of how our Lord Himself tells us that God sends His rain upon the evil and the good and causes His sun to rise on the just and the unjust – it is the same thing. The God who sends rain and sunshine and gives crops to the evil farmer as well as to the Christian farmer, dispenses artistic and scientific gifts in exactly the same way, indiscriminately, to bad and good, saved and unsaved. It is a work of the Holy Spirit.

Then another way in which common grace manifests itself is this. We read in Isaiah 45: 'I form the light, and create darkness: I make peace, and create evil.' What does this mean? Not that God is the creator of sin, nor that He is the author of evil – as such – but that He is the author of the evil consequences that follow certain actions. He controls everything. In that sense He makes peace and creates evil. In other words, it is the Holy Spirit who sees to it that certain actions lead to certain painful and evil consequences. Those, then, are some of the ways in which common grace manifests itself.

But let us look now at the effects of all this. The first is that *the execution of the sentence of judgment upon man and woman in sin was delayed.* Have you not sometimes asked yourself the question: Why was it that God did not immediately punish sin by bringing the world to an end in the Garden of Eden? the answer is that God decided, in His own inscrutable and eternal will, not to do so.

But the further question is: How can the world go on existing at all in sin? The answer is that it is kept in existence by this power that the Spirit puts into it. It is the Spirit who keeps the world going. Human life is prolonged both in general and in particular. 'The goodness of God,' says Paul in Romans 2:4, 'leadeth thee to repentance.' Peter says the same thing in his second epistle: 'The Lord . . . is longsuffering to us-ward, not willing that any should perish that all should come to repentance' (2 Pet. 3:9). God is patient and long-suffering; to Him a thousand years are as one day and one day as a thousand years.

4

The Significance of Pentecost

We are still considering, you remember, the apparent conflict in the Bible over the coming of the Holy Spirit, and we are looking now at the biblical evidence for the fact that He had been at work in the world before the Day of Pentecost. We have seen three aspects of His working: that He was operative at creation, that He sustains the universe and that the work of common grace is His.

Let me give you further evidence. The fourth is this: there is plain scriptural teaching to the effect that the Holy Spirit has given special gifts to certain men. Take, for instance, Samson. He was a man of unusual strength and physical vigour and power. Now that strength, we are told, was given to Samson by the Holy Spirit (Judg. 13:25) and it was because he had not realised that the Lord, or the Spirit, had left him after his hair had been shaved that he was finally captured and overpowered by his enemies the Philistines (Judg. 16:20). Then there is a very interesting incident in the life of Moses when he complained that the work was too much for him, and we are told in Numbers 11:17 that God said to him, 'I will take of the spirit which is upon thee, and will put it upon them,' namely, the seventy elders who were going to share the work with Moses. Now that is very striking. It was the Spirit who had enabled Moses to do the work and some of that Spirit was now taken and put upon the seventy elders in order that they might assist Moses in the carrying out of this work.

Then there was a man called Bezaleel who had certain abilities in connection with the building and furnishing of the tabernacle. You will read about him in Exodus 31:2–5. It was the Holy Spirit who gave him the skill to do that work. And the same thing, of course, is true of Joshua. Joshua's military strategy and ability was the result of

He keeps the world going by the Holy Spirit instead of pronouncing final judgment.

The second effect of common grace is that *the Holy Spirit strives with men and women*. Take that statement in Genesis 6:3: 'My spirit shall not always strive with man.' It does not exhaust the meaning of those words, but it does, at any rate, mean that a time was coming when instead of keeping men and women alive, in spite of their sin, God would stop and the flood would come and they would all be destroyed. The striving, in other words, has two meanings. It means 'keeping in existence, keeping going', and it also means that God was there, as it were, pleading through His Spirit, trying to get men and women to see the enormity of their sins and of their actions before it was too late. You find the same idea in Stephen's sermon recorded in the seventh chapter of Acts. He says, 'Ye do always resist the Holy Ghost' (Acts 7:51). The Holy Ghost is there, with this general work of conviction, but people resist it instead of yielding to it.

And, again, in Romans 1, we see the same thing. Paul there teaches that 'God gave them over to a reprobate mind' (Rom. 1:28). Read again in the second half of that chapter the terrible description of the moral iniquity, the horrible, foul perversions, of the world at the time when Paul was writing. Why was this? Paul's answers is, 'God gave them up unto vile affections' (v. 26). Now up to a point He did not do that. Up to a point, God, by the Holy Spirit, restrained men and women from these vile affections and that is why the world is not always as bad as it might be. God, through the Holy Spirit, restrains the foulest manifestations of sin, but there are times when He gives people up to them. Are we, I wonder, living in such an age? Compare the twentieth century with the nineteenth. It is obvious that the moral level is very much lower today. That does not mean that everybody was a Christian in the Victorian era, but it does mean that even people who were not Christians were better men and women, speaking generally, than people now. Why? It was because of the general influence of the Holy Spirit. But it does look as if again, today, God is giving humanity over 'unto vile affections' as Paul outlines in Romans 1.

Therefore I deduce that one of the results of the operation of the Holy Spirit in common grace is that God does *restrain* men and women. He does specifically restrain sin. That is why God has appointed governments, authorities, magistrates and powers: it is to keep sin within bounds. Though God knows that there are certain people in the world who will never be saved, He does not allow them to live just as they please and to give fuller manifestation to sin; He restrains it in them.

In others words, there is a general sense of morality and right and even of religion in the world, apart from a saving knowledge of the Lord Jesus Christ. We all know many people, do we not, who are religious but who are not Christian. There are many people who would say that they believe in God and who are concerned about practising religion, and some of them make great sacrifices for their religion. They do not believe that they are so sinful that nothing but the death of Christ can save them. They are not Christian in our sense of the term, but you have got to grant that they are religious. What is it that makes a person religious? It is nothing but the operation of common grace. It is one of God's ways of restraining sin, of keeping it within bounds. So every sense of morality and rightness and religion, the belief in goodness, beauty and truth, such as you have in the Greek philosophers – it is all the result of the operation of the Holy Spirit. Paul puts it clearly in Romans 2:14, 'For when the Gentiles, which have not the law, do by nature the things contained in the law, these, having not the law, are a law unto themselves.' That is the basis and the authority for saying all that.

And then lastly, under common grace, we have, as I have already mentioned, those common blessings which God gives – the sun and the rain. Our Lord spoke about it in the Sermon on the Mount – Matthew 5:44–5. Paul spoke about exactly the same thing at Lystra, where he healed a man who was lame and then made this remarkable statement:

> Sirs . . . we also are men of like passions with you, and preach unto you that ye should turn from these vanities [these gods] unto the living God, which made heaven, and earth, and the sea, and all things that are therein: who in times past suffered all nations to walk in their own ways. Nevertheless he left not himself without witness, in that he did good, and gave us rain from heaven, and fruitful seasons, filling our hearts with food and gladness.
>
> Acts 14:15–17

And, lastly, we have that statement of the apostle Paul in 1 Timothy 4:10 where he talks about Christ as 'the Saviour of all men, especially of those that believe'. That phrase, 'the Saviour of all men', does not mean salvation in the sense of the soul being saved but that He is the sustainer, the one who is kind and good to men and women.

Let me, then, remind you of what we have been doing. facing this great problem as to what happened exactly on th Pentecost. It is a turning point. You read your Bible and you first that everything says that the Holy Spirit had not yet com He was going to come. But you go back again and you find th Holy Spirit had been active and that He had already been ope in the world. So then, having looked at the two bits of evidenc shall attempt to give what we regard as the biblical explanatic what exactly happened on that important and vital occasion recor for us in Acts chapter 2.

the operation of the Holy Spirit upon him. Now I simply take those examples at random to illustrate the point that, away back there in the old dispensation, the Holy Spirit came upon these men and gave them these particular powers.

Then, fifthly, we have to deal with the whole gift of prophecy; it is the teaching of Scripture everywhere that prophecy is made possible by the activity of the Holy Spirit. The first instance of this is the case of two men called Eldad and Medad. These two men began to prophesy, causing some of the people to become rather jealous for Moses' reputation, and this led Moses to make one of the greatest statements he ever made. He recognised that Eldad and Medad were able to prophesy because God had put His Spirit upon them and he said to his supporters, Don't be jealous for my sake – 'Would God that all the Lord's people were prophets, and that the Lord would put his spirit upon them!' (Num. 11:29).

The same thing is true, of course, even of a hireling prophet like Balaam. Balaam was enabled to say, and had to say, what he said because the Spirit of God was upon him (Num. 22–24). Furthermore, we read about Saul – the first king of Israel – that the Spirit came upon him and people said, 'Is Saul also among the prophets?' (1 Sam. 10:12). That was because Saul, under the influence and the power of the Holy Spirit, had been prophesying. And this is obviously true of all the prophets whose works are recorded in the Old Testament canon. Indeed, when we were dealing with the doctrine of Scripture we went further. We said then that all the writers of the Scriptures, both of the Old Testament and the New, were under the influence and the power of the Holy Spirit. These 'holy men of God' – that refers especially to the prophets – 'spake as they were moved by the Holy Ghost' (2 Pet. 1:21); but 'All scripture is given by inspiration of God' (2 Tim. 3:16) – *all scripture*. So it is good to include that under this particular heading of prophecy and it is, therefore, another very powerful argument for showing that long before the Day of Pentecost the Holy Spirit had been coming upon these men and enabling them to act as they did.

But for the sixth piece of evidence, I refer you to something that seems to take us even further. In Psalm 31:11, David says, 'Take not thy holy spirit from me.' Now here was a man under the Old Testament dispensation, a man before Pentecost, and he prayed that God would not take His Spirit from him. And what was true of David was, of course, equally true of all the Old Testament believers such as

Abraham, Isaac and Jacob. All these Old Testament saints were believers and citizens of the kingdom of God, and obviously you cannot be either of these things without the Holy Spirit. But David's striking statement focuses attention upon this matter: 'Take not thy holy spirit from me.'

But now, coming on to the New Testament – I am taking this, as you can see, in a chronological order – we come to John the Baptist. And the statement that the angel made to Zechariah the father of John the Baptist is this: 'And he shall be filled with the Holy Ghost, even from his mother's womb' (Luke 1:15). Now that is a very important statement but there is also another which says, 'Among them that are born of women there hath not risen a greater than John the Baptist: notwithstanding he that is least in the kingdom of heaven is greater than he' (Matt. 11:11). Yet we are told of John that he would be filled with the Holy Spirit even from his mother's womb.

Then it is said about John's mother Elisabeth: 'And Elisabeth was filled with the Holy Ghost' (Luke 1:41). Now this was all before Pentecost, remember, so we must test any theory we may have about the coming of the Spirit at Pentecost by a statement like that. And we are told the same thing about Zacharias in Luke 1:67: 'And his father Zacharias was filled with the Holy Ghost, and prophesied, saying . . .'; and then follows the account of what he said. Furthermore, we have a similar statement about Simeon, the old man who held the infant Lord Jesus in his arms. In Luke 2:25 we read, 'And the Holy Ghost was upon him,' and in verse 26 we are told, 'It was revealed unto him by the Holy Ghost . . .'. Then, verse 27 reads, 'And he came by the Spirit into the temple'.

And as you read in the Gospels about the disciples sent out by the Lord to preach and to cast out devils, you realise that they were enabled to do all that they did by means of the Holy Spirit. Their ability to preach and the power to exorcise devils was given to them by the Lord through the Holy Spirit. So that everything they did was by, and in, and through the power of the Spirit.

But there is the final statement in John 20:22, which is so important as one considers this doctrine of Pentecost. After His resurrection our Lord appeared to the disciples in the upper room. The doors were all shut, but suddenly He appeared among them, and eventually we are told this: 'And, when he had said this, he breathed on them, and saith unto them, Receive ye the Holy Ghost.'

There, then, is the evidence. Now the previous evidence was all to the effect that the Day of Pentecost had not yet come, that 'the Holy Ghost was not yet given; because that Jesus was not yet glorified' (John 7:39). Our Lord also said, 'It is expedient for you that I go away: for if I go not away, the Comforter will not come unto you' (John 16:7), and He gave them this injunction: 'Behold, I send the promise of my Father upon you: but tarry ye in the city of Jerusalem, until ye be endued with power from on high' (Luke 24:49). In Acts 1 Luke writes, '[He] commanded that they should not depart from Jerusalem, but wait for the promise of the Father, which, saith he, ye have heard of me' (v. 4). So that is the problem which seems to confront us – statements which imply that the Holy Spirit had not come and statements which teach plainly that He was active and operative and that mighty things were happening in Him and through Him.

So how do we reconcile these things? Obviously there cannot be a contradiction and there must be some way of understanding these two groups of statements. Let us try to approach the solution by putting it like this. There are certain things which are abundantly plain and clear. First: The coming of our Lord and Saviour Jesus Christ into the world made a vital difference in this whole question of the work and the operation of the Holy Spirit. Indeed, we must go further, and say that His death, and especially His resurrection and His ascension, made a still more vital difference. The moment you turn to the New Testament, the moment the coming of the Lord begins to be talked about, there seems to be something new, something special and additional. As we have seen, He Himself often says, 'Yes, but there is going to be more,' and there is the prophecy of John: 'He shall baptize you with the Holy Ghost, and with fire' (Matt. 3:11).

The second thing we notice is that in chapter 2 of the prophecy of Joel, which was quoted by Peter in his sermon on the Day of Pentecost, the emphasis is placed upon the word *pour out*: 'It shall come to pass in the last days, saith God, I will pour out my Spirit upon all flesh' (Acts 2:17). Now that is surely significant. The emphasis is upon the extent, the giving of the Holy Spirit is going to be more general. Also there is an emphasis upon the fact that it is going to be upon all types and kinds: '. . . your sons and your daughters . . . your young men . . . your old men . . . and on my servants and on my handmaidens, [on all these] I will pour out in those days of my Spirit; and they shall prophesy' (Acts 2:17–18). Now in the Old Testament the giving of the Spirit is something unusual, and these people on whom the Spirit came were exceptional persons. But the emphasis here is upon the generality; upon this whole idea of pouring out, the largeness, and the freeness, and the fulness of the gift. Not only that, there is an emphasis upon a further fact, which is that it is no longer going to be confined to the Jews. You will actually find that in the prophecy of Joel, at the end of that chapter. And, of course, you will find it worked out still more fully in the book of Acts. The gift of the Spirit is no longer confined to the Jews but is for all nations. There is this largeness and this freeness – He will pour out His Spirit upon all people. There is an all-inclusiveness which we must note.

So we notice those bits of evidence which are perfectly clear. But there is one other to which I must refer, and that is a word spoken by our Lord Himself. You will find it in John 14:17. Referring to the Holy Spirit, He says, 'He dwelleth with you, and shall be in you.' Now a distinction is made there by our Lord which obviously must be of vital importance. 'He dwelleth with you,' He says, and there has been proof of that, of course, in the works that the disciples have been enabled to do. But He says, 'He dwelleth with you, *and shall be in you.*' He makes this prophecy with regard to what will happen after the Day of Pentecost.

In order to make our evidence still more complete and that we may now come to a suggested synthesis of these two groups of statements, I must call your attention to three incidents. One took place in the house of Cornelius (Acts 10), another in Samaria (Acts 8), and the third in Ephesus (Acts 19). Now I shall take chapters 8 and 19 together; chapter 10 I put in a category on its own. But first I would like to look at the three together because there is one factor which is common to them all, and that is the element of unity which is emphasised in all three in exactly the same way as it is emphasised in the events of the Day of Pentecost recorded in Acts 2.

Unity is the big thing in Acts 2, is it not? There were these different people up at the Feast of Pentecost in Jerusalem. They were 'Parthians, and Medes, and Elamites, and the dwellers in Mesopotamia, and in Judaea, and Cappadocia, in Pontus, and Asia, Phrygia, and Pamphylia, in Egypt, and in the parts of Libya about Cyrene and strangers of Rome, Jews and proselytes, Cretes and Arabians (vv. 9–11). There were all these different nationalities, these different tongues and languages, but they all said, 'We do hear them speak in our tongues the wonderful works of God' (v. 11). That obviously stands out, that amazing oneness, that extraordinary unity. And of course the same unity was displayed in the apostles themselves. There was a coming together, a drawing together. And you find the same unity in Samaria, among the Gentiles in the household of Cornelius, and among the believers who were in Ephesus.

Now surely it is there that we find the key to the solution of this problem. When the Holy Ghost descended on the Day of Pentecost, when the Lord Jesus Christ baptised with the Holy Spirit, as He had said He would do, what was happening was the formation of the Church as the body of Christ. Now, before this there were believers. The apostles were obviously believers before the Day of Pentecost; you must not regard them as unbelievers before then. We know perfectly well that though they were imperfect and unclear in many respects, nevertheless they did believe in our Lord, and when He appeared to them, you remember on the day he rose from the dead, He breathed upon them and said, 'Receive ye the Holy Ghost.' So if you do not believe that they were believers before that, they must have been believers then. But that was before the Day of Pentecost.

So, then, what was it that happened on the Day of Pentecost? Well, I would suggest that the believers were welded together as members of the one body of Christ. Before that they were separate believers, even as the believers in the Old Testament were believers and were citizens of the kingdom – Abraham, Isaac and Jacob, and David and the patriarchs and so on – but they were not members of the body of Christ. On the Day of Pentecost the primary event was that all these became one. This is something which we can understand if we see that it could only happen after our Lord's ascension. While He was here in the flesh and teaching his followers, the Church as His body had not yet been formed. In the book of Acts, we read a statement, do we not, that He has 'purchased [the Church] with his own blood' (Acts 20:28). Thus the Church in that sense could not have existed before our Lord had completed the work which He had come to do. And He only completed that work as He ascended into the presence of the Father, but the moment He did that, He completed the work which was necessary for the purchase of the Church. He was made the head of the Church and as the head of the Church, the Holy Spirit was given to Him that He might give it to the Church which is His body.

So the point I am emphasising is that all that could not have happened before the ascension, but you would expect it to happen after it. And that is precisely what happened – ten days after the ascension, our Lord, now the head of the body which is the Church, sent His Spirit into and upon the body, to fill it. It was the gift that He gave, the promise of the Father was sent by the Son who had completed the work that was necessary in order that it might happen. So on the Day of Pentecost the Church was established as one unity, as the body of Christ.

Now, let me give you a verse which will explain all this: 'For by one Spirit are we all baptized into one body, whether we be Jews or Gentiles, whether we be bond or free; and have been all made to drink into one Spirit' (1 Cor. 12:13). Now, there it is, *'by one Spirit'* – the Holy Spirit – we are all 'baptized into one body'. And it was on the Day of Pentecost that all these believers were baptised into one body, all the apostles together with the three thousand other people from different parts of the world, who believed their preaching. Later, in the house of Cornelius, and again, in Samaria and Ephesus, all people, Jew and Gentile, were baptised into one body. The Church is one and there is only one Church, this invisible Church, the mystical body of Christ – that is where the division between the visible and the invisible Church becomes important – but what I am emphasising here is that there is a unity in the Church and that unity was brought into being when all these people were baptised into the one body on the Day of Pentecost.

Let me put it in different language. You can say that the Day of Pentecost was the day of the public inauguration of the Church as the body of Christ. There was something new there which had never been before. There is a sense in which you can speak of the Church in the Old Testament, yes, but it is not the same as the Church was subsequent to the Day of Pentecost. The unity was established. Then you see the significance of what happened in the house of Cornelius, and how important that was. Peter, of course, as a Jew would obviously have found it very difficult to believe that Gentiles could really come into this unity. That was why the vision was given to him as he was there on the top of the house. As he was praying he saw a great sheet coming down with clean and unclean animals and birds upon it and he heard God's voice telling him to kill and eat. God said, 'What God hath cleansed, that call not thou common' (Acts 10:15). But is there not a further suggestion that even that vision was not enough? Certainly it was enough to take Peter to the house of Cornelius and to preach as he did. But you will notice that, even while Peter was yet preaching, the Holy Spirit descended upon Cornelius and his household. And Peter and the Jews, especially, were amazed at this. They could not quite understand it but they had to face the facts as they heard these other people speak with tongues and magnify God. 'They of the circumcision which believed were astonished, as many as came with Peter, because that on the Gentiles also was poured out the gift of the Holy Ghost' (Acts 10:45).

Not only that, the next chapter tells us that when all this was reported in Jerusalem, the believers there were a little troubled about it, so when Peter went up he was cross-examined. 'When Peter was come up to Jerusalem, they that were of the circumcision contended with him' – 'they of the circumcision', remember, means the Jewish Christians – 'saying, Thou wentest in to men uncircumcised, and didst eat with them. But Peter rehearsed the matter from the beginning, and expounded it by order unto them . . .' (Acts 2:2–4). But the thing that Peter emphasised was that while he was speaking the Holy Spirit had descended upon them:

> As I began to speak, the Holy Ghost fell on them, as on us at the beginning. Then remembered I the word of the Lord, how that he said, John indeed baptized with water, but ye shall be baptized with the Holy Ghost. Forasmuch then as God gave them the like gift as he did unto us, who believed on the Lord Jesus Christ; what was I, that I could withstand God? When they head these things, they held their peace, and glorified God, saying, Then hath God also to the Gentiles granted repentance unto life.
>
> Acts 2:15–18

Now you see what was happening. God was declaring that they were to be baptised into this same body, that the Church was to consist of Jews and Gentiles. That is the great theme of Paul, is it not, in Ephesians? The mystery that had been hidden from the previous generations was that the Gentiles were to be made fellow heirs, that they were to be brought into the kingdom, that they were to be welded, baptised into the body, and that, therefore, as one body, they would be there for Him to function through them in this world of time.

But for me to complete my evidence, let me give you one further most significant scriptural quotation and this time it is from Hebrews 11:39–40. You remember the great list and gallery of the heroes of the faith in the Old Testament that appears in that chapter? Then this is what the writer says: 'These all having obtained a good report through faith, received not the promise: God having provided some better thing for us, that they without us should not be made perfect.' Oh yes, he says in effect, they were believers but everything was not given to them; they were held back, as it were, until this should happen, so that they and we together should be made perfect. They were believers but they had not been baptised into the body of Christ. The Church had not yet come into being in this sense, because Christ had not yet ascended, He had not done the work, He had not returned to the Father. But they were believers, they were being reserved, they were being held, they were being kept, so that when our Lord did ascend, then they were welded, baptised into the body; and the Church is one and has remained one ever since. Now that, I suggest to you, is the real meaning and significance of what happened on the Day of Pentecost, and what happened in the household of Cornelius is comparable to it. It is really the same thing, as Peter argues in that eleventh chapter of Acts. And indeed you will find that he had to bring out the same argument in the fifteenth chapter, at a great council of the Church in Jerusalem.

Then, finally, what about the events recorded in Acts 8 and 19? You notice that I separate them from Acts 10, and it is for this reason: in the household of Cornelius, just as Peter began to preach the Holy Spirit was poured out. But that is not what happened in Samaria and Ephesus. In Samaria Philip went down and preached and evangelised and a number of people believed and were baptised into the name of the Lord Jesus Christ. But Peter and John had to go down and pray for them and lay their hands upon them before they received the gift of the Holy Spirit. When Paul visited Ephesus, he asked the people the question which in the Authorised Version reads: 'Have ye received the Holy Ghost since ye believed?' In the Revised version it is: 'Did ye receive the Holy Ghost when ye believed?' It does not really make any difference; they mean the same thing. And these men said, 'We have not so much as heard whether there be any Holy Ghost' (Acts 19:2). In other words, they had received John's baptism only. And there Paul preached to them and baptised them in the name of Christ. He placed his hands upon them and they received the gift of the Holy Spirit.

Now you see that we must put these events in a different category because the Holy Spirit was received by these people in a different way. The question is often asked: 'Why did it happen like that in Samaria and Ephesus? What is the difference between those two groups and Cornelius and his household?' Well, I suggest to you, it is this: Cornelius and his household were Gentiles; they were not actually proselytes, but they were Godfearing and they were seeking. The people in Acts 8 were Samaritans. You will find the history of the founding of the Samaritan country in the Old Testament. They were, in a sense, neither Jews nor Gentiles. They had the five books of Moses but none of the remainder of the Old Testament. But they regarded themselves, you see, as being equal to the Jews. The woman of Samaria said to our Lord, 'Our fathers worshipped in this mountain, and ye say, that in Jerusalem is the place where men ought to worship' (John 4:20). There was a great feud between the Jews and the Samaritans for that reason. The Samaritans felt they had a perfect religion, but the Jews knew that it was imperfect. Now it seems to me that is the key to the understanding of what happened.

The Holy Spirit did not fall upon the Samaritans as Philip preached; envoys, emissaries, had to be sent down from the church – the headquarters at Jerusalem – to give them the gift of the Holy Spirit. Why? Well, surely, to establish the fact that the Samaritans must recognise their allegiance to the church at Jerusalem. The church at Jerusalem was the logical sequence and outcome of the Old Testament faith in its completeness, in its fulness. The Samaritans had to recognise that their religion was incomplete and that the Christian Church had come out, as it were, of the Jewish Church, the Church in the Old Testament. They had to realise that there is a continuity in God's way of salvation, that you have to accept the whole of the teaching of the Old Testament if you are to be truly Christian. You cannot suddenly come in into the New Testament, as it were; you cannot come in by some other way into the kingdom. No, *this* is God's way. So the Samaritans had to submit themselves to all of this teaching and to the church at Jerusalem which was first of all a Jewish church – to the Jew first, then to the Gentiles. They had to recognise and submit to all that and then they were given the gift of the Spirit.

In the same way, the people at Ephesus, in Acts 19, had a religion which was all right as far as it went. They were disciples of John and had been baptised into the name of John, but they were not clear about the gospel. So in their case again, this had to be made clear, it had to be put straight. In the case of Gentiles, like Cornelius, there was no error to correct – they had nothing – so as Peter preached the Holy Spirit descended, but in these other cases there was an incomplete religion, an imperfect understanding. That had to be put right before the gift of the Holy Spirit was given, and that is a very important distinction. In the case of Cornelius and his household God was simply making this great demonstration to the effect that the Gentiles had to come in and to be baptised into the body. In these other cases what was necessary was that they should believe the truth clearly and get rid of certain prejudices and false ideas.

We sum it up by saying that the great purpose of Pentecost is to give the final proof of the fact that Jesus of Nazareth is the Son of God and the Saviour of the world. That is declared. The second thing is the great inauguration of the Church as His body, and thirdly it is a proof of the fact that these various people who are added to the Church are members of the body. In addition, there are various other things which we shall have to come to later but the main one is this: in the Old Testament we are told that the Holy Spirit was with the men, or that He came upon them. He worked upon them from without, as it were, and what David even said, you remember, was, 'Take not thy holy spirit from me' (Ps. 51:11), as if the Holy Spirit was *with* him – that is the Old Testament terminology. The New Testament terminology is *in, within*; He works from within, and He abides. In the Old Testament He came upon men and left them. He comes, in the New Testament, because we are members of the body of Christ and because the Spirit is in Him in His fulness and comes from Him through the whole body. Because we are members of the body, the Spirit abides in us – perfectly; and that, it seems to me, is the essence of the teaching with regard to this matter.

Confusion has often arisen because, in addition to all this, on the Day of Pentecost the disciples in the upper room were at the same time filled with the Spirit, and as the result of the filling with the Spirit, they were able to witness, but you notice that that was repeated several times. I hope to come back to the teaching concerning the filling with the Holy Spirit at a later point – it must obviously come after justification and sanctification – I just mention it at this point. There is often confusion because of the term *filling*. They were filled with the Spirit, but they were repeatedly filled with the Spirit, and, because of that, were enabled to witness with boldness.

But on the Day of Pentecost the rushing mighty wind and the cloven tongues as of fire specially emphasised, not the filling with the Spirit, but the baptising into the unity of the body, the inauguration of the Church – that is why you have the special phenomena. The cloven tongues of fire were never repeated again. The walls were shaken on another occasion, but this particular sound, this noise, the gathering together of the special phenomena, places a uniqueness upon the event on the Day of Pentecost which was never repeated. It was never necessary to repeat it because it was something once and for all. The filling with the Spirit is something which can be, and often is, repeated, but that is not the vital thing which happened at Pentecost. As we have said, what happened there was something that could only happen when our Lord had finished the work for His people and risen and become the Head of the Church. The Church became His body and the Spirit was given to fill the body – that is what is emphasised at Pentecost. And so, having dealt with that, we shall now be in a position to go on to consider in detail the work of the Holy Spirit as He comes to deal with and to apply the work of redemption completed by our Lord and Saviour.

5

The Work of the Holy Spirit in General

Having looked at the work of the Holy Spirit in general and having considered what happened on the Day of Pentecost, it is important and interesting for us, before we move on to look at the great work of the Holy Spirit in the application of redemption, also to consider briefly His work in connection with our Lord Himself.

First with regard to His birth, we read how the angel of the Lord appeared to Joseph in a dream and said to him, 'Joseph, thou son of David, fear not to take unto thee Mary thy wife: for that which is conceived in her is of the Holy Ghost' (Matt. 1:20). Then Luke, in his Gospel, tells us that when speaking to Mary, the angel Gabriel told her, 'The Holy Ghost shall come upon thee, and the power of the Highest shall overshadow thee: therefore also that holy thing which shall be born of thee shall be called the Son of God' (Luke 1:35).

Then, secondly, when Peter preached to the household of Cornelius, he told the people about the ministry of our Lord which, '. . . began from Galilee, after the baptism which John preached: how God anointed Jesus of Nazareth with the Holy Ghost and with power' (Acts 10:37–38); and we are told in John 3:34 that 'God giveth not the Spirit by measure unto him'. We know, too, that after 'the Holy Ghost descended in a bodily shape like a dove upon him' (Luke 3:22) at His baptism, He was then 'led up of the Spirit into the wilderness to be tempted of the devil' (Matt. 4:1).

And more than that, thirdly, He was crucified in the power of the Spirit. 'Who, through the eternal Spirit', says the writer to the Hebrews, 'offered himself without spot to God' (Heb. 9:14); and then He was raised by the power of the Spirit as Paul tells us in Romans 1:4.

Finally we learn that He gave commandments to the apostles 'through the Holy Ghost' (Acts 1:2).

And now, let us move on to what, after all, is the main work and function of the Holy Spirit – His work in connection with the application of the redemption that has been achieved and worked out by the Son of God, our Lord and Saviour Jesus Christ. Notice the importance of proceeding with these doctrines in a logical manner. We obviously had to take the person and work of our Lord first; there we have seen what He has done. The whole question now is *how* that work is applied to men and women like ourselves.

In this series of discourses, we have often had to refer to that great meeting that was held in eternity, when God the Father, God the Son, and God the Holy Spirit met in council, and the work of salvation was divided up between them. The Son volunteered to take unto Himself human nature, to give a perfect obedience to the law, and to die for the guilt and punishment of the sins of men and women. And the Holy Spirit volunteered to take upon Himself the work of applying that redemption. That is His special work, and we must now pay attention to it.

Here again we must divide the subject into two main headings: the Holy Spirit's work in general, and His work in particular. There is a work of the Holy Spirit in connection with the application of redemption to all people, and He has a special work in the application of redemption only to those who are redeemed experientially. I am not dealing with the latter yet, but with the work that the Holy Spirit does in connection with Christ's redeeming work before that and apart from that.

First, I would suggest that His very coming and presence in the Church and in the world is, in itself, a part of this work; and in this connection I want to call your attention to John 16:8–11: Our Lord says, 'And when he is come [referring to the Spirit], he will reprove the world of sin, and of righteousness, and of judgment: of sin, because they believe not on me; of righteousness, because I go to my Father, and ye see me no more; of judgment, because the prince of this world is judged.'

Those are most important verses, and it is vital that we should interpret them correctly, because frequently they are wrongly interpreted. So often they are interpreted as if they were a description of the work that the Holy Spirit does in the souls of individuals in order to bring them to salvation. They may have some indirect reference to

that, but I want to try to show you that that is not their primary reference, that is not what they are really describing. You notice that the
Authorised Version reads like this: 'When he is come, he will *reprove*
the world . . .'; in the Revised Version, there is a better translation:
'When he is come, he will *convict* the world of sin, and of righteousness, and of judgment,' and that is correct. It is not *convince*, as it is
translated in the Revised Standard Version, but *convict*, and I need
not stress the difference between convicting and convincing. It is possible to convict a person without convincing him. To convince means
that you have persuaded that person. In other words, the Revised
Standard Version supports the false interpretation, which is that these
verses are describing the way in which the Holy Spirit brings a soul to
salvation. Now there is a sense, of course, in which every soul brought
into salvation does come along that way, but that is not the meaning
of this statement.

Let me try to substantiate this. I maintain that John 16:8–11 is a
general statement with regard to the coming of the Holy Spirit, and
with regard to the effect of His coming. You notice that our Lord is
very careful to say that when the Holy Spirit has come He will convict
not individuals, not believers, but the *world*. Now the world includes
everybody, those who become believers and those who do not, but
our Lord is careful to say that the convicting work is something that
the Holy Spirit does to the world. And I think it is because expositors
have so often forgotten this that they have gone so sadly astray in
their expositions.

Another point to notice is this: I wonder whether you have ever been
puzzled as to what these verses mean? For instance, our Lord says that
the Holy Spirit will convict the world of sin, and then He expounds that
– 'of sin, because they believe not on me'. He does not say that the Holy
Spirit will convict the world of sin by teaching it the whole truth about
sin. No! He only specifies one particular thing – 'because they believe
not on me'. That, again, is very significant. The law that God gave
through Moses convicts of sin in that more general sense and there was
no need for the Holy Spirit to come to do that. But the Holy Spirit does
this special work. And, in the same way, when our Lord expounds
'righteousness' and 'judgment', He pins it down to something very particular. In other words, our Lord's teaching here is with respect to the
effect that the actual coming of the Spirit has upon the world, and He
says that the very presence of the Holy Spirit in the Church convicts it
of sin, and righteousness, and judgement.

Now there is a parallel statement in Acts 5:29–32. Peter and the other Apostles are brought before the Court, before the Sanhedrin, where Peter makes his defence, and this is what we read:

> Then Peter and the other apostles answered and said, We ought to obey God rather than men. The God of our fathers raised up Jesus, whom ye slew and hanged on a tree. Him hath God exalted with his right hand to be a Prince and a Saviour, for to give repentance to Israel, and forgiveness of sins – then notice – And we are his witnesses of these things; *and so is also the Holy Ghost,* whom God hath given to them that obey him.

'We,' says Peter, 'are witnesses of these things, and the Holy Spirit is a witness of these things that we are telling you.' The coming of the Holy Spirit into the world witnesses concerning certain things, and, as He bears this witness, He convicts the world of sin, and of righteousness, and of judgment.

How does He do that? Well, let us follow our Lord's own exposition. But in passing we must observe a general point because it is a vital part of the whole doctrine of the work of the Holy Spirit, and it is this: in all three cases, the Holy Spirit is pointing to the Lord. He does not stop at sin. He does not teach about Himself or call attention to Himself or glorify Himself. He is all along calling attention to the Lord, and that is the characteristic of the whole of the work of the Holy Spirit. His one function and business, as our Lord Himself teaches here so clearly, is to glorify the Lord Jesus Christ. The whole of our redemption comes out of Christ, every blessing, every experience – *everything.* John has already said that at the very beginning of his Gospel. In John 1:16 he says, 'Of his fulness have all we received, and grace for grace.' The Holy Spirit can give us nothing whatsoever except it come from Christ. He does not give us anything Himself, but passes on to us, mediates to us, reproduces in us, brings to pass in us that fulness which is in Christ and His redemption. So you notice that as our Lord interprets these three things He does so entirely in terms of what the Holy Spirit will do with respect to Him.

The first thing is that He will convict the world 'Of sin, because they believe not on me'. I have already pointed out that He does not say that He will just convict the world of sin in general. He does not say that He is going to show the foulness of sin, or the evil or the ugliness or the depravity of sin; he will not show how sin is lawlessness or 'missing the mark', or any one of these other things. Our Lord does

not mention them at all. It is only one thing and this one thing is 'because they believe not on me'. Now what does He mean by this? Well,
surely, there is only one adequate explanation, and it must be that the
very coming of the Holy Spirit into the Church on the Day of Pentecost at Jerusalem, with the signs that followed, and the way in which
He used the Apostles, all that in itself convicted the world of its complete error when it had denied Jesus of Nazareth and cried, 'Away
with Him! Crucify Him!' The coming of the Holy Spirit is proof positive and final that Jesus of Nazareth is the Son of God, the Saviour of
the world.

How does the Holy Spirit do this? Well, while He was here in this
world our Lord had said that He was going to send 'the promise of
the Father'. This was something that the Jews had been looking forward to for centuries. They had these prophecies of Joel and others,
and they knew that the Messiah was the One who was going to send
that promise. Then Jesus of Nazareth appeared before them; He
claimed to be the Messiah; and they disputed His claim and denied it.
They would not believe on Him and they finally rejected Him and
crucified Him. But here is the Holy Spirit sent upon the Church,
according to prophecy! What, then, is the effect of that? It proves that
He is the Messiah, and, therefore, the world which rejected Him is
convicted of its sin – the sin of failing to recognise Him, the sin of
rejecting Him and of crucifying Him. That is why He says that the
Holy Spirit in particular convicts the world of sin 'because they
believe not on me'.

I trust I am making this clear: it was the very coming of the Spirit
that did that, it was not the result of a work that He does in the depths
of the soul. I shall be dealing with that later, when we come to the
question of how redemption is applied to those who are redeemed.
But now we are dealing with the way in which the Holy Spirit convicts the world of sin. When He fell upon the Church, when there was
the sound of the rushing mighty wind and the cloven tongues, as of
fire, came upon those disciples and they spoke with other tongues,
that alone convicted the world of sin, the sin of unbelief. That is why
I put this under the heading of 'general'.

But come to the second indictment – '. . . of righteousness, because I
go to my Father, and ye see me no more.' Have you ever been troubled
as you have tried to expound that? It is very interesting to read the commentators and the various sermons on this subject because, forgetting
that our Lord is talking about the world, they tend to misinterpret it.

Some say that by 'righteousness' Jesus meant that God was showing His own righteousness and justifying Himself. They say that the charge against God was that this One who had claimed to be His Son had been forsaken by Him. God had allowed Him to be crucified and God was, therefore, not righteous. Very well, say these commentators, by sending the Holy Spirit God established His own righteousness. He raised Christ again from the dead, and after Christ had ascended to heaven, God sent down the Holy Spirit, in this way establishing the fact that God had not been unrighteous after all, and had been taking care of His Son through everything that happened.

Others say that what is meant by 'righteousness' here is the establishing of the righteousness of Christ the Son. When He was crucified in weakness, men said that He was not the Son of God, and that He was not righteous; that what He claimed was not true, and because it was a lie, He was, therefore, not a righteous person. The sending of the Holy Spirit is therefore said to prove that He is what He said He was, and therefore it establishes His righteousness. But that point has already been dealt with under the previous category, and if it means that, it would be a kind of tautology, a mere repetition of something that has already been established. So it does not mean either of these things.

Now our Lord puts this in a very interesting way. He says, '. . . of righteousness, because I go to my Father, and ye see me no more.' So how does it work out? Well, the fact that our Lord rose again from the dead is proof positive that He has been accepted by the Father. The Father has not only accepted Him, but He has also accepted His perfect work. The Apostle Paul, I think, gives us the key to the elucidation of this problem. In Romans 4:25 he says, 'Who was delivered for our offences, and was raised again for our justification.' It is in the rising again that we see Christ as our justification. The fact that God raised Him from the dead, with His perfect, spotless life of obedience, with His passive obedience in His death upon the cross, as He bore the guilt and the punishment of all the sins of men and women. In the resurrection God is declaring, 'I am satisfied, the law is satisfied. There is nobody who can bring any accusation.'

But the ultimate proof of God's acceptance of Christ as our justification is the sending of the Holy Spirit. That is why it is so important that we should always bear in mind the fact that what happened on the Day of Pentecost at Jerusalem must always be included in the great series of events, the historic events, that establish salvation. This is the last and the ultimate proof that Christ is the Son of God, and the Saviour of the world, for as we have seen it was only to the One who established His righteousness that God gave the gift of His Spirit for His people who are His body, the Church.

And, therefore, the very coming of the Holy Spirit on the Day of Pentecost made the pronouncement that there is only one way of righteousness, and it is that which is in Christ Jesus. You cannot establish a righteousness of your own by means of the law; you cannot establish it by means of your own moral effort or striving. He is our righteousness; He is our peace; He is God's way of righteousness; and the righteousness that God gives us is the righteousness of His own Son. The Holy Spirit proclaims that. When God sent the Holy Spirit He was convicting the world of righteousness; He was telling them, pronouncing to them, that in Christ and in Him alone can we be made righteous. That is the great theme in the book of Acts and in all the New Testament epistles. It is that Christ 'is made unto us . . . righteousness' (1 Cor. 1:30). And nothing proclaims that so powerfully as the descent of the Holy Spirit sent by Christ upon the Church on the Day of Pentecost.

And then it is exactly the same with the third statement – '. . . of judgment, because the prince of this world is judged.' Here again there is much confusion as to why our Lord put it in this way. He says that the coming of the Holy Spirit convicts the world of judgment because the prince of this world is, or has been, judged as the result of His work. Now what does this mean? Well here again I put it like this: the coming of the Holy Spirit on the Day of Pentecost was the final proof of the defeat of Satan and the judgment that is pronounced upon him. I regard this as a most important doctrine at this point. Talking about His death, just before this, our Lord said, 'Now is the judgment of this world: now shall the prince of this world be cast out' (John 12:31). He was referring to what He was going to do in His death: 'And I, if I be lifted up from the earth, will draw all men unto me. This he said, signifying what death he should die' (vv. 32–33).

Then there is the statement of the apostle Paul in Colossians 2:15, where he says that in dying upon the cross our Lord was putting principalities to an open shame, 'triumphing over them in it'. The statement in John 12:31, therefore, means that our Lord in His death upon the cross was judging and defeating Satan. It was a prophecy that the prince of this world was to be cast out by that event. Paul says it has happened. And I suggest that our Lord says the same thing here in

John 16. The death of our Lord upon the cross, His resurrection and ascension, and His sending of the Holy Spirit, was the proclamation of the defeat of Satan. Satan is now cast out, as our Lord had prophesied and predicted that he would be. And, of course, it was the coming of the Holy Spirit that finally proclaimed this. It was the coming of the Holy Spirit on the Day of Pentecost that proved, as I have been repeating, that our Lord is indeed the Son of God, that His work was accepted, and that He had thus done the great deed of redemption which would save men and women out of the dominion of Satan. It is therefore a conviction or judgment, especially because the prince of this world, Satan, is judged.

I wonder whether you have always realised the significance of this statement? Do you not see that it means that Satan has already been judged? He was judged by the work done on the cross; it was proclaimed by the sending of the Holy Spirit. And it is a fact. Our Lord's last great commission to His followers was, 'All power is given unto me in heaven and in earth. Go ye therefore, and teach all nations, baptizing them in the name of the Father, and of the Son, and of the Holy Ghost' (Matt. 28:18–19). He *has* this power. The apostle Paul puts it like this: 'He must reign, till he hath put all his enemies under his feet' (1 Cor. 15:25). The Day of Pentecost, the descent of the Holy Spirit, therefore, was a great proclamation to this effect – that the world will never be the same again as the result of what our Lord has done upon the cross.

Now before the coming of our Lord, Satan had held all the nations of the earth, apart from the Jews, in bondage. They were all pagans. They believed in their various gods, and the knowledge of the true and living God was confined to the one nation of Israel, the Jews. But as the result of our Lord's work upon the cross, and the sending of the Holy Spirit on the Day of Pentecost, that is no longer the case; Satan, in that sense, has not been deceiving the nations ever since then. Christ has been preached, and there are believers in Him in all nations under the heavens. He said, 'I, if I be lifted up from the earth, will draw *all* men unto me' (John 12:32) – like those who had come to Andrew, and others. So in that sense Satan is no longer controlling the world. Christ is controlling it, He is reigning. He is seated at the right hand of God's power. All power is given unto Him in heaven and in earth, and He is going on to disciple all the nations, by the Holy Spirit, through His workers, through His followers. So the very descent of the Holy Spirit on the Day of Pentecost, as our Lord here predicts, convicted the world of judgment.

I am afraid we do not realise this. I confess that I myself had not realised it as I should. I see it most clearly in this way: what was happening when the Holy Spirit descended? Well, among other things, it was a proclamation to the world that the spell of Satan on the world had finished, had been broken. He was cast out, as our Lord prophesied he would be. It does not mean that he is not able to exercise certain powers, but they are all within limits, he is not exercising them as he once did. The kingdoms of this world, in one sense, have already become the kingdoms of our God and of His Christ.

And all that is proclaimed by the descent of the Holy Spirit. 'When he is come, he will convict the world . . . of judgment, because the prince of this world is judged.' And he has been judged. What the Holy Spirit proclaims further is that all who belong to Satan will likewise be judged and condemned with him and cast into the lake of fire. Here, then, is a great work that is done by the Holy Spirit, immediately, by His mere presence in the Church, in connection with our Lord's completed work of redemption.

One other thing I want to mention at this point, in order that we may be free to go on to consider the work in the redeemed, is this: He also does a certain preparatory work in all and sundry – both the redeemed and the unredeemed. This has sometime been called the 'external' call of the gospel. It means that, since the coming of the Holy Spirit, a general call of the gospel has been made to all people. Let me emphasise this: it is made to those who remain unbelievers, as well as to those who become believers.

Perhaps the simplest way of putting that is to ask a question. If you were asked to define the difference between a Calvinist and a hyper-Calvinist, how would you do it? It is a question that is worth asking for this reason: I know large numbers of people who, when they use the term 'hyper'-Calvinist, generally mean Calvinist. In other words, they do not know what a hyper-Calvinist is. A hyper-Calvinist is one who says that the offer of salvation is only made to the redeemed, and that no preacher of the gospel should preach Christ and offer salvation to all and sundry. A hyper-Calvinist regards anyone who offers, or who proclaims, salvation to all as a dangerous person. For what it is worth, there is a society in London at the moment that has described me as a dangerous Arminian because I preach Christ and offer salvation to all!

I have called your attention to hyper-Calvinism in order that we may realise that the Bible teaches that Christ is to be preached to *all*. Let me give you my evidence for saying that. Take the great commission to which I have already referred: 'Go ye,' says our Lord, 'and preach the gospel to all nations.' Take also the statement of the apostle Paul in Acts 17:30: God 'commandeth *all* men every where to repent.' It is a universal command. And take the statement made by Paul about himself and his own ministry in his address to the elders at Ephesus in which he says that they must bear him record that he has testified both to the Jews and to the Greeks – that is to say, to everybody – 'repentance toward God, and faith toward our Lord Jesus Christ' (Acts 20:21). The gospel is a universal proclamation.

Another way I can prove it is this: our Lord Himself, in His parable about the wedding feast, tells us that some people were invited who did not come (Matt. 22:2–14). He recognises that the gospel will be preached to some who will reject it. That proves that it should be presented to all. And you will find the same teaching in Luke 14 in the parallel parable, about another wedding feast. Indeed, the Scriptures tell us quite specifically that certain people do, and will, reject the gospel. Paul at Antioch in Pisidia said that he had been preaching the gospel to the Jews but they had rejected it. So he was going to turn from them and was henceforth going to the Gentiles (Acts 13:46).

This proclamation of the gospel is to be made through the word of God. There is a great statement with respect to this in 1 Peter 1:12:

> Unto whom [the prophets] it was revealed, that not unto themselves, but unto us they did minister the things, which are now reported unto you by them that have preached the gospel unto you with the Holy Ghost sent down from heaven; which things the angels desire to look into.

The Holy Spirit always works through the word of God. Now there are many people who claim that He works directly. That was what caused the Quakers to wander off from the main party of the Puritans. They said that the word was not necessary, that the Holy Spirit spoke directly to each person, in some secret mystical manner, by some 'inner light'. Not at all! The Holy Spirit always uses the word: 'This is the word which by the gospel is preached unto you,' says Peter (1 Pet. 1:25). 'Being born again,' says Peter, 'not by corruptible seed, but of incorruptible, by the word of God, which liveth and abideth for ever' (1 Pet. 1:23).

In order to do His work, the Spirit uses the word of God. And what does He do? Let me give you the headings: first, He reveals, through the word, the great love of God to sinners in general: 'God . . . for his great love wherewith he loved us . . .' (Eph. 2:4) and so on. Secondly, He presents and offers salvation in Christ; through His people, He states the facts about Christ. That is the business of preachers of the gospel. It is to give the record of the life, the death, the resurrection and the resurrection appearances of our Lord. What is preaching? It is proclaiming these facts about Christ. Not only that. It is an explanation of the facts, the meaning of the facts, how these facts constitute salvation and are the cause, the means, of salvation. So in the preaching of the word in the power of the Holy Spirit, these facts and their interpretation are presented.

Then, as I have already reminded you, the Holy Spirit calls us to repentance. He calls everyone to repentance, all men and women everywhere, because of these facts, because of 'that man whom he hath appointed', by whom the whole world is going to be judged in righteousness (Acts 17:31).

And finally the Holy Spirit calls us to faith in Christ. Take again those words of Paul in his farewell message to the church at Ephesus, what did Paul testify? What did he preach? It was 'Repentance toward God, and faith toward our Lord Jesus Christ' (Acts 20:21). He called men and women to faith in Christ in order that they might obtain forgiveness of sins and inherit eternal life. That was the way in which our Lord commissioned Paul on the road to Damascus. He said that He was going to send him to the people and to the Gentiles, '. . . to turn them from darkness to light, and from the power of Satan unto God, that they may receive forgiveness of sins, and inheritance among them which are sanctified by faith that is in me' (Acts 26:18).

That, then, is the work of the Holy Spirit in general, in connection with our Lord's work of redemption. And having dealt with that, we are now in a position to go on to consider in detail what it is that the Holy Spirit does to those who become believers, and only to them, in order to apply the work of redemption.

6

The Work of the Holy Spirit in Redemption

I cannot imagine a better text to bear in mind, as we come to consider the subject that is to engage us now, than verses 6 and 7 of 1 Corinthians 2, where the apostle Paul says, 'Howbeit we speak wisdom among them that are perfect: yet not the wisdom of this world, nor of the princes of this world, that come to nought: But we speak the wisdom of God in a mystery, even the hidden wisdom, which God ordained before the world unto our glory.' Now I am acting on the assumption that we are people whom the Apostle describes in that language, for we are certainly going to look into the wisdom of God. The Apostle said that he could not preach in this way to the Corinthians when he was with them because they were still 'babes' and 'carnal' (1 Cor. 3:1), but, he says, 'We speak wisdom among them that are perfect.' It was not the sort of wisdom that the Greeks had been interested in; it was the wisdom of God in a mystery. We are now going to try to look at this great hidden wisdom of God in which we find things relevant to our salvation and to our eternal destiny.

Now we are considering the work of the Holy Spirit and we have looked at the very general work of the Spirit, and then, in the last lecture, we considered together our Lord's statements about His work which we find recorded in John 16, where He said, 'When he [the Holy Spirit] is come he will convict the world of sin, and of righteousness, and of judgment.' And we have expounded those statements as meaning that that is not a description primarily of the work He does within the soul, but is the work that the Holy Spirit does by His very presence in the world. As I was entering my room from this pulpit last

Friday something occurred to me which I apparently had not seen before, but I put it to you as an additional word for your consideration. Jesus said, '. . . of sin, because they believe not on me; of righteousness, because I go to my Father, and ye see me no more; of judgment, because the prince of this world is judged.' Now, we have seen those three things point to the Lord Jesus Christ, but it did not occur to me, until I was walking into my room, that what our Lord was really saying was that the Holy Spirit in His coming would be the final proof and demonstration that He, Christ, is indeed the one who comes from God to teach us, the very Son of God who is the Prophet and the Teachers and the Revealer of God. Yes, and the Priest also, the one who deals with righteousness, the one who offers us righteousness in the only way possible, by making expiation for sin. And, finally, the King, who rules over all, who has defeated Satan, the god of this world, the prince of the power of the air, and who is now seated and ruling at the right hand of God and who will rule; all power is given unto Him. So the presence of the Holy Spirit is the final demonstration of the fact that the Lord Jesus Christ is Prophet, Priest, and King.

We have seen also that the Holy Spirit is concerned about giving the general call of the gospel, and we emphasised that it is a call that is given to all, to those who remain unbelievers and to those who become believers. The Holy Spirit sees to it that that message is delivered and that that proclamation is made, that general, external call.

But at once, of course, we come up against a problem. That call, that offer of the gospel, is made to all, but we realise that it causes a division. We see that in the second chapter of Acts: some believed and some did not. Indeed, our Lord had prophesied that that would be the case when He said, 'For many are called, but few are chosen' (Matt. 22:14). A congregation sits in church and listens to the gospel: some are saved by it, some are not. Now that is a fact which is recorded in the Scriptures, which our Lord predicted, and which has been abundantly demonstrated in the history of the Christian Church from the very beginning right until today. Children of the same parents are brought up in the same home, in the same circumstances, attend the same place of worship, yet one is saved and one is not.

So the question at once arises: Why this difference? And in dealing with the work of the Holy Spirit, of necessity we have to face that problem. It is one of the most mysterious problems in connection with the Christian life, the Christian faith, but that is no reason for avoiding it. It is a very real problem, but it is a fact and it is our business to examine it – as long as we do so, of course, carefully; as long as we do so with wisdom; and as long as we do so with a desire to know the truth, and not in order to confirm our own prejudices. Many answers have been given to this question, many solutions have been put forward to explain the astounding fact that though the same general call is made to all, there is nevertheless this division in the response.

Now it seems to me that it is of value to us to look at some of the historical answers that have been given to this question. There is an answer which generally goes by the name of the *Pelagian* answer. Pelagius happened to be a man who was brought up in Britain. I do not say that because I am proud of him, but as a fact! He was the man with whom the great St Augustine dealt so effectively. The only reason I personally have for being grateful to Pelagius is that he caused Augustine to write much in correction of his erroneous teaching!

For Pelagius's teaching was that there is no such thing as original sin. The Pelagian view holds that men and women are born and live in a kind of neutral state, that every person has a perfect free will, and is able to choose good or evil, and can believe God's word or reject it. The Holy Spirit does nothing within the person at all. The only work of the Holy Spirit, according to that view, is that He did produce the Scriptures by using men, but having done that, He does nothing further: so anyone reading the Scriptures may decide to agree with it or to reject it. That is the view of Pelagius, and he has many followers even at this present time, in the Church, alas, as well as outside.

Then there were others who were sometimes called *semi-Pelagians*, because they were not as extreme as that. They said that the Holy Spirit helps men and women, but the love originates in the people themselves. People desire to know God, they want to know truth, and because of that, the Holy Spirit comes to them and helps them. On this view, Pelagius went too far. Men and women cannot do it all by themselves, they do need assistance; and if they show this desire, then the Holy Spirit will assist them. That is called semi-Pelagianism, and you see the reason for giving it that designation – it teaches a kind of co-operative grace. All the Holy Spirit does is co-operate with us, and graciously help us to arrive at a knowledge of truth and salvation.

Then next – I am taking the theories in the order in which they appear in history, with slight variation, perhaps, at this point – there is what is generally known as *Arminianism*. It originated with a man called Arminius, who was a Dutchman living at the beginning of the seventeenth century. Arminius taught, as did one of his great followers, John Wesley, that human beings are totally depraved, and therefore are quite hopeless when left to themselves. But what Arminians then go on to teach is that the Holy Spirit gives a sufficient measure of grace to everybody born into this life to accept and to believe the gospel. Therefore, of course, what people have to do is to co-operate with that.

'Well then,' someone may say, 'if it is given to all, why is it that only some believe and others do not?'

'Ah,' is the reply, 'the explanation is that the ability to believe is given to all by the Holy Spirit, but it is only some who choose to use it, while the others do not.'

That is the Arminian teaching and again, you see, there is a kind of co-operation, but put rather differently. The semi-Pelagian says that it is man who desires it first and the Holy Spirit comes and helps him. But this Arminian view says that man desires nothing, he is dead in trespasses and sins, totally depraved, but the grace of God comes, in the Spirit, and gives the ability to all to desire, to believe and to accept. But it all depends upon whether or not men and women co-operate with the Spirit. If they do, they will be saved; if they do not, they will be lost. And that is virtually the view that was taught by John Wesley and by all who have followed him ever since.

Now the *Lutheran* view is different, and I put it here because, though it came before the Arminian teaching, it approximates more closely to what is commonly called the *Reformed* view. The Lutheran view is, again, that men and women are totally depraved, that they are dead in trespasses and in sins, that in and of themselves they can do nothing at all, but that grace is again operating in all men and women in the early stages of regeneration. Why, then, are some saved and some lost? Well, for this reason, say the Lutherans – that men and women have the capacity to resist the operation of God's grace. If they resist it they remain unbelievers and stand condemned. If they do not resist it, they will be saved by it. You see the difference between that and Arminianism? Arminianism says that people must co-operate. The Lutheran does not say that; he says that they are incapable of co-operating positively, but they are capable of resisting negatively. That is the historic Lutheran teaching with regard to this matter, and it is what is taught by Lutherans in all parts of the world to the extent that they are indeed orthodox Lutherans.

So there we have four views that have been put forward in history. The fifth and last is what is called the *Reformed* view and that is the view of this matter which is taught in the Thirty-nine Articles of the Church of England. Let us be careful to note that. It is taught plainly and explicitly in the Thirty-nine Articles, in the Westminster Confession of Faith and in the great historic Reformed Confessions of the continental churches, such as the Heidelberg Confession, the Dutch or Belgic, and the other classic statements of Reformed doctrine. Again, the teaching here is that men and women are totally depraved, utterly helpless and incapable. How is it, then, that one is saved and the other is not? The answer is that it is due to the special work of the Holy Spirit in the saving. This view says that the Holy Spirit of God does a work in those who are saved which He does not do in those who are not saved. It talks about *prevenient grace*: a grace that goes before and does its work in men and women, enabling them to believe. In other words, it amounts, ultimately, to the doctrine of the absolute necessity of regeneration before anything else can happen at all.

There, then, are some of the classic attempts which have been made to deal with this problem with which we are all familiar. 'Many are called, few are chosen.' The only comment I would make is that the theory we espouse, and are prepared to contend for, will be determined by our view of what happened to humanity in the fall, and by our view of the condition of men and women in sin, as the result of the fall. Now when we dealt with those doctrines,[1] of necessity I committed myself to the Reformed view.

I would add that here, more perhaps than anywhere else in the consideration of doctrines, it is vital that we should all realise that there is a limit to our understanding, and that we must come to the Scriptures with open minds and not be led over much by our own ideas and by our own philosophy. We must come to the word of God and we must ask certain questions: Why do I believe this? Would man ever have invented such a doctrine? Is it or is it not taught in the Scripture? Fortunately we are not saved by our understanding of these things. I

---

1. See Volume 1, *God the Father, God the Son*, chapters 16–18.

thank God for that, because I am quite sure that there will be Pelagians in heaven and I am quite sure there will be Arminians and Lutherans as well. By the grace of God, men and women, who may be muddled in their thinking and in their understanding of the mechanism of salvation, can still be saved. What a wonderful thing that is! If we were saved by our understanding, some people would have an advantage over others because they have greater intellect, greater ability. We are not saved by that.

'Well then,' says someone, 'if we are not saved by our understanding of these matters, why bother with them?'

Ah! Now that, I think, is a foolish question. We 'bother', to use the term, because the Scripture has a great deal to say on the subject. Not only that. All children of God should be anxious to understand as far as they can. I will go even further. If I were to give my own experience, I should have to put it like this: I know of nothing that is so strengthening to faith, nothing which so builds up my assurance, nothing which gives me such certainty about the blessed hope for which I am destined, as the understanding of Christian doctrine, the understanding of the way, yes, the mechanism of salvation. And that is why I personally 'bother' with it. It is not an intellectual interest, although it is entrancingly interesting from the standpoint of intellect, but I confess frankly that I am concerned about it primarily for a most practical reason: it is so comforting, so strengthening, so upbuilding.

In other words, you will find, as I have indicated many times before, that the people who are 'carried about with every wind of doctrine' (Eph. 4:14), are the people who have been too lazy to study doctrine. They say, 'I am not interested in doctrine,' and that is precisely why they believe a wrong doctrine. They have no method of discriminating; they have no tests by which they can evaluate teachings. 'The only thing that matters,' they say, 'is that I am saved,' and then you will find them running after the latest cult or heresy. So we consider these things, though they are not essential to salvation, because in the actual living and practical details of the Christian life they are of very great importance indeed.

Having said that, then, let me announce that my conclusion, therefore, at this point is that the Holy Spirit does a special work in those who are going to be saved which He does not do in those who will remain lost.

Then, I come to another question, which in a sense is still more baffling and perplexing. That was why I told you at the beginning that I could quote to you the words of Paul: 'Howbeit we speak wisdom among them that are perfect'; that is my assessment of your standing and of your ability, and of your desire to know the truth. I do not know whether you realise it, but I am paying you a great compliment! The next question, therefore, which we go on to consider is this: If there is this special work which is done in the souls of those who are to be saved, in what order does the Holy Spirit do that?

Have you ever thought of that? Now the great authorities, the great doctors of the Church, the great theologians of the centuries, those saintly men of God, have written volumes on this and they have disputed about what they called the *ordo salutis* – the *order of salvation*. I confess frankly again that I find it a most entrancing theme, and I have spent a great deal of my time in preparing this lecture, in considering this great question. I find it difficult to understand people who have to resort to crossword puzzles and things like that in order to find a fascinating matter of arrangement! Think of this: What are the steps and the stages? How does the Holy Spirit proceed to do this work? And the answers that have been given have been almost endless.

Now the Scripture itself does not give us any precise order. In a way, the nearest approach is Romans 8:28–30, where we read: 'We know that all things work together for good to them that love God, to them who are the called according to his purpose' – notice – 'For whom he did foreknow, he also did predestinate to be conformed to the image of his Son, that he might be the firstborn among many brethren. Moreover whom he did predestinate' – Paul is going on with it now – 'them he also called: and whom he called, them he also justified; and whom he justified, them he also glorified.'

That is the order, is it not? Predestined, called, justified and glorified, too. Yes, it is an order but, unfortunately, it is not a complete list. The Apostle was not interested there in giving us a complete list, he had a special object in view. He was interested in this glorification and wanted to guarantee that, so he just put in the essential steps. You notice he does not mention sanctification at all.

That is one passage; there is one other, and the Lutherans are very fond of using this. In Acts 26 you will find a suggested order in the commission that was given by the Lord Jesus Christ to the apostle Paul on the road to Damascus: 'Delivering thee from the people, and from the Gentiles, unto whom now I send thee' – what for? – 'to open their eyes, and to turn them from darkness to light, and from the power of Satan unto God, that they may receive forgiveness of sins, and inheritance among them which are sanctified by faith that is in me' (Acts 26:17–18). But, again, that is obviously not a complete and a perfect list. It does not deal with it sufficiently *in extenso*. There is a suggested order, but it does not go far enough.

Now as I have suggested, it is almost impossible to find two people who agree about this question of the order of salvation. What is very interesting is that even people who belong to the five different schools I mentioned earlier do not agree among themselves. You can consult the Reformed authorities and you will find that scarcely two of them will put all these items in precisely the same order. So here again, we cannot arrive at precision. Why not? What is the difficulty? Well, of course, the difficulty is due to the fact that it depends entirely upon how you approach the question.

Now there are, at any rate, two main ways in which you can approach it. You can think of this order of salvation in the mind of God: God in His holiness looking down upon men and women in sin as the result of the fall, and thinking out the plan of salvation. There must have been an order. You can think of that, if you like as the kind of logical order in the mind of the Eternal. Then another obvious approach, and it is almost the exact opposite, is to think of these things in a temporal manner, in the way in which they happen in time and in experience.

Or you can think of this order in a purely objective way. Instead of thinking of what is happening to you experientially, you can say, 'Now what are the things that must happen to men or women before they can be saved, and in what order are they likely to take place?' That is an objective view. And then you can take the subjective view, and say, 'All I know is that in practice this is the way in which it happens.' Now our view of this matter will, once more, depend upon our view of the fall, and the condition of men and women in sin as the result of the fall. And I would suggest that it would be an interesting exercise for you to work out your order of salvation according to that doctrine. It would be very interesting to see the result!

Once more I say that this is not something which is essential to salvation. None of us will be saved because we put these things in the right order, in the correct sequence. But, again, though it is not essential to salvation, it is indeed something which is of great profit and value, and a wonderful spiritual exercise.

Now let me, therefore, suggest to you certain possible orders. I shall not keep of necessity to any one of them, but if you look at it from the logical and objective standpoint you might very well take them like this. You might say that the first and the fundamental thing is union with Christ, that we are ultimately saved by union with Christ, so you start with that. Then, because of that, you put justification next, and then, because of that, you follow with regeneration. Out of that comes faith, and out of that adoption. Then you can put conversion, which includes repentance and a turning away, and a believing, then sanctification, and then perseverance.

If, on the other hand, you are more anxious to stress the subjective element and still try to keep some theological order, you might put it like this: You might start with what is called 'effectual calling', that which makes the offer, the call, effectual in men and women. That is the first thing. Then you could go on to regeneration, and then to faith, followed by justification, then union with Christ, then repentance and conversion, then adoption, then sanctification, and then perseverance.

But if you were anxious to take it in a purely subjective and experiential manner, you might very well put it like this: conviction, conversion, faith, justification, regeneration, adoption, sanctification, union and perseverance. However, though I suggest that those would be the three main classifications, you can vary the positions of individual items almost endlessly. And I repeat that it is of great value as a spiritual exercise.

But let me end by saying this: the danger in doing all this is to become too chronological. The danger is to bring in the time element with too great a prominence and to say that each one of these must follow the other in a very rigid, mechanical time sequence. Now that is the danger, indeed, it is the thing that always leads to error, because ultimately God's action is outside time, and that is where our difficulty comes in. We tend to think of everything as it occurs to us, as we experience it in time. But the fact that we experience things in time, in a given order, does not of necessity mean that that is the order in which they have happened.

Let me give you an illustration. The first evidence we have of the fact that a child is born, is that it may cry or scream, but we do not say that, because of that, screaming comes first. Not at all. Birth is essential before the child can scream. In other words, we tend to pay attention to the *evidence* of life, and to say that that comes before life, but obviously it does not. There is very little doubt in my mind that some of these things happen to us at exactly the same time, and that, therefore, from the standpoint of time, you must not say that one is prior to the other. And yet obviously you cannot speak about these things without giving them a certain order.

I have been making a number of confessions in this lecture; let me make still another! I was a bit concerned as to whether or not I should say everything I have said tonight. I tested this idea on my wife and she said to me, 'You know, if you do that you will cause confusion. It is difficult. It is a mystery.' I confess it was a late hour of the night and she confessed to being confused by it herself!

My reply is this: I agree that it is difficult, but, you see, the only alternative was that instead of taking you through all we have been considering, I should begin lecturing on the work of the Holy Spirit in the saved, and start by saying that first of all we consider this, and then we go on to that, and so on, without giving you my reasons.

But then, I imagine, somebody would have said, 'Surely the first thing is conviction, and surely you do not put regeneration before faith!' And that person would have become perplexed and would have said, 'Now, why did he start with that? Why did he put that second and the other third?'

So I have taken you through this consideration, this brief consideration of the order of salvation, in order to try to give you some justification for what I am doing. It seems to me to be very wrong that any man should just stand in a pulpit and speak to others and not explain as far as he can what he is doing and why he is going it. In other words, I am not a pope. I do not believe in popes, and I do not believe in making *ex cathedra* statements. It is the business of any man who tries to expound biblical truth and doctrine to justify what he is doing, and that is why I say it is important for us to consider this question of the order. And as we go on now to consider the various details in the order, I think you will realise that you have not been wasting your time, but that we are basing the order upon our understanding of what happened when man fell, the result of original sin, the condition of man in a fallen and lost condition. We cannot claim that one order is of necessity perfect rather than another, but, all the same, I think it is our business and our duty to see that our order of taking these things, as we come to consider them and to grasp them, conforms to the teaching of the Scriptures.

7

Effectual Calling

As we now proceed to consider in detail what exactly it is the Holy Spirit does to us in the application of redemption, I would remind you that I am not insisting that the order which I shall follow is of necessity the right one, and certainly not of necessity the chronological one.

'So how do you arrive at your order?' asks someone. My answer is that I mainly try to conceive of this work going on within us from the standpoint of God in eternity looking down upon men and women in sin. That is the way that appeals to me most of all; it is the way that I find most helpful. That is not to detract in any way from experience or the experiential standpoint. Some would emphasise that and would have their order according to experience, but I happen to be one of those people who is not content merely with experience. I want to know something about that experience; I want to know what I am experiencing and I want to know why I am experiencing it and how it has come about. It is the child who is content merely with enjoying the experience. If we are to grow in grace and to go forward and exercise our senses, as the author of the epistle to the Hebrews puts it (Heb. 5:14), then we must of necessity ask certain questions and be anxious to know how the things that have happened to us really have come to take place.

My approach therefore is this: there is the truth of the gospel, and we have seen already that it is a part of the work of the Holy Spirit to see that that truth is proclaimed to all and sundry. That is what we called the *general call* – a kind of universal offer of the gospel. Then we saw that though the external or general call comes to all, to those who will remain unsaved as well as to those who are saved, obviously some new distinction comes in, because some are saved by it. So the question we must now consider is: What is it that establishes the difference between the two groups?

And the way to answer that question, it seems to me, is to say that the call of the gospel, which has been given to all, is *effectual* only in some. Now there is a portion of Scripture which is a perfect illustration of this. The followers of Christ who were even described as 'disciples' were divided up into two groups. One group decided that they would never listen to Him again. They left Him and went home. And when He turned to the others and said, 'Will ye also go away?' Peter said, 'Lord, to whom shall we go? Thou hast the word of eternal life' (John 6:67–68). The one group disbelieved and went home, the others, who had heard exactly the same things, stayed with Him, wanted to hear more, and rejoiced in it. What makes the difference? It is that the word was effectual in the case of the saved in a way that it was not effectual in the case of the unsaved who refused it.

This, then, is something that is quite obvious. We can say that in addition to the external call there is this effectual call, and that what makes anybody a saved person and a true Christian is that the call of the gospel has come effectually. Let me give you some scriptures that establish that. The first, Romans 8:28–39, is a great statement of this very thing. 'We know,'says Paul, 'that all things work together for good to them that love God . . .' Not to everybody but *to them that love God*. Who are they? 'To them who are called according to his purpose,' and Paul goes on: 'For whom he did foreknow, he also did predestinate to be conformed to the image of his Son, that he might be the firstborn among many brethren. Moreover whom he did predestinate, them he also called: and whom he called, them he also justified: and whom he justified, them he also glorified.' The saved are described as those who are *called*. And they have been called in a way that the others have not. That is, therefore, a scriptural statement of this effectual call.

Then, another one is to be found in 1 Corinthians 1:2. It is a statement that you will find in other places as well: 'Unto the church of God which is at Corinth, to them that are sanctified in Christ Jesus, called to be saints . . .'. It is not simply that they are called saints, they are *called to be* saints. And then, in that same chapter, the Apostle repeats it. He says, 'We preach Christ crucified, unto the Jews a stumblingblock, and unto the Greeks foolishness' – then notice – 'but unto them which are called, both Jews and Greeks, Christ is the power of God, and the wisdom of God' (1 Cor. 1:23–24). Now there are people to whom the preaching of Christ is foolishness; they are the unsaved. But the saved he again describes as those who are *called*.

And let me give you one other example. Take that great statement made by the apostle Peter: 'But ye,' he says, referring to Christian believers, 'are a chosen generation, a royal priesthood, an holy nation, a peculiar people; that ye should shew forth the praises of him who hath called you out of darkness into his marvellous light' (1 Pet. 2:9– 10). God has called them out, and because they are the saved, He has called them effectually. The call of the gospel has gone to many others but they are not the people Peter is talking about. He is talking about these people who correspond to Israel after the flesh in the Old Testament. He applies to them the very terminology that was applied to the Children of Israel, just as the Ten Commandments and the moral law were given to them. Peter uses the same words – they are the called, the 'Israel of God', called to show forth His praises. Now it is obvious therefore that in these people the call has been effectual; that is the teaching of these scriptures.

But there is another argument which states this perfectly. What is the meaning of the term *church*? We are members of the Christian Church. But what is it – what does it mean? What is the connotation of the term? Well, the word church translates the Greek word, *ecclesia*; and the *ecclesia* means the 'called forth ones'. A church is a gathering of people who have been called forth, called out, separated out as the result of this call. As Peter puts it: 'Who hath called you out of darkness into his marvellous light'. That is the meaning of this term *church*. And therefore that very word in and of itself is sufficient to establish the statement that there obviously is such a thing as an effectual call, because the same message has gone to others but they have been called from the world into the Church.

What, then, is the difference between the external call and this call which has become effectual? And the answer must be that this call is an internal, a spiritual call. It is not merely something that comes to a person from the outside – it does that, of course, but in addition to that external call which comes to all, there is an internal call which comes to those who are going to be Christians, and it is an effectual call. The contrast, therefore, is between external, and internal and spiritual.

Now I want to go even further and again give you scriptural proofs of the fact that there is such an internal and spiritual call. We have only looked at it in general in the scriptures that I have given you so far, they are simply designations, descriptions. So I want to give you scriptures which specifically state that this is something that happens within; and first of all I go to the sixth chapter of John's Gospel. Incidentally, this particular doctrine is taught much more clearly, if I may use such a comparison, by John than it is by the apostle Paul. People sometimes tend to think that this is a doctrine conjured up only in Paul's mind, but it is much more evident in John's Gospel and particularly in this great sixth chapter.

Here, in verse 45, is one statement of it: 'It is written in the prophets, And they shall be all taught of God.' That is it; God gave the prophet this information and he recorded it. There will be certain people who shall be taught by God Himself, not taught by men only but in addition to that taught by God, taught by the Spirit. Some internal work is going to take place. 'Every man, therefore, that hath heard, and hath learned of the Father, cometh unto me' (v. 45). You see the people who come to Christ are those who have been taught of God, who have learned of the Father by the Spirit, and they alone. Now that is a crucial statement. But our Lord repeats it later on in verses 63–65. His listeners have stumbled at His words and He says to them, 'It is the spirit that quickeneth; the flesh profiteth nothing: the words that I speak unto you, they are Spirit and they are life. But,' He says, 'there are some of you that believe not.' And John adds, 'For Jesus knew from the beginning who they were that believed not, and who should betray him.' They had responded to the external call and thought that they were Christians. Here it becomes evident that they were not; they had never been taught of God. They had held on to the shell, the external word, and they had not got the Spirit. John continues, 'And he said, Therefore said I unto you, that no man can come unto me, except it were given unto him of my Father.' And the Father had not given it to these people so they did not come and they went home. But He had given it to the others, so they remained and they rejoiced in it. That is a proof that there is this spiritual, this internal call. And that is what makes the call effectual.

Or take another statement. It is from Ephesians 1:17. Paul prays for the Ephesians, 'That the God of our Lord Jesus Christ, the Father of glory, may give unto you the spirit of wisdom and revelation in the knowledge of him.' In other words, we cannot have knowledge of Him unless He gives us the Spirit of wisdom and of revelation – they are absolutely essential. And that was why Paul prayed that they might have the Spirit, it was in order that they might grow increasingly in this knowledge of God. Without this work of the Spirit we cannot attain unto such knowledge. Or again, in Ephesians 2:8, we read, 'For by grace are ye saved through faith; and that not of yourselves: it is the gift of God.' And then, of course, there is Philippians 2:12–13, where Paul says the same thing: 'Work out your own salvation with fear and trembling. For it is God which worketh in you both to will and to do . . .' God does an internal work and it is as the result of that that we are enabled 'to will and to do of his good pleasure'.

In 1 Thessalonians 1:5, Paul makes a most important statement in this connection: 'For our Gospel came not unto you in word only, but also in power, and in the Holy Ghost, and in much assurance.' Now if you read that epistle, especially the first two chapters, you will find that the Apostle goes on repeating that statement in different ways. He says that they received the word that came to them 'not as the word of men, but as it is in truth, the word of God' (1 Thess. 2:13). But what did he mean when he said 'For our gospel came not unto you in word only'? It did come in words, of course, the Apostle was speaking, but that was not the thing that had turned those idolatrous Thessalonians into saints. What was it, then? It was that it had come 'in power, and in the Holy Ghost, and in much assurance'. It is this internal work that turns people from sinners into saints; this is preaching in demonstration of the Spirit and of power.

And, indeed, the Apostle makes a very similar statement in 2 Timothy 2:25. Here he is telling the young Timothy how to handle certain people who were opposing him. 'In meekness,' he says, 'instructing those that oppose themselves; if God peradventure will give them repentance to the acknowledging of the truth.' Timothy, says Paul, I want you to instruct these people who are opposing you and my reason for doing so is this: it is not to suggest to you that you by your arguments or logic can convince them. If God does not do this work in them, they will never acknowledge the truth, but if God does work, they will acknowledge it. Indeed there is a statement that we can find more than once in the Gospels and which we have already quoted, which really says it all in one phrase: 'Many are called, but few are chosen' (Matt. 22:14). Take that especially in its context of the wedding feast. 'Many are called' – that is the external call – 'but few are chosen' – that is the effectual call.

So then, the next step which we take is this: we have seen that the Scripture teaches that the saved are the effectually called and that they are effectually called because of the work that goes on within them.

'But,' someone may say, 'why all this?' And the answer is that this is absolutely essential. Without this work within, no one would ever become a Christian; it is an utter necessity. Let me give you my proof for that. 'For they that are after the flesh do mind the things of the flesh; but they that are after the Spirit the things of the Spirit' (Rom. 8:5). Now the Revised Standard Version puts it like this: 'They that are after the flesh are interested in the things of the flesh and they that are after the Spirit, or in the Spirit, are interested in the things of the Spirit.' But the natural man or woman – those 'after the flesh' – are not interested in the things of the Spirit at all. They find them dull and boring and uninteresting. They regard them as a waste of time and they hate them. But they that are after the Spirit are interested in the things of the Spirit: 'For to be carnally minded is death; but to be spiritually minded is life and peace. Because' – and this is the final argument – 'the carnal mind is enmity against God' (vv. 6–7).

Now that is a very strong statement but it is true. Men and women, as they are by nature as the result of the fall, are at enmity against God. 'The carnal mind . . . is not subject to the law of God, neither indeed can be. So then they that are in the flesh cannot please God' (vv. 7–8). To me that is a final statement. Men and women by nature are opposed to God; they hate God and they are not interested in Him, neither are they interested in the things of God. From that statement of the Apostle I deduce that the internal work of the Spirit is an absolute necessity before anyone can possibly believe in the gospel of God and accept it and rejoice in it.

However, let us go on and consider other statements to the same effect. Take the famous statement in 1 Corinthians 2:14: 'But the natural man receiveth not the things of the Spirit of God: for they are foolishness unto him: neither can he know them, because they are spiritually discerned.' That is a categorical statement, but do not suddenly become a philosopher and say, 'Well, if that is true I do not understand this and that.' No, let us face the statements of Scripture. We are dealing with things beyond our understanding. We are dealing with the inscrutable purposes of God, and if we are going to be foolish enough to put up our understandings or our philosophy against these categorical statements, then we deserve to remain in darkness. We must not approach the Scripture with such a conceit of ourselves that we think we can understand everything – we cannot. 'Great is the mystery of godliness' (1 Tim. 3:16), and especially in this matter. But here is the statement that the natural man or woman not only does not receive it, but *cannot* receive it because these things are spiritually understood, judged and discerned.

Then there is the statement in 2 Corinthians 4:3–4: 'If our gospel be hid,' says Paul, and it is quite clear that the gospel is hid to certain people; they hear it like everybody else but they see nothing in it, they do not want it, they blaspheme it, they treat it with scorn. 'If our gospel be hid, it is hid to them that are lost.' And who are they? They are the people, 'In whom the god of this world' – the devil – 'hath blinded the minds of them which believe not,' lest they believe this glorious gospel. Could anything be plainer? They cannot believe because Satan has blinded their minds 'lest the light of the glorious gospel of Christ, who is the image of God, should shine unto them' (2 Cor. 4:4).

And then, finally, we find the statement in Ephesians 2:1: 'And you hath he quickened, who were dead in trespasses and sins' – dead! You cannot have anything stronger than that; that is their position spiritually. All these are statements to prove the absolute necessity of this internal work of the Spirit before the call – the external, general call of the gospel – can possibly be effectual.

So, then, what is this effectual, internal call that we are speaking about? Well, the most we can say about it is – and this must of necessity be true in the light of these scriptures – that it is the exercise of the power of the Holy Spirit in the soul. It is a direct operation of the Holy Spirit within us. It is immediate, it is spiritual, it is supernatural, miraculous. And what it does is to make a new mode of spiritual activity possible within us. Without this operation we are incapable of any true spiritual activity but as the result of this operation of the Holy Spirit upon us, we are rendered capable, for the first time, of spiritual activity and that is how this call now becomes effectual, that is what enables us to receive it.

Now this is very important and I want to emphasise the immediacy, the direct action. You see, what happens when the call comes to men and women effectually is not simply that the moral influence of the truth is exercised upon them. Some people have thought that; they have said that the gospel is preached and that the truth has a kind of general moral effect upon people. For instance, to take a human theme, a capable orator, a man wanting to persuade men and women to vote at an election for a given party, can put the case so well that he can exercise a moral influence upon his listeners. But it is not that. It is an operation of the Spirit upon the men and women themselves, in the depths. It is not merely that the Holy Spirit heightens our natural faculties and powers. it is more than that. It is the Spirit acting upon the soul from within and producing within us a new principle of spiritual action.

Now it must be that; it cannot be less than that. Because these things, says Paul, are all spiritual. And that is why the natural man does not understand them; and that is why, as I have often reminded you, we should never be surprised, or to the slightest extent disappointed or put out, when somebody brings us the argument that 'Christianity cannot be right because look at this great man and he doesn't believe it!' How often have you heard that argument! Someone says, 'You know, I cannot believe this, because if Christianity were true, it could not be possible that all these philosophers and scientists and all these great statesmen and other men do not believe it.'

In the light of these things, it is very natural and we can understand it perfectly well. The greatest natural intellect cannot receive this, he is 'a natural man'. And you need a spiritual faculty to receive the wonderful truth about the two natures in the one Person; the outstanding doctrine about the Trinity; the whole doctrine of the incarnation and the atonement, and so on. This is spiritual truth and to the natural person it is utter folly, it is foolishness, as Paul says. So when the Holy Spirit does enable us to believe it, it must be something beyond the heightening of our natural faculties. It is not simply that He brings the truth of His great moral suasion to us. No, no. We need some new faculty, some new principle, and that is the very work that He does. He implants within us this new spiritual principle, this principle of spiritual vitality and activity, and it is as the result of this that the general call of the gospel comes to us in an effectual manner.

So, then, let me again give you some scriptural proofs of this, because I do have them. You will find a practical illustration in Acts 16:14. Here is Paul, preaching in the town of Philippi. It is a very crucial passage for us because it was the Apostle's first visit to Europe and it was the first time that the Christian gospel was ever preached there. And do not forget that the first convert that the Christian gospel obtained in Europe was a woman called Lydia. She was the first person in the history of Europe to whom the call of the gospel came. How did it happen? We are told: 'A certain women named Lydia, a seller of purple, of the city of Thyatira, which worshipped God, heard us' – as many others did. The Apostle sat down and preached the word. There was the external call; he told them the gospel, the facts about the Lord Jesus Christ and the meaning of the facts. He said all this and we are told that among those listening was a woman called Lydia and that she heard this, as many have heard the gospel preached in a church or a chapel but have gone home in an unbelieving condition and have died as unbelievers. What was it, then, that made the difference with Lydia? Notice! '. . . whose heart the Lord opened, that she attended unto the things which were spoken of Paul.'

Now there it is perfectly. The word is preached, yes, but people do not pay attention to it. They look at one another while it is being preached, or they write in their books or they recite poetry to themselves or they are smiling at one another. In a sense they hear it, but they do not attend to it and you cannot be saved until you attend to it. What made Lydia attend? The answer is, *whose heart the Lord opened*. The Lord put something in her heart, this internal work, and the result of that was that she paid attention, and she saw the gospel and received it. The external call became the internal call, the general became effectual. She believed and was baptised and also her household. It is unmistakable – it was the Lord opening her heart that made the difference; but for that, she would never have believed.

And then, of course, we have a great theological statement in 1 Corinthians 2:10–15. Paul has just been saying that the princes of this world do not know God's secret wisdom, 'for had they known it, they would not have crucified the Lord of glory' (v. 8). The princes had heard about these things but they had not believed. But we believe, says Paul. Why? What is the difference between us and the princes of the world? It is this: 'But' – and there is the contrast – 'God hath revealed them unto us by his Spirit: for the Spirit searcheth all things, yea, the deep things of God. For what man knoweth the things of a man, save the spirit of man which is in him? Even so' – notice this – 'the things of God knoweth no man, but the Spirit of God.' No man can know them, it is the Spirit of God alone who can know them. 'Now we have received' – we the believers, the Christians – 'we have received, not the spirit of the world, but the spirit which is of God' – Why? – 'that we might know the things that are freely given to us of God. Which things also we speak, not in the words which man's wisdom teacheth, but which the Holy Ghost teacheth; comparing spiritual things with spiritual. But the natural man receiveth not the things of the Spirit of God: for they are foolishness unto him: neither can he know them, because they are spiritually discerned. But he that is spiritual' – and we are that, thank God – 'judgeth' – discerns, understands – 'all things, yet he himself is judged of no man. For who hath known the mind of the Lord, that he may instruct him? But we have the mind of Christ.'

And again I could refer you to Ephesians 1:18 and to 1 Thessalonians 1:5 once more, and to Philippians 2:13. In other words, there are proofs positive of this statement that it is the internal operation of the Holy Spirit upon the soul and the heart of men and women that brings them into a condition in which the call can become effectual. And when the Spirit does it, of course, it is absolutely certain, and because of that some people have used the term – which I do not like myself – *irresistible grace*. I do not like the term because it seems to give the impression that something has happened which has been hammering at a person's will and has knocked him down and bludgeoned him. But it is not that. It is that the Holy Spirit implants a principle within me which enables me, for the first time in my life, to discern and to apprehend something of this glorious, wondrous truth. He works upon my will. 'It is God that worketh in you both to will and to do.' He does not strike me; He does not beat me; He does not coerce me. No, thank God, what He does is operate upon my will so that I desire these things and rejoice in them and love them. He leads, He persuades, He acts upon my will in such a way that when He does, the call of the gospel is effectual, and it is certain, and it is sure. God's work never fails, and when God works in a man or woman, the work is effective.

So let me plead with you to consider those great passages of Scripture that I have put before you. Study them, pray over them, meditate with them. And as you do so, I think you will agree with me that there is only one thing to say and it is this:

> A debtor to mercy alone,
> Of covenant mercy I sing.
> Augustus Toplady

I am what I am by the grace of God and by that alone.

8

Regeneration – a New Disposition

In the last lecture, we saw that the Bible teaches that in the case of the saved there is an effectual call. That call comes in such a way that they accept it and we realised that this is the result of the work of the Holy Spirit in each person; it is a supernatural work which makes the call effectual in believers, in the saved. But of course even that does not bring to an end our consideration of this question.

We must now ask: What is it that the Holy Spirit does to enable those who become believers, who are saved in this way, to believe the truth? What exactly does He do in order to make the general call effectual? And the answer is, *regeneration*. Now you notice the order in which we are taking these doctrines. Earlier, we spent some time in considering the order of salvation, the order in which these things should be considered, and this seems to me to be the inevitable order: the general call; yes, but effectual in the saved. What makes it effectual? The Holy Spirit regenerates.

It is interesting to notice the relationship between this effectual call and regeneration. There is a sense, of course, in which regeneration precedes the effectual call.

'Well, why didn't you put them in that order?' someone may ask.

It was for this reason: having started with the general call we notice that there is this division into the two groups and it is clear that it must be effectual in some and not in others. When you ask what it is that makes it effectual, the answer is, regeneration. But looked at from the eternal standpoint, they come in the other order, and what happens is that the general call is responded to by the regenerate. In other words, the call becomes effectual because they are regenerate. That is largely a technical matter and yet I think it is good for us to have these things clearly in our minds.

Here, then, is this great central and vital doctrine of regeneration. There can be no question at all but that from our standpoint this doctrine, together with the doctrine of the atonement, is incomparably the most important doctrine of all, and there is a sense in which we simply cannot understand Christian doctrine and Christian truth without being clear about the doctrine of regeneration. And yet I would suggest that this doctrine is seriously and sadly neglected amongst us. Oh, I know that lip service is paid to it and that people talk very glibly and generally about being 'born again'. But to what extent do people study it? To what extent have we really looked into it and discovered what exactly it means?

No, there is undoubtedly a failure in this respect. Search the various hymnbooks and you will, I think, be struck by the paucity of good hymns on this theme of regeneration. We have seen that there is a defect in most hymnbooks with regard to strong doctrinal hymns on the Holy Spirit. The hymns we have are superficial, subjective and generally sentimental. And it seems to me that exactly the same thing can be said with regard to this great doctrine of regeneration. This is significant, I feel, because there is no doubt, as I hope to show you, that this doctrine is absolutely pivotal. Why is it that we persist in stopping with the idea of forgiveness only, and fail to realise that this other doctrine is as essential to us as the doctrine of the atonement leading to the forgiveness of our sins?

The only other general remark I would make is this: I have always been convinced, and I am now more convinced than ever, that people who are in trouble about these great doctrines of grace are generally so because they have never clearly grasped the significance and meaning of the doctrine of regeneration. If we only grasp this clearly, most of the other problems solve themselves. But of course, if we are not clear about this, if we do not realise exactly what happens to us in regeneration, then it is but natural that we should be in difficulties about the effectual call and many other subjects.

Let us, therefore, approach our subject by first of all simply looking at the various terms that the Bible itself uses with regard to this great event that the Holy Spirit produces within us. First, there is the word *regeneration* itself. In Titus 3:5, the apostle Paul speaks about 'the washing of regeneration'. That is actually the only instance in which the word 'regeneration' is used in the New Testament to describe this great, climactic event in the history of the saved soul.

Then there is a second group of terms which mean *to beget* or *to beget again, to bear* or *to give birth*; and there are quite a number of these. In John 1:13, for instance, in the prologue to this Gospel, we read, 'Which were born, not of blood, nor of the will of the flesh, nor of the will of man, but of God.' Then there are all those instances in our Lord's conversation with Nicodemus, in John 3:3, 4, 5, 6, 7 and 8. And you have the same word in several passages in the first epistle of John: 1 John 2:29, 3:9, 4:7, 5:1. 'Born of God' is a great statement in 1 John.

Next, there is another word which rather conveys the suggestion of *bringing forth* or *begetting*. This is found in James 1:18, which reads, 'Of his own will begat he us with the word of truth.' Then there is a large group of words which carry the meaning of *creating*. We read in Ephesians 2:10, 'For we are his workmanship, created in Christ Jesus. . . .' It is also in 2 Corinthians 5:17: 'If any man be in Christ, he is a new creature' – a new creation. In Galatians 6:15 we read, 'For neither circumcision availeth any thing, nor uncircumcision, but a new creature,' or a new creation; and again in Ephesians 4:24: 'And that ye put on the new man, which after God is created in righteousness and true holiness.' Again, that is a term used to describe this amazing event in the history of the soul: it is a new creation.

And finally there is the word *to quicken*. Now the example of this is in Ephesians 2:5, where we read, 'Even when we were dead in sins, hath quickened us together with Christ (by grace ye are saved).' You may be surprised that I do not say Ephesians 2:1 which reads, 'And you hath he quickened, who were dead in trespasses and sins', but the expression about quickening is not there in the original, but has simply been supplied by the translators for the sake of understanding, and rightly so. And then there is just one other example of that word, and it is in Colossians 2:13, 'And you, being dead in your sins and the uncircumcision of your flesh, hath he quickened together with him, having forgiven you all trespasses.' It is the parallel, of course, to the statement in Ephesians 2:5, something that we constantly find with these two epistles.

Those, then, are the actual terms which are used in the Scriptures to denote and to convey the teaching concerning this great climactic change. So, what do we mean by regeneration? Now if you read the history of the use of this term in the history of doctrine or of the Church, you will find great confusion, because it is a term that has been used loosely and even individual writers are not consistent in their use of it. Sometimes it has been used in a very restricted sense, but sometimes in a wide sense to include almost everything that happens to the believer – justification and sanctification as well as regeneration – and this is the practice, for instance, in Roman Catholic writers.

So as we consider what we mean by regeneration, the one important thing, it seems to me, is that we must differentiate it from conversion. And yet how frequently they are confused. But regeneration is not conversion and for this reason: conversion is something that we do whereas regeneration, as I shall show you, is something that is done to us by God. Conversion means a turning away from one thing to another in practice, but that is not the meaning of regeneration. We can put it like this: when people convert themselves or turn, they are giving proof of the fact that they are regenerate. Conversion is something that follows upon regeneration. The change takes place in the outward life and living of men and women because this great change has first of all taken place within them.

You can look at it like this: there is all the difference between planting the seed and the result of the planting of that seed. Now regeneration means the planting of the seed of life and obviously that must be differentiated from what results or eventuates from that. There is a difference between generation and birth. Generation takes place a long time before the birth takes place. Generation is one act. It leads subsequently, after certain processes have been going on, to the actual process of birth. So it is good to hold the two things separately in our minds, and remember that when we are talking about regeneration, we are talking about generation, not the actual bringing forth, the birth.

Now the effectual call comes in in the actual birth, and that is what gives a proof of the fact that men and women are alive. The call is effectual: they believe. Yes, but that means that the process of generation, the implanting of the seed of life, must have already taken place. I find it helpful to draw that kind of distinction because it will help us to differentiate not only between regeneration and conversion, but between regeneration and adoption. For again, people often confuse adoption into sonship with regeneration, and yet, clearly and patently, they are two different things, as we shall see.

'So then, we define regeneration as the implanting of new life in the soul. That is it in its essence. If you like a definition which is a little more amplified, consider this: it is the act of God by which a principle

of new life is implanted in a man or woman with the result that the
governing disposition of the soul is made holy. And then the actual
birth is that which gives evidence of the first exercise of this disposition.

Having put that to you as a precise definition, let us go on to consider
the essential nature of what takes place when we are regenerated. This
is obviously of very great importance and therefore we must start
with certain negatives so that we may be quite clear as to what regeneration does not mean and what it does not represent.

The first thing we must say, negatively, is that regeneration does
not mean that a change takes place in the substance of human nature,
and the important word there is *substance*. The doctrine of regeneration does not teach that the substance, or the raw material, of what
constitutes human nature, whatever it may be, is changed.

Or we can put it like this: we must not think that some actual, sub-
stantial physical seed or germ of life is introduced. Regeneration is not
a kind of injection or infusion of actual physical substance into us. It
is not anything physical, it is a spiritual change.

Thirdly, we must not think that it means that there is a complete
change of the whole of human nature. The regenerate person does not
become something entirely different. It does not mean that (and we
shall see as we go on with these doctrines why all these negatives are
important). In the same way, it does not mean that man becomes
divine or that he becomes God.

'Ah, but,' says someone, 'are we not partakers of the divine
nature?'

Yes, but not in the sense that we suddenly become divine. We do
not become like the Lord Jesus Christ with two natures – human and
divine. We must be very careful to exclude that.

Another negative is that regeneration does not mean addition to or
subtraction from the faculties or the essence of the soul. Now some
people have thought that – and every one of these negatives is put in
to safeguard against things that have been thought and said from time
to time about regeneration. The five faculties of the soul are mind,
memory, affection, the will and conscience and some people seem to
think that what happens in regeneration is that an additional faculty
is put in or that, somehow or another, one or more of the other faculties is taken out or is changed. But that is not the biblical doctrine of
regeneration.

And my last negative is that regeneration does not just mean moral
reformation. Again, some people have thought that. They have

thought that all that happens in regeneration is that people's wills are changed and that, because of this, they reform themselves and live a better life. But that is nothing but moral reformation; it is not regeneration.

Let us, then, come to the positive. What is regeneration? It is, let me repeat, the implanting of a principle of new spiritual life and a radical change in the governing disposition of the soul. Let me explain what I mean by that. The important thing to grasp is the whole idea of *disposition*. In addition to the faculties of our souls, there is something at the back of them which governs them all and that is what we refer to as our disposition. Take two men. They have the same faculties, as regards their abilities there may be nothing to choose between them, but one lives a good life, one lives a bad life. What makes the difference? The answer is that the good man has a good disposition and this good disposition, this thing which is behind the faculties and governs them and uses them, urges him to use his faculties in the direction of goodness. The other man has an evil disposition, so he urges the same faculties in an entirely different direction. That is what one means by disposition.

When you come to think of it, and when you analyse yourself, your life and your whole conduct and behaviour, and that of other people, you will see at once that these dispositions are, of course, of tremendous importance. They are that condition, if you like, which determines what we do and what we are. Let me give you some other illustrations. Take people who have different interests and abilities. Take two people who are more or less opposite; one who is artistic and another who is scientific. What is the difference between them? Well, you cannot say that it is merely a difference in intellectual power, nor is it a difference in the faculties of their souls. No, but there is in every person a disposition which seems to determine the kind of person he or she is. It is this that directs the faculties and the abilities so that one person is artistic and the other scientific, and so on. Now I am making this point to show that what happens in regeneration is that God so operates upon us in the Holy Spirit that this fundamental disposition of ours is changed. He put a holy principle, a seed of new spiritual life, into this disposition that determines what I am and how I behave and how I use and employ my faculties.

Let me give you one great illustration to show what I mean. Take the case of the apostle Paul. Look at him as Saul of Tarsus. There is no question about his ability, nor about his understanding, nor about his will power. There is no question about his memory. His faculties are there and are clear and outstanding; he has always been a remarkable man. But there he is, persecuting the Church, regarding the Son of God as a blasphemer, and he goes down to Damascus, 'breathing out threatenings and slaughter', using all his powers to exterminate the Christian Church. But look at him later, preaching the gospel as it has never been preached before or since, with the same powers, the same abilities, the same personality, the same everything, but moving in exactly the opposite direction. What has changed? It is not the faculties of Paul's soul – they are still the same: the same vehemence, the same logic, the same thoroughness, the same readiness to risk all, out and out, he is the same man, obviously. And yet the whole direction, the whole bent, the whole outlook has changed. He is a different man. What has happened to him? He has a new disposition.

Now, I am emphasising this for this good reason: it is only by understanding this that we are able to understand the difference between regeneration and a psychological change and process. You see, when men and women are regenerated, they do not become all the same, like postage stamps. But when they become the victims of a psychological movement they tend to become identical – a very important distinction. When people are regenerated, the particular gifts which make them the men and women they are always remain. Paul, as I reminded you, was essentially the same man when he preached the gospel as he was when he denounced and persecuted it. I mean by that that he was the same individual and did things in the same way. We are not all meant to be identical as Christians. We are not all meant to speak and to preach and to pray in the same way. The gospel does not make that kind of change, and if you think of regeneration as doing that, then you have a false doctrine of regeneration. What it does is to deal with and to change this disposition that is at the back of everything; this fundamental something that determines direction and way and manner. It is vital that we realise that the change in regeneration takes place in the disposition.

Then, secondly, because of the power of the disposition in us, it therefore follows of necessity that this change is going to affect the whole person. Does anybody think that I am contradicting one of my negatives? I have maintained that the whole person is not entirely changed – am I now saying the opposite? I hold to my negative, but I do say that, *in principle*, because of the change in the disposition, the whole person is affected. The way I use my mind will be affected, the operation of my emotions will be affected, and so will my will, because, by definition, the disposition is at the back of all those and gives direction to them. So when this disposition of mine is changed, then I am like a person with a new mind. Before, I was not interested in the gospel; now I am very interested in it. Before, I could not understand it; now I do.

But the change in my disposition does not mean that I have a greater intellect now than I had before! No, I have exactly the same intellect, the same mind. But, because the disposition governing it is changed, my mind is operating in a different realm and in a different way and it seems to be a new mind. And it is exactly the same with the feelings. A man who used to hate the gospel, now loves it. A woman who hated the Lord Jesus Christ, now loves Him. And likewise with the will: the will resisted, it was obstinate and rebellious; but now it desires, it is anxious, it is concerned about the gospel.

The next thing we say is that it is a change which is instantaneous. Now you see the importance of differentiating between generation and coming to birth? Generation, by definition, is always an instantaneous act. There is a moment, a flash, in which the germ of life enters, impregnates; that is one instantaneous action. In other words, there are no intermediate stages in regeneration. Life is either implanted or it is not; it cannot be partly implanted. It is not gradual. Now, again, I do want to emphasise this point. When I say that it is instantaneous, I am not referring to our consciousness of it, but to the thing itself, as it is done by God. The consciousness, of course, comes into the realm of time, whereas this act of germination is timeless, and that is why it is immediate.

So the next thing – and this again is most important – is that generation, the implanting of this seed of life and the change of the disposition, happens in the subconscious, or, if you prefer it, in the unconscious. Our Lord explained that fully to Nicodemus (John 3). It is a secret, an inscrutable operation, that cannot be directly perceived by us; indeed, we cannot even fully understand it. The first thing we know about it is that it has happened, because we are conscious of something different, but that means that we do not understand it and that we really cannot arrive at its secret.

Now, let me give you the authority for this. Nicodemus, like all of us, was trying to understand it. Our Lord said to him, 'Except a man be born again, he cannot see the kingdom of God' (John 3:3). 'My dear Nicodemus,' He said in effect, 'you are trying to understand the difference between yourself and Me and what I am doing. Stop at once! It is not a question of changing, or of understanding, this or that particular thing, it is the governing disposition of your life that must be changed; you must be born again. it is something at the back of all these faculties that you are trying to use.'

'But,' Nicodemus said, 'How can a man be born when he is old? Can he enter the second time into his mother's womb, and be born?' (John 3:4). He wanted to understand, and our Lord kept on giving the same reply, and Nicodemus continued to argue.

Eventually our Lord put it to him like this: 'The wind bloweth where it listeth . . .' There is something sovereign about it. You do not know when it is going to come and go, it decides its own time. You do not know where it starts and where it ends. 'The wind bloweth where it listeth, and thou hearest the sound thereof' – you are aware that it is happening – 'but canst not tell whence it cometh, and whither it goeth' (John 3:8). You do not see it; you can hear it, you can see things waving in the breeze, but you do not understand it. There is a mystery about the wind, something inscrutable. You cannot fathom it or grasp it with your understanding, but you see the results. 'So' – like that – 'is every one that is born of the Spirit' (v. 8).

Now there are some people who completely miss this because they would translate the wind in verse 8 as 'the Spirit bloweth' – the Holy Spirit. But patently it does not mean that, it cannot mean that, because our Lord is using an illustration. He is talking about the wind, the gale, if you like, not the Holy Spirit, nor any other spirit. '[It] bloweth where it listeth, and thou hearest the sound thereof' – you cannot see it, but you see the effects and the results – 'so is every-one that is born of the Spirit.' There is the essential nature of this great change.

My fourth point is that regeneration is obviously, therefore, something which is done by God. It is a creative act of God in which men and women are entirely passive and contribute nothing, nothing whatsoever. We read in John 1:13, 'Which were born' – you do not give birth to yourself – 'not of blood, nor of the will of the flesh, nor of the will of man but of God' – entirely. God implants this principle, this seed of spiritual life. And again, of course, there are the words our Lord spoke to Nicodemus, 'Except a man be born of water and of the Spirit, he cannot enter into the kingdom of God. That which is born of the flesh is flesh' – and it cannot do anything about it – 'and that which is born of the Spirit is spirit' (John 3:5–6). In other words, the terms are that we are *born again*. It is something that happens to us; we are begotten, we do not beget ourselves, we cannot generate ourselves. It is entirely the work of God in us and upon us.

We have not yet finished our consideration of this great and pivotal and central doctrine, but I do trust that, at this point, the great thought is clear in our minds and in our understanding, that it is there, in the disposition, that God operates, and it is God through the Holy Spirit who does it. We are born of the Spirit.

Now I hesitate to use the illustration, but you remember that our Lord and Saviour Jesus Christ was born of the virgin Mary but He was conceived of the Holy Ghost. Something comparable, similar to that – not the same thing, let me be clear about that – seems to happen here. This principle of spiritual life, this change, therefore, in the disposition, is something that is done by the Holy Spirit of God. Human nature is not entirely changed by it but because the disposition is changed the whole man or woman is like a new creation. In every respect they are different people because this fundamental thing that governs all else has been changed in them.

The faculties, however, remain as before. Never try to be somebody else, be yourself. God wants you to be yourself. He has made you as He has made you, and you can best glorify Him by being yourself. Beware always of Christian people who always talk in the same way and are the same in most respects, that is more likely to be psychological than spiritual. The man or woman, each individual, remains what he or she was, and thus you have the glorious variety in the apostles and in the Christian Church throughout the centuries. All together testify to the same Saviour and the same grace, the same regeneration, the same change in the disposition, but revealed according to the gifts and faculties, the propensities and powers that God has given to each person.

What a wonderful salvation, what a glorious way of redemption! Oh, I like a word which is used by the author of the epistle to the Hebrews in the second chapter. It describes and defines perfectly what I am trying to say. Talking about this great salvation, the author says of God, 'For it *became* him' – it was like Him, it was His way of doing it – '. . . in bringing many sons unto glory, to make the captain of their salvation perfect through suffering' (Heb. 2:10) – it became Him! And I trust that we all, having looked thus briefly and inadequately at this great doctrine, would say the same thing; it is a way of salvation that becomes Him, the almighty God.

9

The New Birth

We have, let me remind you, been asking how it is that the call of the gospel becomes effectual in certain people. And in the last lecture, we began to answer that question by saying that the call becomes effectual in men and women as the result of the Holy Spirit's work of regeneration. It becomes effectual because in these people there is now a principle which was not there before which enables them to respond to this spiritual truth, this divine truth, that comes to them. And that is the difference between believers and unbelievers, those who are saved and those who are not. The latter have the 'natural mind', they are in the flesh, they are not spiritual, and that is why these things mean nothing to them. But they mean everything to the others and that is because they are now spiritual, and they are spiritual as the result of regeneration. So we began considering what the Bible teaches about regeneration. We considered the terms in Scripture and then we came to examine its real nature. It is not a mere change in some of the faculties of the soul, but it something behind that; and this we defined as being a change in a person's fundamental disposition.

Now as we proceed with our consideration, I want to emphasise again the profound nature and character of the change. It is something that is emphasised everywhere in Scripture, which talks about our being given 'a new heart' (Ezek. 36:26), and 'heart' in the Bible generally means, not merely the seat of the affections, as in current usage, but the very centre, the seat, of the whole personality. So when the Scriptures talk about giving us a new heart or a clean heart, they are talking about what I have described as the fundamental disposition, the thing that controls and determines everything else, the change is made there.

This whole question of regeneration, as we saw when we considered what our Lord said to Nicodemus, is, of course, a great mystery. It is a miracle, it is supernatural. Our Lord compared it to the wind in order to get Nicodemus, and all of us through Nicodemus, to see that there is a sense in which we just cannot finally understand it. 'Thou hearest the sound thereof, but canst not tell whence it cometh, and whither it goeth: so is every one that is born of the Spirit' (John 3:8). And yet it does behove us, as I am never tired of saying, to go as far as we can. So, in an attempt to make this wonderful change more or less comprehensible to us, I pass on to you what I, at any rate, regard as the best illustration that I have come across. It is an illustration that is suggested by the Scripture itself, and it is that of the whole process of grafting.

You may be anxious, for instance, to grow a certain type of pear. Now a way in which it is often done is this: you are given just a graft, a portion, a shoot, of the variety you like. Then you take a common wild pear tree and hack into it and into that wound which you have made in the tree, you put this shoot, this sprout. Then you bind them together. And eventually you will have a wonderful pear tree, producing nothing but your chosen variety of pear.

But in the meantime you have many things to do. You do not merely leave it at that. What happens is that the strength and the power, as it were, the life and the sap that comes up through that wild pear tree, will enter into this shoot and it will produce fruit. Yes, but below the level of the grafting, the wild pear tree will still tend to throw out its own wild shoots and branches and want to produce its own fruit. So you have to lop off these natural branches. You have to cut them, prune them right down and, if you do that, a time will arrive when the tree will produce only this wonderful type of pear that you are anxious to grow.

You see, at first you seem to have two natures in the one tree, but if you prune off the old the new will gradually master the whole and you will eventually have a pear tree which is producing the type of fruit that you want. Now that seems to me to be incomparably the best illustration that has ever been used with regard to this matter. You are putting new life in so that at one stage you have got one tree but with two natures – the cultured, cultivated nature, and the wild nature. Yes, but if, by pruning off these wild branches, you see to it that the strength of that tree is only allowed to go into the grafted-in branch, not only will that be strengthened and bear its fruit, it will gradually conquer and master the other. It seems to have a power to send its life down into the old until eventually you have the excellent pear tree that you desired at the beginning.

Now no illustration is perfect, but it does seem to me that that goes as far as we can possibly go. That is what happens, in a sense, in regeneration. There is still only one self, there are not two selves. But this new nature is put within us. We are called upon to mortify our members that are on the earth. We have to go on pruning and keeping under that which belongs to the old nature and, as we do so, this new life will grow and develop and produce fruit and the new nature will be increasingly in evidence. I am anxious to stress this point, because I am afraid we can even go further and say that some people, who regard themselves as truly evangelical, altogether deny the truth and the doctrine of regeneration. So I want to put this very strongly. In regeneration, a real change takes place and that within us. It is more than a mere change in our relationship to truth or to a person. A change takes place in us and not outside us only, and it is as definite as the grafting of a pear shoot into a pear tree.

Nor is this a change that remains only while we remain abiding in Christ. Now there is a very familiar teaching about sanctification which is put to us like this: the illustration is taken of a poker. There is the poker, it is cold, black and hard and cannot be bent. So you take that poker and put it into a fire and leave it there. And in the fire the poker becomes red hot and malleable, so that you can bend it. Ah yes, we are told, that is all right, but the poker remains red and hot and malleable only as long as it is kept in the fire. That is an illustration of abiding in Christ, and as long as you abide in Him there will be this new life, it is said, and this new way of living. But if you take that poker out of the fire and leave it out, it reverts completely to what it was before; it becomes black and cold and hard.

Now all that is taught to show the importance of abiding in Christ. It tells us that if we do not do so, we revert exactly to the condition that we were in before. But that, I suggest, is a denial of the doctrine of regeneration! Those who are Christians and who are born again, may backslide; they may not abide in Christ in this mystical sense, but even then, they do not return to where they were before. They are born again; there is this new principle in them; the change has taken place and the change is still there. They are not manifesting it fully but it is there and we must not describe those people as reverting to the precise position they were in before.

It is exactly the same with that other illustration about the lifebelt. The sinner is compared to a man in the sea who cannot swim, but, we are told, as long as he puts on the lifebelt he is held up. Yes, but if he wriggles out of the lifebelt, he will sink to the bottom. Now there again, it seems to me, is a denial of the doctrine of regeneration because it tells us that when the man is not abiding, he finds himself in exactly the same position in which he was before, as if nothing had happened to him and no change had taken place.

But as we have said, the doctrine of regeneration teaches that the change is one which takes place not merely in our relationship to the Lord or in our relationship to truth, but is something that God does within us. It is a new life put in us, a new principle of life and obedience, and therefore, of course, it is something which grows and develops and becomes progressively greater. Listen to the apostle Paul saying that: 'But we all,' he says, 'with open face beholding as in a glass the glory of the Lord, are changed into the same image from glory to glory' (2 Cor. 3:18). Now there, you see, is development and growth. Why? Because this principle of life has been put in. 'We are changed,' as Charles Wesley puts it, drawing upon that verse, 'from glory into glory, till in heaven we take our place.' The work is within us, and we are changed, we are no longer the same. All these scriptural terms should surely have saved us from the error that is illustrated in the pictures of the poker and the lifebelt. We are talking of a rebirth, a new birth, of being born again, of a new creation. Each of us is virtually a new person.

Now I cannot emphasise that too strongly because it is not only something that is clearly taught in Scripture, but when we come on later to deal with the doctrine of sanctification, we shall of necessity see how important it is that we understand this particular teaching about regeneration. If we do not, we shall unconsciously be denying the doctrine of regeneration altogether in our anxiety to get people to abide in Christ. It is right to exhort people to do that, and we shall do so when we come to that doctrine, but we must never put it in such a way as to give the impression that regeneration simply consists in a new relationship to Christ. That is to introduce a very real confusion.

So, then, having emphasised the profound inward character of the change, let me go on to ask a question: Why is this change absolutely essential? On what grounds have we the right to say that it is? Well, first of all, Scripture teaches that. You remember again what our Lord said to Nicodemus: 'Verily, verily I say unto thee, Except a man be born again, he cannot see the kingdom of God' (John 3:3). Then he also says: 'Except a man be born of water and of the Spirit, he cannot enter into the kingdom of God' (v. 5). The rebirth is an absolute, utter essential. A man cannot even see the kingdom, let alone enter it, unless he has been born again.

Paul teaches the same thing in Galatians 6:15: 'In Christ Jesus,' he says, 'neither circumcision availeth any thing, nor uncircumcision, but a new creature.' That is the only thing that matters: not circumcision, nor the absence of it but the new creature, the new creation. And again, in Ephesians 4:24, Paul says the same thing when he describes the new man, 'which after God is created in righteousness and true holiness'.

But, in many ways, one of the most important texts in this connection is Hebrews 12:14: 'Follow peace with all men, and holiness, without which no man shall see the Lord.' Holiness is absolutely essential and, mark you, holiness there does not merely mean a sanctification that you may or may not receive. Without holiness no man shall – can – see the Lord. So it is no use saying that some Christians have received sanctification and some have not, and that those who have not are still going to heaven – without holiness heaven is impossible. And it is in regeneration that this holiness is implanted in us. This new life is a holy life, a holy principle is placed within us.

There, then, are the explicit statements of Scripture. But there are other statements which teach the same thing by implication. Eternal life is defined as a knowledge of God: 'This is life eternal, that they might know thee the only true God, and Jesus Christ, whom thou hast sent' (John 17:3). Our Lord says that He has come 'that they might have life, and that they might have it more abundantly' (John 10:10). He has come to give us eternal life and eternal life comprises this knowledge of God and of Jesus Christ whom He has sent. And that in itself makes regeneration an absolute necessity. God is holy. God is light and in Him is no darkness at all. So life eternal is to know Him and to have fellowship with Him. And, therefore, it means, of necessity, that my nature must correspond. There must be something in me which corresponds to that and can enjoy that.

Yes, but we know that, by nature, men and women as the result of the fall, and as the result of sin, are the exact opposite of that. And again, that is why our Lord puts it so plainly in speaking to Nicodemus. Nicodemus was trying to understand and thought he could go from where he was to the next position. No, no, says our

Lord, 'That which is born of the flesh is flesh; and that which is born of the Spirit is spirit' (John 3:4), and there is nothing in common between them at all. You cannot mix the flesh and the Spirit, it simply cannot be done. It is no use arguing, He says, the thing is impossible. There is the spiritual, here is the sinful, that which belongs to the flesh, and you cannot bring them together. You must be born again. You must be made spiritual.

So the character of God and the character of men and women as the result of sin makes regeneration essential, because there is no such thing as an innate divine spark in human beings. Of course, the people who believe in a divine spark do not believe in regeneration and they are perfectly consistent. But it does seem rather odd that people who denounce the doctrine of the divine spark nevertheless seem to think that there is something in human nature which can do a great deal and which does not make regeneration an absolute and prior necessity.

So regeneration must come at the very beginning because if it is possible for me to do something which will eventually lead to my regeneration, I do not need regeneration. If I, by myself, as I am as the result of the fall and of sin, can appreciate spiritual truth, if I can appreciate the gospel and say, 'Yes I'm going to pay attention to that,' and then, as the result of my paying attention, I am born again, well then, I do not need the gift of life. If I have already got the ability and the power and the discrimination to recognise truth and to desire it, then I do not need to be regenerated. But the fact is, of course, that I do not have such a power. Men and women, as the result of the fall and of sin, do not desire this truth. They are at enmity against God. They are opposed to God. 'You that were sometime alienated and enemies in your mind by wicked works,' says Paul (Col. 2:21). They hate the law of God. They have nothing to do with Him. They are carnal, carnally minded. They 'mind the things of the flesh' (Rom. 8:5). So regeneration is not only essential, but is essential at the beginning; you can have nothing without it. It is impossible for anything to happen in us which can make us Christians until regeneration has taken place.

Now that brings us on to the next question: How exactly is regeneration brought about in us? This is an interesting subject. It is not merely a question of the moral influence of the truth. Those who are not evangelical say that as people listen to the gospel, as they come under its influence and its power, it changes them. They like the ideas, they take hold of them, and the effect of the ideas and of the truth is such that they become different people; they are changed. But that is not it. We are talking about something that happens down in the depths of the personality, and this is what brings about change.

Moral influence can, of course, make a great difference. It can make people change their ideas. It can make them change their way of living; it can turn a drunkard into a teetotaller – it has often done it. You can present arguments and the argument may go home. Someone may give up drink completely, become very sober, and an advocate of temperance, without Christ being mentioned at all. Under the moral effect of truth, and the moral influence of ideas, people can produce great changes in themselves. But that is not what we are dealing with here.

Secondly, it is not produced by baptism either. This is an old controversy, an old source of discussion. The Roman Catholic Church teaches that regeneration is produced and accomplished through the instrumentality of baptism, and only through baptism. You must be baptised before you can be regenerate. I do not want to anticipate a later lecture, but let us be clear at this point. In baptism, Roman Catholics teach that our sins are forgiven and that our moral nature is changed and renewed within us. We are told that baptism delivers us from the inherent power and defilement of original sin. You remember that, as the result of the fall of Adam and our connection with him, we are all defiled, and the power of sin has entered in upon us. Now Roman Catholics teach that when a child is baptised, it is delivered from the inherent power and pollution of original sin. All that it has inherited from Adam is washed away, blotted out, and not only that, by baptism we are made children and heirs of God.

The Anglo-Catholics also teach baptismal regeneration. And, strange though it may seem, the same is true of the Lutherans. Luther never quite got rid of this view, and neither have his followers. There is one difference between the Lutheran and Roman Catholic views. The Catholics say that you cannot be regenerate without baptism; the Lutherans say that you can but that the usual, normal manner is by means of baptism. Well, we do not teach that. We say that regeneration is not by baptism, that there is abundant scriptural evidence in the book of Acts alone to prove that the people who were baptised were those who gave evidence that they were already born again. Indeed, they were baptised *because* they had been born again. It was given as a sign and a seal to them because they had produced evidence of the new birth.

But to us a much more interesting and fascinating question is this: What is the relationship of regeneration to the word that is preached?

There are a number of texts that suggest that our regeneration takes place through and by means of the word. Let me suggest two to you. James 1:18: 'Of his own will begat he us *with the word of truth*, that we should be a kind of firstfruits of his creatures.' Then there is 1 Peter 1:23: 'Being born again, not of corruptible seed, but of incorruptible, by the word of God.' However, you will remember that in the last lecture I drew a distinction between the act of regeneration and the coming to birth and said that there may be a long interval between the two. Now I suggest to you that both these texts I have quoted are concerned about the bringing to birth. And it is certainly the word that does that. It is the effectual call, coming through the medium of the word, that, as it were, brings the seed of life to life, so that the birth takes place. But if you keep in mind the distinction between the generation and the actual coming to birth, I think you will see the difference. The word is used, not in the act of generating, but in the bringing out into life of that which has already been implanted within.

At this point some would quote the parable of the sower and the different types of ground, and emphasise that the life is in the seed and so on. But surely the whole point of that parable is to emphasise the character of the ground into which the seed is put. It is stony ground? Is it encompassed by thorns? And so on. Or is it good ground? In other words, the teaching in that parable is that what really matters is that fundamental something which we call the disposition. And if that has been changed and put right, then, when the word comes, it will be effectual; it will lead to the result; it will yield the fruit.

Indeed, the Scriptures do seem to teach that quite explicitly. Take, for instance, John 6:65: 'Therefore said I unto you,' says our Lord, 'that no man can come unto me, except it were given unto him of my Father.' Now there were the people, hearing the same word, and as we have already seen, some came, some went away – what was the difference? It is this, our Lord, says, '. . . except it were given unto them of my Father.' And again I would remind you of what we are told about Lydia. It was because the Lord had 'opened her heart' that she attended to Paul and received the word. It was not the word that opened her heart, it was the act of the Lord. It was this that led to her reception of the word. That surely must be the order. And the argument of 1 Corinthians 2, especially verses 12 to 15, obviously teaches the same thing.

But there are two final arguments about this which are not only of great importance, but, it seems to me, of very great interest also. What about the Old Testament saints? Now when we were dealing with the doctrine of the covenant, we were at great pains to emphasise that the Old Testament saints are in the same position as we are. There is only one covenant in the Old and in the New Dispensations. And you and I today are the children of Abraham, Abraham is our father, because we are children of faith. There is a difference, of course, in the administration of the covenant in the Old and in the New, but only one great covenant of grace. Our Lord tells us that Abraham, Isaac and Jacob will be in the kingdom and that others will come from the east and from the west while the Jews will be left outside (Luke 13:28–29). In other words, the Old Testament saints were born again. David was born again, he was a new man, a new creature, and so were the patriarchs and the prophets.

The author of the epistle to the Hebrews puts it like this at the end of chapter 11. He said that those saints did not receive the promise in full. His argument is that it was kept back so that they should not, as it were, run ahead of us. Here it is: 'And these all, having obtained a good report through faith, received not the promise: God having provided some better thing for us, that they without us should not be made perfect' (Heb. 11:39–40). So we are made perfect together. But if those Old Testament saints were regenerate, as they must have been, it is clear that it is not the word that actually performs the act of regeneration. Regeneration is something that is not mediate through the word, but immediate. It was the Spirit of God who dealt with them and operated upon them.

The other argument is that about children, especially about infants. Now we all believe, do we not, that there are infants and children who have gone and who will go to heaven and spend their eternity in the presence of God. Now how can a child be saved? Obviously every infant needs to be saved. If you believe in the doctrine of the fall and in the doctrine of original sin, you must believe that every child is born in sin and 'shapen in iniquity' (Ps. 51:5); every child is dead in trespasses and in sins (Eph. 2:21). They all inherit original sin and original guilt from Adam, every child that is born. How, then, can any child be saved? How can any child ever go to heaven?

Now, if you want to insist upon the fact that regeneration always follows upon hearing the word and believing it and accepting it – how can in infant be saved? The infant cannot receive truth, it does not have the ability; it does not have understanding, it has not awakened to these things. So is there no hope for any infant? We do not believe that, we obviously reject such a suggestion. And the answer is, of course, that a child is regenerated in exactly the same way as anybody else, because it is the action of this almighty being, of God Himself through the Holy Spirit. He can implant the seed of spiritual life in an unconscious infant with the same ease as He can do it in an adult person. Therefore you see why it is important for us to consider whether regeneration is something that happens indirectly through the word or whether it is indeed the direct operation of God upon us. And I am teaching again, as I did in the last lecture, that it is immediate, direct, it is God creating anew as He created the world out of nothing at the beginning.

And, finally, the last thing is that obviously, in the light of all this, regeneration is something that can never be lost. If you are regenerate, you will remain regenerate. It seems to me that this is absolutely inevitable because regeneration is the work of God. Yet there are those who seem to think that people can be born again as the result of believing the truth and then, if they backslide or fall into sin or deny the truth, they lose their regeneration. But if they come back again and believe again, then they are regenerate again – as if one can be born again and die and be born again and die an endless number of times! How important doctrine is! How important it is that we should be clear as to what the Scripture teaches about these things! It tells us that regeneration is the work of God Himself in the depths of the soul and that He does it in such a way that it is permanent. 'No man is able to pluck them our of my Father's hand' (John 10:29).

'I am persuaded,' says Paul, and let us notice this, 'I am persuaded' – he is certain – 'that neither death, nor life, nor angels, nor principalities, nor powers, nor things present, nor things to come, nor height, nor depth, nor any other creature, shall be able to separate us from the love of God, which is in Christ Jesus our Lord' (Rom. 8:38–39). And when Paul says that, he is expounding regeneration. It is not merely the relationship between us, it is because God has put this life in me, that nothing can separate me from Him. And when we come to deal with the mystical union which follows directly from this, we shall see how still more inevitable this must be. This is a permanent work and nothing can ever bring it to an end.

Take those verses from the first epistle of John: 'Whosoever is born of God doth not commit sin' – which means that such a person does not go on abiding in sin. Why? Well – 'for his seed remaineth in him:

and he cannot sin, because he is born of God' (1 John 3:9). He cannot go on sinning because he is born of God. Let us be clear about that. The man or woman who is born of God, who is regenerate, simply does not and cannot continue – abide – in a life of sin. They may backslide temporarily, but if they are born of God they will come back. It is as certain as that they have been born again. It is the way to test whether or not someone is born again.

Or take that other word in 1 John 2:19: 'They went out from us, but they were not of us; for if they had been of us, they would no doubt have continued with us: but they went out, that they might be made manifest that they were not all of us.' They were members of the Church, these people, they appeared to be Christians, they said the right things and up to a point their life seemed to be right, but they 'went out'. Why? They went out 'because they were not of us' – they were not regenerate. They had never been born again. That is why they have gone out, says John, in a sense, to give proof of the fact that they have never really had life.

'But what about Hebrews 6 and 10?' asks someone.

The answer is that there is nothing in either of those chapters to suggest that those people were ever regenerate. They had had marvellous experiences, but there is nothing to say that they were born again. They were not, and that is the explanation. The regenerate abide. They may backslide, they may fall into sin, they may fail, but they abide, because the life is there. The others may appear to be fully Christian but if there is no life they will not abide. Life shows itself, it gives proof of its existence – as we shall go on to see.

10

A Child of God and in Christ

You will remember that we are still considering this great doctrine of
regeneration – the work of the Holy Spirit in regenerating the
believer. It is such a vital and all-important subject that I have deliberately not hurried with it. I have forgotten all about form and precision
and have allowed the great truth itself to lead us and to guide us. Now
we have considered something of its essential nature. We have considered also why it is absolutely essential, and we have seen how it is
brought about and in particular its relationship to the word. We have
emphasised in particular that no means are used in our regeneration;
it is the direct, immediate work of the Spirit upon our souls. Furthermore, it is something that can never be lost; it is a work done by God
and it is a work that is permanent. Ultimately, the security of the
believer, as we shall see when we come to deal with the doctrine of
final perseverance, rests specifically upon this great doctrine of regeneration.

We come now to the consideration of a subject which, while it is
essentially doctrinal, is also more practical. The essential purpose of
these lectures is to look at doctrine, but I have tried throughout to
show that this is not something dry and arid, theoretical and abstract.
My concern with doctrine is because of all things, it helps me most in
the living of the Christian life. So we must, perforce, turn occasionally
to consider the practical application and therefore I want to deal now
with the results to which regeneration leads, or to put it another way,
the proofs of the fact that we are regenerate. I know that this troubles
large numbers of people and that is why I am turning to it. 'My difficulty is,' they say, 'how may I *know* that I'm regenerate?' Now that is
an essential part of the doctrine of regeneration and that is why I have

called this the *results* to which regeneration leads. It is a subject about which the Bible has a great deal to tell us.

We can start from this general principle: regeneration, we have shown, is the implanting within us of a principle of spiritual life. Very well, life is something that always shows itself. A baby gives proof of the fact that it is born alive and not still born, by screaming or moving. You cannot have life without some kind of manifestation of that life and that is as true of spiritual life as it is of any other form of life. So the Bible has many tests which it puts before us in order to help us to know whether we are truly regenerate or not. The classic passage of Scripture on this is the first epistle of John. One man who wrote a book on 1 John very rightly, I think, gave it the title *The Tests of Life*. And that is precisely what the first epistle of John is. But I always feel that the Beatitudes are also a test of life and of regeneration and they are the tests put forward by our Lord Himself.

Now let us look at this briefly. In the first epistle of John there are four main tests which John constantly repeats. (There are other subsidiary tests, but we will not be dealing with these.) 1 John is an epistle which can be divided up with comparative ease on condition that we realise that it depends upon the recognition of these four major tests of spiritual life or of the fact that we are regenerate. I shall not take them precisely in the order in which they appear but they are to be found in every section of the epistle.

The first test is *believing that Jesus is the Christ*. John says, 'Beloved, believe not every spirit, but try the spirits whether they are of God . . . Hereby know ye the Spirit of God: every spirit that confesseth that Jesus Christ is come in the flesh is of God' (1 John 4:1–2). Now that is a tremendous statement. It means the full doctrine about the Lord Jesus Christ. It means that you believe that He is indeed eternal God, one of the three Persons of the blessed Holy Trinity. Apply that test to some of the cults around today and you will see what a vital test it is. It is not enough that you praise Jesus Christ, not even enough that you say He is the Son of God. You must say that He is Jehovah, that Jesus Christ is come in the flesh – the eternal Son of God, co-equal, co-eternal with the Father – that the second Person in the blessed Trinity has come in the flesh. It was not a phantom body, 'The Word was made flesh, and dwelt among us' (John 1:14). It is all that we said earlier[1] about the great doctrine of the person of our

---

1. In Volume 1, *God the Father, God the Son*.

Lord and Saviour Jesus Christ. John is very fond of repeating this. He says it again in chapter 5 in the first verse: 'Whosoever,' he says, 'believeth that Jesus is the Christ is born of God: and every one that loveth him that begat loveth him also that is begotten of him,' and so on. And, you remember, Paul has said the same thing. He said, 'No man can say that Jesus is Lord, but by the Holy Ghost' (1 Cor. 12:3). You cannot say it otherwise. The man who tells me that Jesus is Lord, and puts the right content into that statement and is not merely repeating it mechanically, is giving proof of the fact that the Holy Spirit is in him, that he is regenerate.

The second test is the test of *keeping the commandments*. That is actually the first test that John introduces: 'And hereby we do know that we know him, if we keep his commandments' (1 John 2:3). And John constantly repeats that also; you will find it in every section of the epistle. He says it again in the very last section: 'For this is the love of God, that we keep his commandments: and his commandments are not grievous' (1 John 5:3). He sometimes refers to it as 'doing righteousness' (1 John 2:29). That is the way to distinguish between the child of God and the child of the devil, John says. And not only that; not only does this child of God, this person who is born again, keep the commandments, to him the commandments are a delight. God's commandments, says John, are not a burden; they are not against the grain. Christians are not always kicking against them and wishing they were not there; they enjoy keeping the commandments. You will find that again elaborated by Paul in Romans 7. So keeping the commandments is a most important test. Our relationship to the commandments of God and of Christ proclaims at once whether or not we are recipients of this blessed new life.

The third test is that *He has given us His Holy Spirit*. 'Hereby we know,' says John, at the end of the third chapter, 'that he abideth in us, by the Spirit which he hath given us' (v. 29).

'But,' says someone, 'how do I know that I have received the Spirit?'

Well, we shall have to deal with that later on as we continue in our consideration of this doctrine, but one aspect of it is certainly this: there is such a thing, says the apostle Paul, as 'the Spirit of adoption, whereby we cry, Abba, Father' (Rom. 8:15). Paul says that again in Galatians 4:6: 'God hath sent forth the Spirit of his Son into your hearts, crying, Abba, Father.' The Spirit is 'the Spirit of adoption' and one of the proofs, therefore, that the Holy Spirit is in us is that, though we may not understand it fully, we have a feeling, a consciousness, that God is our Father. He is no longer a God afar off, but is our Father. We say, 'My God, my Father.' There are also other manifestations of the presence of the Spirit but we must leave these to a subsequent lecture.

The last test is that we *love the brethren*. 'We know that we have passed from death unto life, because we love the brethren' (1 John 3:14), and this is a wonderful test. It is a test that points on to the next theme that we shall consider, namely the mystical union of all believers with the Lord Jesus Christ and therefore with one another. This is inevitable, you see. If we are all joined to Him and joined to one another, we are related to one another and we inevitably love one another. In other words, we recognise Christians when we meet them. In a sense, we don't need to be told that people are Christians, we recognise them at once and we feel that we have always known them. They belong to the same family, we are related to one another. We prefer their society to any other. If you offered us the choice of spending our evening with the so-called great people of this world or with some humble unknown Christian people, we would prefer to spend our evening with the unknown Christian people. There is something in common; we love them; we know that we belong together; nothing can ever separate us. 'We know that we have passed from death to life because we love the brethren.' If we do not recognise Christians, even at their worst, and love them, then we had better examine the whole foundation of our position. The children of the family love one another.

Those, then are the four main tests given by John in his first epistle, but there are other tests suggested elsewhere in Scripture and I just want to note them. Here is one which I regard as of great value and which has, many a time, been a great comfort to me: the consciousness of a struggle within. That is an extremely valuable test. Paul puts it perfectly in Galatians 5:17 where he teaches us that 'the flesh lusteth against the spirit, and the spirit against the flesh: and these two,' he says, 'are contrary the one to the other: so that ye cannot do the things that ye would.' The Spirit and the flesh. They are warring or 'lusting' against one another. What it means is that Christians, by definition, are people in whom a great competition is taking place. The Holy Spirit, as it were, wants them for God, but the flesh – this other spirit that is worked by the devil – wants them for the kingdom of darkness. So they are fighting for possession and Christians are aware of the fact that they are the seat of conflict, that a kind of internecine warfare is taking place within them. They are conscious of these two forces, these two powers, and men and women who are conscious of that have a right to know that they are Christians.

But be very careful. I am not merely talking about the consciousness of good and evil, right and wrong; they have a sense of moral decency and have a code of ethics and may feel that they let themselves down. I am not referring to that. What I am referring to is very different. In the old unregenerate life, you are aware of the fact that you are handling the whole situation, everything depends upon what you do. *You*, as it were, are dealing with the conflict. But what I am describing now is that you become aware of the fact that there is another Spirit apart from yourself, in you, dealing with you, working in you, drawing you, weaning you from the world and indicating truth to you. You are aware of the operation of the Holy Spirit and you are aware of the power of Satan in a sense that you never were before.

A very good sign, therefore, that people are born again is that they become more acutely aware of the existence and the working of Satan than they have ever been hitherto. There is no need for Satan to busy himself very much with the unregenerate. They can be left, as it were; they are already bound; they are already in his kingdom and they cannot escape. But once people are transferred to the kingdom of God and the kingdom of light, the devil makes a new effort and in a spiritual way comes to them and attacks them. And they are aware of this other presence that is fighting for their life and for their very existence. Flesh and Spirit – the conflict is a proof of regeneration.

Another very good test is this: anybody who is aware of a desire to know God and not merely a desire to be blessed by God, can be quite happy and certain of being a child of God. Everybody wants blessings, of course. Yes, but the peculiar mark of children is that they are interested in the person. They want their Father. They want to know their Father better. They are more interested in the Giver than the gift, the Blesser than the blessing. They begin to know something of a hunger and thirst for God Himself, as the psalmist puts it, 'for the living God' (Ps. 42:2). Their soul thirsts for the living God. And whatever may or may not be true about you, if you have a desire to know God Himself, you can be quite happy that you are regenerate. That is something that the unregenerate is incapable of, because the natural mind is 'enmity against God' (Rom. 8:7) and we are all by nature, as Paul says, 'alienated and enemies' (Col. 1:21), away from God. Unregenerate men and women are haters of God and do not want Him, and are always ready to believe anything they may read in the newspaper which purports, however vaguely, to prove that there is not a God. They are against God, but the children desire to know God.

The last test I would mention at this point – and again I regard this as very important – is that children of God do not merely desire forgiveness of their sins and an avoidance of the consequences of sins, but they also know what it is to hate sin. In other words, in Paul's words in Romans 7, they say, 'O wretched man that I am! who shall deliver me?' (v. 24). Now sinners, unregenerate men and women, do not like the consequences of sin, they do not want to be punished for sins, but they know nothing about a sense of sin, they do not know a true conviction of sin. They have not seen sin in all its vileness and foulness, in all its ugliness, they do not hate it. But the children of God do. That is why our Lord says concerning them: 'Blessed are they which do hunger and thirst after righteousness' (Matt. 5:6). Why are they blessed? It is because they are already children of God. Unbelievers cannot know, the unregenerate cannot experience, this hunger and thirst after righteousness and true holiness. They may want to live a good life and keep up to their standards, but Christians go beyond all that. They have a positive hunger and thirst for a positive righteousness. They want to be like Christ. They want to be like the saints of whom they have read. They are not content merely with not committing certain sins but want a clean heart. They want to be pure. They want to be holy. They want to be like God. They hunger and thirst after righteousness.

Those, then, it seems to me, are some of the main tests. They are not the only ones but I regard them as the most important tests which we can apply to ourselves in order to discover whether or not we are truly born again.

However, in dealing with this whole subject of regeneration in his first epistle, John also introduces something else and that is *our union with Christ*. That appears many many times in that epistle. For instance, 'He that keepeth his commandments dwelleth in him, and he in him' (1 John 3:24). In other words, John sometimes writes in terms of regeneration, of the seed of life, and at other times he puts it in terms of the union of the believer with his Lord. Now this doctrine is quite inseparable from the doctrine of regeneration with which we have just been dealing, and that is why we have to take it at this point. I think you will agree that there is no more vital, sublime and glorious doctrine than this.

Now some may be surprised at the fact that we are taking this doctrine now. Indeed, you will find that many would take it as possibly the last doctrine of all, the final doctrine, the one to which all the other doctrines lead up. They believe that the union of the believer with Christ is something that we only attain when we have arrived at an unusual degree of holiness and of sanctity and therefore would not include it here, comparatively at the beginning. Their confusion is entirely due to the teaching of the mystics. The mystics have their gradation of the manner in which one travels along the mystic way, and, according to their teaching, the ultimate end of the believer is to become absorbed in and 'lost in' the divine.

That is characteristic of practically all the mystics – and when I say 'the mystics' I am putting the term in inverted commas. The apostle Paul was a mystic but not in the sense of which I am now speaking. I do not want to call them professional mystics but I think you know what I mean by that. I refer to the mystics who are more philosophical than spiritual or the mystics who are more philosophical than scriptural. These mystics, particularly among the Roman Catholics, have a view of these matters that is closer to philosophy than to biblical truth. And as I understand his writing, even a great Englishman like William Law has to go into this category. He was a man to whom John and Charles Wesley owed a great deal in the early stages, but they broke with him. They left him, and very rightly so, because they found that he was too philosophical and not sufficiently scriptural. All these philosophical mystics tend to think of the union of the believer with Christ as a kind of absorption into the eternal. This same kind of thing is also characteristic of the teaching of many of the eastern religions.

Furthermore, unfortunately, that kind of teaching has often influenced Christian people and even, indeed, evangelical Christians. So they tend to think that the only people who really experience this union with Christ are those unusually and exceptionally holy, sanctified people who, by tearing themselves away from the world and mortifying themselves, have at last attained this mystical union. But I want to try to show that that is an utterly false doctrine, and that the doctrine of the union of the believer with Christ must come at this particular stage in our consideration of the doctrines.

Why is this? Because, as I think I shall be able to show you, all the benefits of Christ's redemptive work come to us through this union. I will go further and say this still more strongly by putting it negatively. We cannot receive any blessing whatsoever from the work of the Lord Jesus Christ unless we are joined to Him, unless we are in union with Him, every one of us. Let me give you one verse straightaway which will establish the position. Take this statement: 'Blessed,' says Paul, 'be the God and Father of our Lord Jesus Christ, who hath blessed us with all spiritual blessings in heavenly places in Christ' (Eph. 1:3). That is it. All these blessings, all these spiritual blessings in the heavenly places, are all ours in Christ and we have nothing at all apart from that.

Let me give you one other verse, which I shall quote again later on, which says the same thing. John puts it in the very prologue of his Gospel: 'And of his fulness have all we received, and grace for grace' or 'grace upon grace' (John 1:16). We have all received His fulness. How? By being joined to Him. You receive nothing unless you are joined. You must be joined to the source before you can receive anything whatsoever. Therefore, you see, we are constrained to say that even regeneration itself, which we have already been considering, is, logically, an outcome of our union with Christ.

Chronologically, as regards time, of course, there is no doubt but that the two things happen simultaneously. The moment we are joined to Christ, we are born again. The moment we are joined to Him we receive this principle of life. If you look at it from the strict standpoint of time you cannot put one before the other; but, logically, you almost have to put the union before the regeneration. I have taken them in this slightly different order because starting, as I have done, with the whole idea of the call, it seemed to me that as we emphasised the effectual call, we then had to go on to regeneration, but then say that this union of the believer with Christ is the cause of the regeneration.

Now in many ways, of course, it can be said that *the* special and particular work of the Holy Spirit is to produce this union. Was that not what our Lord meant when He turned to the disciples and said, 'It is expedient for you that I go away; for if I go not away, the Comforter will not come unto you; but if I depart, I will send him unto you' (John 16:7)? It is out of this union, you see, that all the blessings proceed. Here is a bit of homework, a task for Bible students! You will find that this doctrine of the union of the believer with Christ seems, in many ways, to be the doctrine of all doctrines given to the apostle John to emphasise. Of course it is elsewhere – you find it in the apostle Paul – but it does seem to be the doctrine particularly emphasised by John. Now work through his Gospel and note carefully the point at which he begins to talk about this union. I think you will discover that it is the point at which John specifically introduces the teaching of our Lord concerning the Holy Spirit. In other words, you will find it beginning in John 14. The moment our Lord begins to tell His disciples about the Holy Spirit, He begins to tell them about the union. In many ways, the classic passage on this whole doctrine of the union of the believer with Christ is to be found in that section of John's Gospel which runs from chapter 14 to the end of chapter 17. What a glorious portion of Scripture it is! And yet, you see, it comes in precisely in connection with the doctrine of the person and the work of the Holy Spirit.

That is what I meant when I said that the particular work of the Spirit does seem to be to unite us to our beloved Lord. There are those who would teach – I do not know to what extent they are justified scripturally, but at any rate it is a thought that is worth repeating – that that is the special work of the Holy Spirit in the Godhead, in the blessed Holy Trinity. They say that the third Person is, as it were, the kind of connecting link between the Father and the Son. That may be pure speculation, we do not know, but we do know that it is He who unites us to the Son and to the Father, and that this work of communion and of union seems to be His particular office.

Now, then, as we approach this great, glorious and transcendent doctrine, let us start again by considering some of the terms that are used in the Scripture itself. And first and foremost we have to put that expression which, alas, so many of us tend to slip over in our reading, whether in private or in public, but which, in many ways, is the greatest term ever used concerning anybody in the Scripture: 'in Christ', 'in Christ at Corinth', 'in Christ at Colosse'. Paul uses it in that list of names which he gives in the sixteenth chapter of Romans, a chapter which so many people do not read because they say, 'It's nothing but a list of names!' Read it again and you will find that Paul refers to Andronicus and Junia who, he says, 'were in Christ before me' (v. 7). And what a thing to say! The Christian is a man or woman who is *in Christ*. 'The saints', wherever they may live, are *'in Christ Jesus'*. The phrase varies but there it is, it really says everything; and the point I am emphasising is that there is no such thing as being a Christian unless you are in Christ. You cannot be a Christian just by believing certain things and saying, 'Now if I keep on, one day I shall be in Christ and joined to Him.' Not at all! You are either in Him now or you are not a Christian.

Let us take another passage. In John 15, our Lord compares this union to the union between a branch and a tree. He says, 'I am the vine, ye are the branches' (v. 5). That is something which will help us to understand this mystical union. It is comparable to that which exists between a tree, the trunk and the branches which are a vital part of that tree. That is a vital relationship, a union.

But then the Bible also says that this union is comparable to that between the head and the members or parts of a body. 'Ye are the body of Christ, and members in particular,' says Paul in 1 Corinthians 12:27. And Paul says the same thing in Ephesians 4:15–16:

> But speaking the truth in love, may grow up into him in all things, which is the head, even Christ: from whom the whole body fitly joined together and compacted by that which every joint supplieth, according to the effectual working in the measure of every part, maketh increase of the body unto the edifying of itself in love.

Then in Ephesians 5: Paul has still another comparison – and, incidentally, the apostle has a greater variety of illustrations and analogies with regard to this question of the union of the believer and Christ than with regard to any other subject. In Ephesians 5 he says, 'For we are member of his body, of his flesh, and of his bones. For this cause shall a man leave his father and mother, and shall be joined unto his wife, and they two shall be one flesh. This is a great mystery: but I speak concerning Christ and the church' (Eph. 5:30–32). The union, he says, existing between the believer and the Lord is the same as the union between a husband and wife, it is that kind of union.

But then we have another picture in 1 Peter 2:4–6 where Peter says, 'To whom coming, as unto a living stone, disallowed indeed of men, but chosen of God, and precious, ye also, as lively stones, are built up a spiritual house . . .' You see the idea? The relationship is compared to a building, and in verse 6 Peter goes on to say that our relationship to Christ may be likened to the relationship between individual bricks or stones and the chief cornerstone: 'Ye also, as lively stones, are built up a spiritual house, an holy priesthood, to offer up spiritual sacrifices, acceptable to God by Jesus Christ. Wherefore also it is contained in the scripture, Behold, I lay in Sion a chief cornerstone, elect, precious.' And that is a very important relationship in the erection of any building.

And then finally there is one other comparison. It is a comparison which Paul makes and it is a vital one from the standpoint of doctrine. He draws a contrast between the union of the unbeliever with Adam and the union of the believer with Christ. It is the great argument in Romans 5, which is repeated in 1 Corinthians 15:22 and 49. In Romans 5 the whole argument is that death passed on to all people because of Adam. Why? Because of their relationship to Adam; that is the whole doctrine of original sin. We are all condemned in Adam because of Adam's sin. He was our representative, you remember,[1] he was our federal head and, not only that, we are bound to him, we were in the loins of Adam when he fell. In Adam all died. In Christ all shall be made alive again. That is it. The relationship of the believer to Christ is the same sort of union and relationship as that old relationship of the whole of Adam's posterity to Adam. We are all born in Adam and we are related, we are joined in that way. Yes, but, being born again, we are in the same sort of relationship to Christ. What a vital doctrine that is when we come to consider the results of the union! We shall see that it is the most precious truth we can ever grasp. Read it again for yourselves in Romans 5 and 1 Corinthians 15 from verse 21 onwards.

So I trust that I have made the connection between these things plain to you. Regeneration and union must never be separated. You cannot be born again without being in Christ; you are born again because you are in Christ. The moment you are in Him you are born again and you cannot regard your regeneration as something separate and think that union is something you will eventually arrive at. Not at all! Regeneration and union must always be considered together and at the same time because the one depends upon the other and leads to the other; they are mutually self-supporting. And now, as we have looked at the Scriptures, and on the basis of these Scriptures, we shall go on to try to consider something of the nature of this union, then something of how the union is established and then some of the glorious results of the union. May God give us grace and ability to lay hold of these profound and precious practical doctrines! There is nothing, I say at the end as I said at the beginning, that so strengthens my faith and fills me with a longing to be pure as He is pure, and to live even as He did in this world, as the realisation of what I am and who I am because I am a Christian. I am a child of God and I am in Christ.

---

1. See Volume 1, *God the Father, God the Son.*

11

Union with Christ

In our consideration of the work of the Holy Spirit in the application of redemption – the redemption that has been worked out and purchased by our Lord and Saviour Jesus Christ – we have now arrived at a consideration of the doctrine of the union of the believer with Christ. I was at pains, in introducing this doctrine in the last lecture, to emphasise the fact that it is a doctrine which, of necessity, must always be taken in conjunction with the doctrine of regeneration. The two things are almost simultaneous. Logically, the union should be put first, but not chronologically. We are regenerated because of our union with Christ; it is from Him we derive our life; it is from Him we derive everything. Therefore we are looking together at one of the most glorious of all the doctrines of the Christian faith. There is none which is more sublime than this, in which we are reminded that we really are made partakers of Christ, that we are partakers of the divine nature, so it goes naturally and inevitably with the doctrine of regeneration. And in the last lecture, having given the reasons why this doctrine must come at this point and not at the end of a series of doctrines, we simply gave the scriptural terms used to describe the nature of the union. So now we are in a position to proceed to a more detailed consideration of this doctrine.

The first thing, clearly, to consider is the nature of the union. Now the very terms that are used in the Scriptures with respect to it, and which we have looked at, give us the key to the understanding of the character of the union. But again, perhaps we had better start with a negative. We must not think of this union between the believer and Christ as if it involved a kind of confusion of persons. It must not be thought of in the sense that our substance, or the essence of our being, becomes merged and lost in the substance, or the essence of the being, of our Lord. Now I emphasise that because of the teaching of the mystics who always tend to think of this union in those terms. Ultimately, their conception of complete salvation is that we become lost, absorbed, in the eternal.

That is the idea in certain eastern religions and there is a sort of kinship between a great deal of mysticism that goes by the name of Christian with the more general mysticism that characterises those eastern religions. In all of them one finds the idea of what is called *Nirvana*. You become lost. You go out of existence altogether by being absorbed into the divine and into the eternal. Now the scriptural doctrine of the union of the believer with Christ does not mean that at all. The Bible teaches very clearly that you and I will exist as individuals throughout the countless ages of eternity. We do not become lost or merged and absorbed into God. We, ourselves, as persons, will not only always be and exist, but we shall enjoy the beatific vision. We shall enjoy seeing God, and we shall enjoy being in His glorious presence.

When we considered the doctrine of the person of our Lord we had to emphasise exactly the same thing. The two natures in our Lord – his human and divine natures – are separate and distinct, but they are joined. There is not a new nature which is partly human and partly divine. No: He is God, and He is man; He is divine and He is human. The two remain separate and yet they are together. They are not intermingled. They are not fused in a materialistic sense. So the union of the believer and his Lord must likewise not be thought of in terms of a confusion or intermingling of substance.

But, on the other hand, I am equally anxious to stress another negative which is that the union between the believer and Christ is not merely a union of sympathy or a union of interest. It is not merely a loose, general, external association of separate persons who happen to have the same interest, or the same enthusiasm. No, that again is important because there are some who, in their anxiety to avoid the errors of mysticism, have represented this union in just that way. You know what I mean by that? You can have people joining together to form societies. They may be interested in music or in some particular musician, so you have a Beethoven society or a Mozart society, and so on. Or people may have an interest in art and they form a society. They have a common interest which brings them together and they call it a union. Well, of course, in a sense it is a union, but my point is that that is not the kind of union that binds together the Lord and any one of us His followers. It is not merely that we are interested in salvation. It is not merely that together we are interested in God and in His kingdom. We are, but the union is much bigger and deeper than that. So I am anxious to emphasise those two important negatives, though they happen to be at opposite extremes.

What, then, is the nature or the character of the union? First, it is *a spiritual union*. Now this is where the doctrine of the Holy Spirit is so vitally important. We are joined to Christ and we are in union with Him by means of the indwelling of the Holy Spirit in us. It is the function, the special work of the Holy Spirit to join us thus to Christ, and we are joined to Christ by the Holy Spirit's presence in us. Let me give you some Scriptures to substantiate that. Take the statement in 1 Corinthians 6:17: 'But he that is joined unto the Lord is one spirit.' Here the Apostle is reminding the Corinthians that their bodies are the temples of the Holy Spirit, and that is why they must avoid certain sins of the flesh. Paul says, 'He which is joined to an harlot is one body' with that harlot (v. 16). Then he adds the opposite truth: 'He that is joined unto the Lord is one spirit.' So it is a spiritual and not a materialistic union. Or take again 1 Corinthians 12:13: 'For by one Spirit are we all baptized into one body, . . . and have been all made to drink into one Spirit' – the same idea again. We are joined to Him in this amazing and mysterious manner by the Holy Spirit.

Secondly, it is *a mystical union*. Now what do we mean by this very difficult term? Well the best way to explain it is to take the comparison which the Apostle himself uses in the last portion of Ephesians 5. These verses are sometimes read at marriage services, and rightly so. In some marriage services we are told that the relationship between a husband and a wife signifies unto us the mystical union that is between Christ and His Church. Certainly there in Ephesians 5, the Apostle does say that the union between the Lord and the Christian believer is comparable and similar to the union between a husband and a wife. Now that is what I mean by a mystical union. It is very difficult to put this in language. There is a union, and you cannot find a better term for describing it than this term *mystical*. Not only are the two made one flesh but they are bound together in an intimate manner and the two really become one – it is a mystical union.

Then the next way of describing the union is to say that it is *a vital union*, and this is obviously of the greatest importance. It means that our spiritual life is drawn directly from the Lord Jesus Christ. We are sustained by Him through the indwelling Holy Spirit. There is nothing more important in the Christian life than to realise that our union with Him is a vital one. It is a living thing. It is not something mechanical or conceptual; it is not a thought or an idea; it is really a vital, spiritual union.

Look at some of the statements of Scripture which demonstrate that. Take the great statement in John 1:16, one of the most amazing and marvellous statements in Holy Writ: 'And of his fulness have all we received, and grace for grace.' That says it all. That is our relationship to Him, says John; something of His fulness and of His life is passing into us and we are receiving it. And many other statements say the same thing. Take John 14:19–20 where our Lord says in this very connection, 'Because I live, ye shall live also. At that day ye shall know that I am in my Father, and ye in me, and I in you.' You see how vital a relationship it is, and all because of the indwelling Holy Spirit. Or, again, take John 17:22–23: 'That they may be one, even as we are one: I in them, and thou in me, that they may be made perfect in one.' What sublime teaching!

The trouble with all of us is that we do not realise the truth of these things. But this is the truth given by the Lord Himself. It is His prayer for His people that they may know the meaning of this vital spiritual relationship. And he does not hesitate to compare it with the relationship that subsists between the Father and Himself: as the Father is in Him so He is in us and we are in Him. But take the statement of this truth which is made by the apostle Paul in Galatians 2:20: 'I am crucified with Christ: nevertheless I live; yet not I, but Christ liveth in me.' There is nothing greater than that, and what it does teach is that this is a life-giving relationship; it is a union of life, 'not I, but Christ liveth in me'. And then Paul goes on to say, 'And the life which I now live in the flesh I live by the faith of the Son of God, who loved me, and gave himself for me.'

The next term, therefore, that I must use is the term *organic*. Now the difference between organic and vital is that the term 'organic' suggests a kind of two-way traffic, it is a union in which we give as well as receive. In many ways, the best statement of this is to be found in Ephesians 4:15–16: 'But speaking the truth in love, may grow up into him in all things, which is the head, even Christ: from whom the whole body fitly joined together and compacted by that which every joint supplieth, according to the effectual working in the measure of every part, maketh increase of the body unto the edifying of itself in

love.' What a statement! But you see how it brings out this organic
element. We are to grow up into Him who is the head, yes, but you
notice that Paul says that the whole body is 'fitly joined together and
compacted by that which every joint supplieth'. So that we do not
only receive, we also give; we all are active members. Every part of the
body is playing a vital role in the life of the body. We are not simply
passive. There is an organic relationship, an organic union. There is
an activity and a vitality in the parts as well as in the head. They all
make their contribution.

Now that is the concept of the Church as the body of Christ and it
is a tremendous idea. Nothing, surely, is more stimulating to our
faith, nothing more encouraging, nothing more stimulating to our
practical holiness, than the realisation of this wonderful and exalted
truth about ourselves. I say once more that I am increasingly convinced that what chiefly accounts for the low state of spirituality in
the Christian Church is the failure to grasp these doctrines. We think
so much in subjective terms, and we spend so much time in trying to
work something up, that we fail to see that the way to become holy is
to understand the truth about ourselves and to realise our high calling
and our privileged position.

Then the other statement of the organic union is again in that same
passage in Ephesians 5 where Paul compares it to the relationship
between the husband and the wife. Each has his or her duties, each
has a separate function, but in the union the two play their part, and
that is the relationship between Christ and the Church. We have our
part to play, our lot to contribute.

The next term is personal: this union is *a personal union*. Now I use
that word in order to emphasise that every one of us, separately, is in
union with Christ. This needs to be emphasised because there is a
teaching which is very popular, especially among Roman Catholics
and Anglo-Catholics, and, indeed, I notice that it is insinuating itself
into those who like to call themselves 'liberal evangelicals', a teaching
which maintains that we have no direct union with our Lord as individuals but that we are only connected to Him through the Church.
This teaching does away with the individual aspect, and emphasises
the corporate aspect. Indeed, therefore, it goes on to say that in a
sense we cannot be born again except in and through the Church,
which is a complete denial, not only of scriptural teaching, but particularly of the evangelical emphasis. The evangelical emphasis is that
we all have a personal relationship with our Lord, and it is only

because of that that we are members of the body.

Of course, in a sense you cannot separate these things, but I am anxious to emphasise that I do not derive my life from the Church, I derive it from the Lord. Because we all share His life at the same time, we are all member of His body, and we are all in the Church. You cannot be a Christian without being a member of the mystical body of Christ. But the right order is to put the person and individual first and the corporate second. So that I am not born of the Church – the Church is not my spiritual mother – I am born of the Spirit. And the moment I am, I am in the Church, the unseen, the mystical Church. So let us emphasise the personal aspect, and let us make certain that we will never allow any specious teaching to rob us of that individual element. We do not have to go to Him through the Church; we can go to Him one by one, and we are united to him singly as well as in a corporate manner.

The last term is that it is *an indissoluble union*. I need not emphasise that. It follows of necessity from everything we have been considering together during the past lectures. It is inconceivable to me that we can be joined to Christ in this way by the Spirit and then go out of that union, and then come back and enter into it again, and then go out again, and keep on coming in and going out. This is once and forever. Nothing, no one, 'nor things present, nor things to come, nor height, nor depth, nor any other creature, shall be able to separate us from the love of God, which is in Christ Jesus our Lord' (Rom. 8:38–39). It is an indissoluble union. Thank God for it.

So let us go on now to consider how the union is established. If that is the nature and the character of the union, how is it brought about? Clearly we are face to face here with a very great mystery and we must tread very carefully. But at any rate we can say that two main elements are involved. First and foremost, it is clearly the work of the Holy Spirit. Ephesians 2:5 puts it like this: God 'hath quickened us together with Christ'. It is the work of the Spirit to quicken us. We have already looked at that. And He quickens us 'together with Christ' – that is the union. So in the effectual call, in our regeneration and in all that we have been considering, the main work is done by the Holy Spirit.

But then we must also emphasise that as the result of that, our faith comes into operation, and our faith is a vital part of the union. It is not the first thing, it is the second, and quite inevitably this leads us on to the consideration of the biblical doctrine of faith. Our faith helps to sustain the union, to develop it and to strengthen it – this union that is primarily established as the result of the work of the Holy Spirit. It is only as faith becomes active that we become aware of this union and of our regeneration and all the other things that we have been considering. It is only as our faith comes into operation that we rejoice in it and desire it more and more. So in the biblical passages dealing with the union of the believer with his Lord, the element of faith is of necessity emphasised. It must be. The Spirit establishes the union and leads to faith, and faith, as it were, desires it more and more and keeps it going. So we eat of His flesh and drink of His blood and as we do so, the union between us becomes closer and dearer and deeper. Faith draws increasingly on His fulness and the more we realise the truth about the union, the more we shall draw upon it. You see the difficulty of establishing an exact chronological order in these things, indeed, it is almost impossible, but that is the way in which the union is established and maintained.

But, again, let us be careful about our negatives in this section. We must repeat that the union is not established by or through the Church. We have shown how the Roman Catholics would teach that without mother Church you can never be born again at all, you can never become a Christian, the Church, they say, is absolutely essential at that point. We deny that strenuously. There is nothing to indicate it in the Scriptures. And equally, we must be at pains to emphasise that the union is not established by the sacraments. It is not established by baptism; let us emphasise that again. We do not believe in baptismal regeneration in any shape or form. Nor is it brought into being by the sacrament of the Lord's supper. Both these sacraments can be invaluable in maintaining the union, and in stimulating our desire that the union may be deeper and greater, but they do not bring it into being.

You will be familiar with that false sacramental teaching which would have us believe that grace is actually transmitted mechanically, in the water or in the bread or in the wine, and that these sacraments act – I must use the technical term, because it is used so frequently that it is good that we should all be familiar with it – *ex opere operato*, which means that they act and operate in and of themselves. We deny that completely. Without our faith there is nothing in the sacraments. The act of christening or baptising an infant does not transmit life or join a child to Christ. No, it is impossible. Nowhere do you find that conception in the Scriptures, and we must resist the teaching in a most strenuous manner.

So, then, we have seen the way in which the union is established. Next we come to something in which we should all delight and for which we should praise God – the *consequences of the union*. What a glorious, endless subject this is! It should always be the great theme of preaching to believers and yet how infrequently do we hear sermons on the consequences of the union of believers with their Lord.

We can subdivide this under two main headings: you can think of this great subject objectively or subjectively. Let me give you parallel terms. Put by the side of objective: *federal*; put by the side of subjective: *spiritual*. I cannot do anything more at this point than just give you a number of headings. When we come to deal with the doctrine of sanctification, I trust we shall be able to elaborate some of them. But for now let us try to look at it as a whole, that we may see something of what our union with Christ must of necessity mean with regard to us.

Here are some of the things which are taught in the Scriptures. Take the federal and the objective aspect first; we must start with that. I am almost tempted to stop there and digress! We must always put the objective before the subjective. We do not like doing that, of course. We are all interested in the subjective; we want the feeling of the experience, and in our concern about that, we are not careful about the grounds. The result is that as our feelings come and go, we become unhappy, and all because we have not based our understanding on the objective truth. Certain things result from our union with our Lord, quite outside the realm of our experience, and these apply to our status, our standing, our position.

Now the term *federal* is the term that Paul has in mind in Romans 5. By nature, all of us are joined federally to Adam. God made Adam the representative of humanity. He is the federal head. Take the illustration of the United States of America. That country consists of a number of different states and each state has its own legislature – its own government, in a sense – but then in addition to that there is what they call the federal government which includes them all. They are all related in this federal union. Now the teaching of the Scripture is that the whole of mankind is in that kind of federal union with Adam and, as we have seen, it was because of that that Adam's sin is imputed to us. Because we are joined to Adam federally, in this legal sense, what he did applies to us. He sinned – we sinned; he fell – we fell. That is the doctrine of original sin and original guilt.

But now, on the other side, we are told – and you will notice the parallelism in the teaching – that we who are Christians are in precisely the same relationship to the Lord Jesus Christ. We are

federally related to Him. What does that mean? It means that we have
been crucified with Him. We must not interpret Romans 6:6 in a subjective or experiential sense. It is not, it is objective. It says that
because I am joined to Christ federally, when He was crucified I was
crucified. That is a statement of fact. God regards it like that. We are
told that, 'We have been planted together in the likeness of his death'
– that is Romans 6:5. Romans 6:8 says we are 'dead with Christ'. We
have died with Him. More, 'we are buried with him by baptism into
death' (Rom. 6:4). And Romans 6:11 adds, 'Reckon ye also yourselves to be . . . alive unto God through Jesus Christ our Lord.'

Now all these things are true of all of us who are Christians, all of
us who are in Christ. Because of this federal relationship I must
believe that I have been crucified with Him. In exactly the same way
that when Adam sinned, I sinned, so when Christ was crucified I was
crucified. I died with Him, was buried with Him, and rose with Him.
Go on to Ephesians 2:6: 'And hath raised us up together, and made
us sit together in heavenly places in Christ Jesus.' Now Paul is not
talking here about something that is going to happen to us. What Paul
says there is that, federally and in terms of this relationship, though
we are still on earth, we who are Christians are in Christ seated with
Him in the heavenly places *now*.

But we have not finished. We are told that we are 'complete in him,
which is the head . . .' (Col. 2:10). That is obviously, again, a federal
statement, a legal statement, or a *forensic* statement. I hope that
nobody feels that all this is bewildering and baffling. My dear friends,
I am telling you the greatest things you will ever hear, I am telling you
the truth about yourself and about myself, thank God! Do not be
thrown by these terms, these are the scriptural statements. Of course
they are difficult, but anything worth having is difficult. And if you
are not interested in it because it is difficult, I say that you had better
make sure that you are a Christian at all. We are seated in the
heavenly places, we are complete in Him. Listen again: 'But of him
are ye in Christ Jesus,' Paul says in 1 Corinthians 1:30, 'who of God
is made unto us wisdom, and righteousness, and sanctification, and
redemption.' Already that has happened. Of course, actually and
experientially it has not all been worked out. But I am already finally
redeemed in Him. That is why in Romans 8 Paul jumps from justification to glorification and says that those who have been called have
already been glorified. That is why the union is indissoluble. But let us
hold on to these things one by one. He 'is made unto us wisdom, and

righteousness, and sanctification, and redemption.' So, what this teaching really says is something like this: our sins were imputed to Him; His righteousness is imputed to us. When we come to the doctrine of justification I shall elaborate that, but that is what it means at this point, that all that is in Him is put to my account because of our union.

The next thing, therefore, that I must emphasise is that *we are sealed by the Holy Spirit* because of our union with Him. It is by the sealing, in a sense, that the union comes about; but the two are separate. Because I am joined to Him, I am sealed by the Spirit. It is because I am one with Him that I receive the Spirit which He received without measure.

The next consequence of this union is that we receive the adoption. That is a separate doctrine and we shall be dealing with that. The union of the believer with Christ is not the same thing as the adoption, as we shall see, but the adoption is one of the consequences of the union.

And the last thing is this: because we are adopted, Paul argues, again in Romans 8, that we are 'heirs of God' and, therefore, 'joint-heirs with Christ' (v. 17). Christ is an heir, so we must be joint heirs, and we are joint heirs of the glory which God has prepared for those who love Him. So there in that list I have been giving you the federal and the objective results of our union with the Lord Jesus Christ.

Finally, let me just give you the list of the vital subjective and spiritual results. It means that we have fellowship with Him. That is a term that includes it all. This is elaborated in John 17 and in the first epistle of John. Again, you find it in John 1:16: 'And of his fulness have all we received, and grace for [upon] grace.' It also means, as we are told in 2 Corinthians 3:18, that we 'are changed into the same image from glory to glory'. What a concept! Because we are joined to Him, we become like Him. That is the purpose of salvation – to make us 'to be conformed to the image of his [God's] Son' (Rom. 8:29). As we are joined to Him, and as we look at Him with unveiled face, we become changed into His image.

That is the Christian life. That is what is happening to all of us. That is what must happen to all of us if we are truly Christian. We are not static. I am referring, of course, to our likeness to Him in His human nature. We do not become divine, but we do become as He was when He was living in this world. We become like God's dear Son. He is the firstborn among many brethren in that respect. And then, of course, it has the consequence that we bear fruit and become people He can use. That is the great teaching of John 15.

And then the last thing that I would emphasise is *our fellowship in His sufferings, and our fellowship even in His death*. 'That I may know him' says Paul in Philippians 3:10–11, 'and the power of his resurrection, and the fellowship of his sufferings, being made conformable unto his death.' What great thoughts! We must work them out, think them out and pray them out. Paul puts that in another way in Colossians 1:24: 'Who now rejoice in my sufferings for you, and fill up that which is behind of the afflictions of Christ in my flesh for his body's sake, which is the church.' I do not pretend to understand that fully, but I do know that there is no higher statement of the doctrine of the union of the believer with His Lord. The Apostle interprets his own sufferings in the flesh and in the body as, in a sense, filling up what remains of the sufferings and the afflictions of Christ Himself. Paul is bearing that in his own flesh. The result of the mystical union is that he enters into this mystical fellowship of the sufferings of Christ. There were people living in the Middle Ages of whom it is said that they so meditated upon and contemplated their Lord and all that He had done for them, that some of them even developed in their physical hands the imprint of nails, the *stigmata*. I do not know, it is not impossible. Such things do happen.

But all I am concerned to emphasise is that the more deeply we realise the truth about this union between us and our Lord, the more we shall know something of the fellowship of His sufferings. In this world He was 'a man of sorrows, and acquainted with grief' (Isa. 53:3). That was because of the sin of the world. And because He saw the enmity of the human heart against His Father, it hurt Him, it grieved Him and He suffered. There is no more delicate test of our relationship to Him and our union with Him than the extent to which you and I know something about this suffering. It is not a glib talking about 'wanting souls to be saved'. No, no. It is much deeper than that. That can be purely carnal. But this is something that is always spiritual; we really suffer because of the sin of men and women and their lost condition. Because of our union with Him, we may know something of groaning in the spirit as He knew it; this deep concern, this pain, this agony of soul. It is one of the subjective consequences of our union with our blessed Lord and Saviour.

May God through the Holy Spirit open our eyes to this wondrous doctrine of the union of the believer with His Lord, and may we be at great pains to work it out in detail, to apply it to ourselves, to tell ourselves, 'I am crucified with Him. I am planted into the likeness of His death. I have died with Him. I have been buried with Him. I have risen with Him. I am seated in the heavenly places with Him. That is my position. It is true of me because I am in Christ and joined to Him.'

12

Conversion

We come now to a kind of turning point in our consideration of the work of the Holy Spirit in the application of redemption. So far we have been looking at His work as He does various things to us, in the depths and recesses of our being. All that we have considered so far in terms of the effectual call and regeneration and our union with Christ can be described in that way. It is something that the Spirit does and of which, at the time, one may not be actively conscious, or at least our consciousness is not essential to the work being done.

Now we come to what we may describe as the manifestations and the results of that work. But though I put it like that, we must again be very careful in the use of chronological sequence. So many of these things really cannot be divided up in terms of time like this. We must keep them clear in our minds, we must keep them clear as ideas, but so many seem to happen at almost exactly the same moment. It has been argued by some of the greatest teachers of the Church that a person may be regenerate for a number of years without its manifesting itself. I find it very difficult to subscribe to that, but I hesitate to pit my opinion against such great authorities. Again, I say that simply to show the kind of distinction that I am drawing.

So we must now consider the manifestations of all that we have considered together and here, too, the question of the order of these doctrines is most interesting. Once more, people disagree as to which doctrine should be put next, but for myself, the next is the biblical doctrine concerning *conversion*. Here is the regenerate person, the regenerate soul. Now that person is going to *do* something, and that action marks the moment of conversion.

What do we mean by conversion? It is the first exercise of the new nature in ceasing from old forms of life and starting a new life. It is the first action of the regenerate soul in moving *from* something *to* something. The very term suggests that: conversion means a turning from one thing to another. The term is not used very frequently in the Scriptures but the truth which the word connotes and represents appears constantly.

You will find that in the Scriptures the term itself is sometimes used in a more general way for any turning. For instance, it is sometimes used even of a believer. Our Lord rebuked Peter on one occasion and said, 'When thou art converted, strengthen thy brethren' (Luke 22:32). He meant: When you come back again, when you have turned back. Here the word does not refer to Peter's original coming into the Christian life, he was already in it, but he was going to backslide, he was going to go astray and then come back. That is described as conversion, but in the consideration of biblical doctrines, it is well to confine the word 'conversion' to the sense which is normally given to it when we talk together about these things, that is, it is the initial step in the conscious history of the soul in its relationship to God, it is the first exercise, the first manifestation, of the new life that has been received in regeneration.

This, of course, is something which is essential and there are many statements to that effect. It is stated specifically in Matthew 18:3: 'Verily I say unto you,' says our Lord, 'Except ye be converted, and become as little children, ye shall not enter into the kingdom of heaven.' But all the texts which we have already considered in dealing with the doctrine of regeneration are equally applicable here, texts such as, 'The natural man receiveth not the things of the Spirit of God' (1 Cor. 2:14), and, 'the carnal mind is enmity against God' (Rom. 8:7). Men and women must come from that before they can be Christians; they must turn from that to this other condition. So conversion is essential. Nobody is born a Christian. We were all born in sin, 'shapen in iniquity' (Ps. 51:5); we were all 'the children of wrath, even as others' (Eph. 2:3), we are all subjects of original sin and original guilt, so we must all undergo conversion; and the Bible is quite explicit about this.

The next question, therefore, to ask is: How does it take place? What is the agency in conversion? And here the answer is quite simple. It is first of all and primarily the work of the Holy Spirit, and the Holy Spirit does it through the effectual call. We have considered that doctrine and that is how this process of conversion takes place.

people say; I don't care what science says, I *know* because of what's happening to me.'

Now my response to that was, 'Yes, and every psychologist in your audience would smile. They would say, "We agree that you have had a psychological change and experience. But, of course, many things can do that." And they would continue to dismiss the whole of Christianity.'

No, the defence of the Christian faith must never rely simply upon some experience that you and I have had. The defence of the Christian faith is objective truth. So unless we are careful at this point in defining conversion the danger is that we shall have nothing to say to those who have undergone one of these counterfeit experiences.

Then there is one other thing – and here we leave the counterfeit and the temporary and come to something which is more immediately practical. There are variable elements in connection with conversion, and because of these we must be very careful that we know what the essential elements are. Let me illustrate what I mean. Take the *time element*, the time factor in conversion. Must it be sudden? Is it impossible for it to be gradual? Well, I would say that the Scripture does not teach that it must of necessity be sudden. The great thing is that it has happened, whether sudden or gradual. The time element is not one of the absolute essentials; it may have its importance, but it is not vital.

Secondly, must one's conversion of necessity be *dramatic*? We all tend to emphasise these, do we not? They have human interest, we say, and we must be interesting. But must conversion be dramatic? Now if you read just one chapter in the Scriptures – Acts 16 – you will see that you have no right to say that. Of course, if you only read the story of the Philippian jailer, then you will say conversion must be full of drama. But I am equally interested in the story of Lydia and there is nothing to suggest that about her conversion. Not at all! It may have been quite quiet, but it was equally a conversion. So here we have another variable element. Dramatic quality may be there, but it may not be. It is not essential.

Then there is the old vexed question of the place of feelings. Of course, they must be there, but there are feelings and feelings. They may be very intense, or they may not be, but they are still feelings. We all differ by nature and temperament, and in this matter of feelings we differ very much indeed. The most demonstrative person is not always the one who feels most.

The call becomes effectual and it is that which leads to the next step – what you and I *do*. You notice that we are mentioning this for the first time, but in any definition of conversion you must bring in the human as well as the divine activity. The call comes effectually and because it comes effectually we do something about it. That is conversion: the two sides, the call – the response. We have seen how all this becomes possible, but in dealing with conversion, of necessity we must give equal emphasis to the activity of human beings. Now in regeneration and in the union, we are absolutely passive; we play no part at all; it is entirely the work of the Spirit of God in the heart. But in conversion we act, we move, we are called and we do it.

We come, then, to consider the characteristics of conversion and this, I sometimes think, is one of the most important topics that Christian people can consider together. Why is that? Well, it is vital that we should consider the biblical teaching about conversion because there is such a thing as a *'temporary conversion'*. Have you noticed how often that is dealt with by our Lord Himself in His own teaching, how at times He almost seems to discourage people from going after Him? There was a man who said, 'I will follow thee whithersoever thou goest,' and our Lord, instead of saying, 'Marvellous!' said, Wait a minute. 'The foxes have holes, and the birds of the air have nests; but the Son of man hath not where to lay his head' (Matt. 8:19–20). 'Do you realise what you're doing?' he said in effect. 'It's a very foolish man who goes to war without making sure of his resources. It's an equally foolish man who starts building a tower without making certain that he's got sufficient material to finish it.'

Our Lord, because He knew the danger of a 'temporary something' happening, was constantly dealing with it, and seemed to be repelling people. Indeed, they charged Him with making discipleship impossible. Take that great sixth chapter of John where the people were running after Him and hanging on to His words because of the miracle of the feeding of the 5000, and our Lord seemed to be trying deliberately to repel them. So a large number, who thought they were disciples, went back, we are told, and walked no longer with Him. It is quite clear that our Lord was giving that teaching quite deliberately because He was drawing a distinction between the spirit and the flesh. He knew that they were carnal and He was anxious to stress the vital importance of grasping the spiritual.

Take also the parable in Matthew 13 – the parable of the sower – and our Lord's own exposition of it. Notice particularly verses 20 and

21: 'But he that received the seed into stony places, the same is he that heareth the word, and anon with joy receiveth it; yet hath he not root in himself, but dureth for a while: for when tribulation or persecution ariseth because of the word, by and by he is offended.' But notice what our Lord says about this same man: he, 'anon with joy receiveth it [the word]'. That is what I mean by a temporary conversion. He seems to have received the word, he is full of joy but he has no root in him and that is why he ends up with nothing at all. Now that is our Lord's own teaching; there is the possibility of this very joyful conversion and yet there is nothing there in a vital, living sense, and it proves temporary.

There is also further teaching in the Scriptures about this same thing. Take Simon the sorcerer in Acts 8. We are told in verse 13, 'Simon himself believed also: and . . . was baptised.' And yet look at the end of that man's story. He was 'in the gall of bitterness' (v. 23), and Peter simply said to him that he had better ask God to have mercy and grant him repentance. He seemed to be a true believer, but was he?

Then Paul speaks, in 1 Timothy 1:19–20, of 'Holding faith, and a good conscience; which some having put away concerning faith have made shipwreck.' Now that is very serious teaching and he says the same thing in 2 Timothy 2. Here Paul is writing to Timothy about certain people who seemed to have been believers but were now denying the resurrection, as a result of which, some frightened Christians thought that the whole Church was collapsing. It is all right, says Paul: 'Nevertheless the foundation of God standeth sure, having this seal, The Lord knoweth them that are his' (v. 19). God knows; He is not deceived or deluded. There is such a thing as temporary conversions, temporary believers, but they are not true believers. That is why it is so vital that we should know the biblical teaching as to what conversion really is.

What about the case of Demas, I wonder? There are many who would say that Demas was never a believer at all. I would not like to go so far. He may have been backsliding: 'Demas hath forsaken me, having loved this present world' (2 Tim. 4:10). But at any rate he is a doubtful case. And then you come to that great classic passage in this connection in Hebrews 6, with a similar passage in the tenth chapter of that epistle. 'It is impossible for those who were once enlightened . . . if they shall fall away, to renew them again unto repentance' (Heb. 6:4, 6).

Therefore I deliberately use this heading of 'temporary convers[i]. There is obviously something wrong with these people, so we n[ust] ask questions. We must consider, we must have definitions, bec[ause] 'All that glisters is not gold.' All that appears to be conversion is n[ot] certainly not conversion according to our Lord's own teaching a[nd] the teaching of the inspired apostles. So I know nothing that is [so] dangerous, reprehensible and unscriptural as to say, 'But you must[n't] ask these questions.' No, no, let them come. Always ask: Does t[he] Scripture entitle us to say that? If we are to be true teachers of t[he] word, and helpers of others, and concerned about the glory of Go[d] we must realise that there is such a thing as a temporary conversio[n] which is based upon misunderstanding.

My second reason for being concerned about precise definitions i[s] that there are not only temporary conversions but even *counterfei[t] conversions*. Now I draw a distinction, you will notice, between the two and the difference is that in the case of a temporary conversion, conversion is something that has happened as the result of the presentation of the biblical truth. In the case of a counterfeit conversion, it is a phenomenon which, though closely resembling and simulating Christian conversion, has been produced by some other agency that is not the truth. So we must draw the distinction.

This was never more necessary than today, because there are so many people who seem to think that as long as there is a great change in the person's life, it must be a true conversion. If a man gives up sins and lives a good life and does good, that, they say, is Christian. But it may not be. It is possible for a man to undergo a great, profound, climactic change in his life and way of living and experience which has nothing to do with Christianity. People may even come out of the world and join a church, and their whole life from the outside may apparently be different, but it may be a counterfeit conversion. It is a conversion in the sense that they have left one thing and have come to another, have given up sins and are now doing good but it is counterfeit because they lack the necessary essential relationship to truth. If you are only interested in phenomena, if you are only interested in someone who can get up and say, 'My whole life is absolutely changed,' then you need only go to books on psychology. Psychology has been very popular now for many years, and it makes a most powerful attack upon the Christian faith – that is why I am so concerned about it. I heard a man say that if his Christian faith were attacked, it would not worry him. He would simply reply, 'I don't care what you

To me the meanest flower that blows can give
Thoughts that do often lie too deep for tears.
W. Wordsworth

So it is not the one who is weeping the most copiously who is of necessity the most intensely feeling. Another person may be feeling so
deeply that his feelings are down beyond the very possibility of tears,
as it were. Feelings are variable and express themselves variously in
different people. They must be present, but God forbid that we should
insist upon a particular intensity or display of feelings.

And then there is the whole question of age. Some have said that
unless you are converted when you are an adolescent, you will never
be converted at all, because the requisite psychological factors can
never be there again. What utter rubbish! How unscriptural! I have
never seen a more striking conversion than I once saw in a man aged
seventy-seven: thank God for that! No, there is no age limit; age does
not make the slightest difference. We are talking about something the
Holy Spirit produces. There is as much hope for the man who is shiver-
ing on the brink of the grave and of hell as for the adolescent – if you
are interested in true conversion, that is. If you are interested in
psychological experiences, then I agree, adolescence is the right time
for it. Everything is very explosive at that point; you merely strike a
match and there it is. But we are not interested in psychological
changes; we are talking about true, Christian, spiritual conversion.
And there age, thank God, is a complete irrelevance.

Now we have considered these things because there is always a
tendency to standardise the variable aspect of conversion. Sometimes
it works out in the evangelist, in his desiring everybody to become a
Christian in the same way, and he is doubtful of the converts unless
they are all the same. But it may happen in us, too, we all desire to be
the same. That is always one of the dangerous things about reading of
somebody else's experiences; consciously or unconsciously we tend to
reproduce them. It is a part of our make-up and of our nature, we are
imitators, and if we like a thing that we see in someone else, then we
wish that to be true of us, too.

Then we also tend to concentrate on particular manifestations of
conversion. The feelings, for instance, are only one aspect, yet we put
all our emphasis on them. This can be extremely dangerous because
feelings, as I have indicated, are one of a number of variables, and this

way may lead to tragedy. Some people are always insisting upon the presence of a variable quality, which is not essential. Thinking it was essential, and not having experienced it, they say that they have never been converted. And this can lead to untold and unnecessary unhappiness. In a way, the great instance of that is John Wesley who thought, immediately after his experience in Aldersgate Street, that that was his conversion, that he had never been a Christian until that moment. Years later he said that he had been quite wrong about that and that he was a Christian already but was 'more like a servant than a son'. All that happened to him there, he said, was that he *realised* his faith.

Well, Wesley may have been right or not; we do not know. But all I am indicating is that if we postulate something that is variable, and insist upon it, we may do ourselves or somebody else great harm. We may tell other people that they are not converted because they do not conform to our particular standard. So we must be very careful that we do not go beyond Scripture and say things which the Bible does not say. Therefore, how vital, how essential it is, that we should have clear definitions in our mind.

What, then, are the permanent and essential elements in conversion? Now these are made quite plain in Scripture, but not only there. We know that what we shall now be considering must be true because of the previous doctrines. This is something that really thrills me! There is such a consistency in the scriptural teaching. These doctrines are all consistent with one another, and if we allow ourselves to be led by the Bible, we shall not be denying at one point what we have said at another. And the doctrines we have already considered make the truth of these permanent and essential elements in conversion inevitable and clear.

Another argument – and I do want to emphasise this – is that what the Scriptures tell us about the permanent and essential elements in conversion has always been repeated in all great revivals in the long history of the Christian Church. That is most important. If you start saying that, because this is the late twentieth century, we can expect something different or that things need not be the same, you are being unscriptural. If this is the work of God, I do not care what century it happens in, it will have the same marks upon it, the same stamp. Read the history of revivals and you will find that they have always reproduced similar characteristics. It has often been said that every revival is nothing but a return to the book of Acts. Every true sign of religion is first-century religion coming up again. Always! There is a standard pattern, and all the histories show that the revivals conform to these great essential elements.

It is not only true in the history of revival. It is equally true in the history of persons, individuals, the saints who have been converted. Men and women of God are always the same. I do not care where they are, from what country, what century, or what time – it makes no difference. The fact is that they are men and women of God, and it is their relationship to God that determines what they must be. And that does not change throughout the centuries because God does not change. There is no special type of man or woman of God for the twentieth century, and do not believe it if anybody tells you there is. They must be the same, they always have been. You can read of them in the early centuries, in the Middle Ages, at the time of the Reformation, in the period of the Puritans, the evangelicals of the eighteenth century – they are always the same. And each one reminds you of the others.

What, then, are these permanent elements? There are two essential elements in conversion, and these are emphasised everywhere in the Scripture, in the Gospels, in the book of Acts and in the epistles. Paul, fortunately, has put it all in a phrase for us, in Acts 20:21, on that moving occasion when he said farewell to the elders of the church at Ephesus. I have sometimes thought that if there was one scene in history more than any other at which I should like to have been present, it was just that. 'I'm going,' Paul says, in effect, to the elders, 'you'll never see me again, and I want you to hold on to the things I've told you, and to remember what I did when I was with you.' What was this? 'Testifying both to the Jews, and also to the Greeks, *repentance toward God, and faith toward our Lord Jesus Christ.*' That is conversion. Those are the essential and the only essential elements in conversion. Repentance and faith. Sudden or gradual, it does not matter. Repentance must be there; faith must be there. If one is missing it is not conversion. Both are essential.

At this point, let me ask a question. In which order do they come? Which comes first, repentance or faith? Now that is a fascinating question. There is a sense in which faith is bound to come before repentance, and yet I shall not put it like that, and for this reason: when I am talking about faith, I mean it in the sense that the apostle Paul used it – faith in the Lord Jesus Christ, not faith in general. There must be faith in general before you can repent, because if you do not believe certain things about God, you do not act upon it and there is no repentance. But I am referring to faith in the special sense of faith in the Lord Jesus Christ. In that case, repentance comes before faith and Paul puts them in that order: 'Testifying both to the Jews, and also to the Greeks, repentance toward God, and faith toward our Lord Jesus Christ.'

Why must repentance come first? Well, you will find that it always comes first in Scripture. Who was the first preacher in the New Testament? The answer is John the Baptist. What did he preach? The 'baptism of repentance for the remission of sins' (Mark 1:4). This was *the* message of the forerunner and the forerunner always comes first. Then the second preacher was the Lord Jesus Christ and if you turn to the Gospels and observe the first thing He ever said you will find that He again exhorted the people to repent and to believe the gospel (Mark 1:15). So, exactly like John the Baptist, the first thing He taught was repentance.

Then what did Peter preach? Take the great sermon on the day of Pentecost in Acts 2. Peter preached and the people cried out saying, 'Men and brethren, what shall we do?' This was the reply: 'Repent, and be baptized every one of you in the name of Jesus Christ for the remission of sins, and ye shall receive the gift of the Holy Ghost' (Acts 2:37–38). *Repent.* And, as I have already quoted to you, repentance was the message of the apostle Paul. He started with repentance. He did it in Athens: God '. . . commandeth all men every where to repent' (Acts 17:30).

Repentance is of necessity the first message, and it surely must be. It is scriptural, yes, but Scripture also enables us to reason. Let me put it to you like this: Why should men and women believe on the Lord Jesus Christ? It is no use just asking them to believe in Christ. They are entitled to ask, 'Why should I believe in Him?' That is a perfectly fair question. And people do not see any need or necessity for believing in the Lord Jesus Christ if they do not know what repentance is. Of course you may be inviting them to Christ as a helper, or as a friend, or as a healer of the body, but that is not Christian conversion. No, no, people must know *why* they must believe in the Lord Jesus Christ. The law is our schoolmaster (Gal. 3:24) to bring us there and the law works repentance.

In other words, the primary point about conversion, the primary thing in the whole of Christian salvation, is to bring us into the right relationship with God. Why did Christ come? Why did He die? The answer is that He did it all to bring us to God. And if we think about these things in any way except in terms of being reconciled to God, our view is entirely false. I say it hesitatingly because I know the danger of being misunderstood, but there is far too much Christianity today, it seems to me, that stops at the Lord Jesus Christ and does not realise that He came and did everything in order to reconcile us to God. Indeed, it was God who was 'in Christ, reconciling the world unto himself' (2 Cor. 5:19). I think the greatest weakness in evangelical Christianity today is that it forgets God. We are interested in experiences, we are interested in happiness, we are interested in subjective states. But the first need of every soul, as we shall see, it to be right with God. Nothing matters but that. The gospel starts with God, because what is wrong with everybody is that they are in a wrong relationship to Him.

So we *must* put repentance first; it is the original trouble, the main consequence of the fall and original sin. God is orderly in His working, and He starts with the big thing, the first thing. Therefore, in the next lecture, we shall go on to deal with repentance.

13
Repentance

Repentance, as we have seen, always comes before faith in our response to the gospel, so we will now look at repentance. The best way to start when considering all these doctrines – a method we have consistently adopted – is to notice the meaning and the connotation of the terms that are used. Now the word *repentance* means 'to think again', 'to think once more'. So whereas you had dismissed this whole subject of religion, and had given up thinking about it, repentance means that you think again. 'Repent' is, of course, a Latin word which we have taken over into the English language and as far as it goes it is all right. Yet in many ways it is a great misfortune that this particular word is the one that we use most frequently and the one that we find in our various translations of the Scriptures because the original Greek word, *metanoia*, used in the New Testament is a much bigger word than its Latin equivalent. *Metanoia*, repentance, does not merely mean to think again. It carries with it a much more significant element, which is that this thinking again results in our changing our minds. And that is a vital addition.

Jesus told a parable which states this perfectly.

A certain man had two sons; and he came to the first, and said, Son, go work to day in my vineyard. He answered and said, I will not: but afterward he repented, and went. And he came to the second, and said likewise. And he answered and said, I go, sir: and went not. Whether of them twain did the will of his father? They say unto him, The first. Jesus saith unto them, Verily I say unto you, That the publicans and the harlots go into the kingdom of God before you. For John came unto you in the way of righteousness, and ye believed him not: but the publicans and the harlots believed him: and ye, when ye had seen it, repented not afterward, that ye might believe him.   (Matt. 21:28–32)

Now the point I am making is shown very clearly in the case of the first son. When the father asked him to go and work in the vineyard, he refused: but afterwards he repented and went. So what happened to him? Well, he obviously reconsidered it. Having said in that brusque, impolite manner, 'I will not,' and having walked away, probably in a rage because his father was interrupting his plans, he came back to it again and he thought again about it. It does mean that – that is the first step. You go back and re-examine the thing you have already dismissed. You think again. Ah yes, but not only that: he thought differently. He changed his mind. He now went and worked in the vineyard, which he formerly had refused to do.

But that does not exhaust the full content of this great term. You change your mind, yes, but in changing your mind, you must be conscious of a sense of regret for the wrong view that you had taken previously and the wrong conduct that had emanated from that wrong view. So clearly, this element of regret is also present. This young man, when he thought about it again, must have said, 'It was very wrong of me to have spoken like that to my father.' Not only did he change his mind, he regretted that he had said and thought the wrong thing. So we see that generally the best way to discover the meaning of New Testament terms is not so much to consult dictionaries as to consult the context. Our Lord defines what He means by His terms in a parable like this.

Then there is another element which is vitally essential in repentance and that is *a change of conduct*: 'Afterward he repented, *and went.*' The action was a part of the repentance. If the son had merely changed his point of view and had felt sorry that he had spoken to his father in the way he did, but then had just sat down, or had gone to spend the afternoon at the seaside with his friends, he would not really have repented. That would have been remorse. It is a vital part of the process of repentance that we *do* the thing that we formerly were refusing to do. There, then, are the essential elements of this condition, this attitude, this new something that comes into being when people hear the call of the gospel effectually and respond to it.

The next question is: What leads to repentance? In a sense, we have already answered by saying that it is the effectual call. Yes, but that is not enough. We must analyse it still more. What produces repentance in us? And the answer of the Bible to that question is the blessed word *grace*. Repentance is a gift of God which leads to an activity on the part of men and women. Take Zechariah 12:10 where God says that 'the spirit of grace and of supplication' will be poured out on His people. That is it. Without grace and supplication there cannot be repentance.

Then come to the New Testament. 'Him' says Peter, 'hath God exalted with his right hand to be a Prince and a Saviour, for to give repentance to Israel, and forgiveness of sins' (Acts 5:31). Had you ever noticed that Christ gives repentance quite as much as He gives forgiveness of sins? Then in Acts 11:18 we read about the reaction of the people who had listened to Peter's story of the conversion of Cornelius. They were amazed that the Holy Spirit had descended upon these Gentiles exactly as He had done on the Jews on the Day of Pentecost. And, we are told, 'When they heard these things, they held their peace, and glorified God, saying, Then hath God also to the Gentiles granted repentance unto life.' Repentance is the gift of grace, the gift of God.

Moving on to Paul, he writes to Timothy, 'In meekness instructing those that oppose themselves; if God peradventure will give them repentance to the acknowledging of the truth' (2 Tim. 2:25). Paul is telling Timothy what to do with people who have become heretical, people who have gone astray and Paul says that Timothy must instruct them in meekness. And this is Paul's reason: 'if God peradventure will give them repentance'. You notice where repentance comes from.

So repentance is a gift of grace, leading to action on our part. And the way in which God does this is through the teaching, the preaching, of the Word. The Bible is full of this. The gospel is preached, the word is proclaimed, calling men and women to repentance. '[God] commandeth all men every where to repent' (Acts 17:30). How? By the preaching of the word. You have a great instance of that in the book of Jonah where Jonah's preaching produced repentance in the Ninevites. There is another in Acts 2 when the apostle Peter, filled with the Holy Spirit, was preaching at Jerusalem on the Day of Pentecost. And as he preached, and as the Holy Spirit applied the word, the people cried out saying, 'Men and brethren, what shall we do?' (Acts 2:37). That is an indication of repentance, and it was the preached word that did it. It is the presentation of the truth that produces this condition of repentance.

And Paul again, in reminding the Thessalonians of what had happened to them, tells them that the gospel that he had preached had come 'not unto you in word only, but also in power, and in the Holy

Ghost, and in much assurance'. And what was its effect? They 'turned to God from idols to serve the living and true God' (1 Thess. 1:5, 9). It produced repentance.

Now that brings us on to our third principle. We have considered the terms, and how repentance is brought about, and now we must ask this question: *What is it in men and women that is engaged or involved in repentance?* We are now trying to measure and to estimate the greatness of repentance and my reason for doing this is not only that it is something that is plainly taught in Scripture but that furthermore while these lectures are called discourses and addresses (and I call them that myself), I cannot forget that I am a preacher. And a man who can forget that he is a preacher when he is handling the word of God needs to repent, because this is not to be considered theoretically, it is something very practical. We must consider this matter because, surely, the thing that accounts more than anything else for the state of the Church, as well as the state of the world today, is our failure to realise the full content of what is meant by repentance. This is the note that is missing. Very often people are rushed to decisions without knowing what repentance means. We have not taken the biblical view of repentance in its height and depth and length and breadth.

Let me show you, then, what is engaged in a man or woman in repentance, what is involved. And the answer is, of course, the whole person. Repentance must include the whole person or it is not really repentance. Now the classic statement of this is in Romans 6:17: 'But God be thanked,' says the Apostle, 'that ye were servants of sin, but ye have obeyed from the heart that form of doctrine which was delivered you.' Or 'the form of sound words', it does not matter which way you translate it.

So let us analyse that. What is engaged? Well, first and foremost, the mind, the intellect. So many people seem to think that the way to call people to repentance is just to press them to *do* something. They address the will only. But the will comes last, not first. Again, there is another statement of this in Romans 3:20: 'By the law,' says the Apostle, 'is the knowledge of sin.' That is what the law is for. Now I do trust that nobody gets tired of my constant references to the Puritans; it will be a sad day when people do tire of them! But I refer to them for this reason: they always believed in doing what they called 'a thorough law-work' before they applied the message of the gospel. They took time, in other words, to see that people were truly convicted of sin.

This preliminary law-work was equally characteristic of the preaching of George Whitefield and of John and Charles Wesley. Indeed, it continued to be the characteristic of true evangelical preaching until the end of the nineteenth century.

Now 'law-work' meant just this: 'By the law is the knowledge of sin.' And that is the function of the law. The law 'was added because of transgression' (Gal. 3:19). It was never introduced in order to provide people with a way of salvation, it could not do that because it was 'weak through the flesh' (Rom. 8:3). So, then, why the law? Well, it was introduced to show the exceeding sinfulness of sin (Rom. 7:13). Men and women do not like this idea of sin, they rebel against it, they hate it. And that is the very reason why they need to be held under the law. They need to be convicted of sin, they need to have their mind addressed and enlightened with regard to their condition. So preaching about repentance starts with the intellect and the understanding. It you exclude the intellect and the mind, it means you are excluding the law as well, and that is a terrible thing; for it is God Himself who gave the law and He gave it for this specific purpose.

'Wherefore I abhor myself, and repent in dust and ashes,' says Job (Job 42:6). Consider also Psalm 51 and notice the deep feeling expressed by David. Then take the famous parable spoken by our Lord about the Pharisee and the tax collector. We are told that the tax collector, 'smote upon his breast' (Luke 18:13). He not only felt that he could not look up into heaven, that he had no right to speak and could only stand afar off, but he smote his breast. Romans 7:24 says, 'O wretched man that I am! who shall deliver me from the body of this death?' And in 2 Corinthians 7:11 there is an extraordinary description of the emotions involved in true repentance. But our blessed Lord Himself has said the whole thing in one of His beatitudes, in the Sermon on the Mount: 'Blessed are they that mourn' (Matt. 5:4); they are not only poor in spirit, they mourn. Now is this not something that somehow or other has been overlooked by us? How often at the present time do you see people in agony because of sin? How many of our converts know anything about an anguish of soul? How often today are men and women seen to be shedding tears because of their conviction of sin? How many people have you known who have groaned because of their sinfulness? Have *we*, I wonder? But all these are to be found in the Scriptures.

Repentance includes the heart and the feelings. It is not a passing sorrow; it is not some desire for something. No, no, this law-work leads to profound emotion. As I have said, the intensity of the emotional manifestation will vary from case to case. We differ emotionally as we differ in every other respect, but what I am concerned to emphasise is that there always must be this powerful element of emotion; and it is not true repentance if it is not there. Think of Charles Wesley's great hymn: 'Jesu, lover of my soul'. Let us never forget that it was that godly, moral and religious young man who said,

> Just and holy is Thy Name,
> I am all unrighteousness.
> Vile and full of sin I am.

You feel the emotion; he is conscious of it. There must be a kind of anguish, a sense of fear and dread. The emotions are always engaged in repentance; as Paul says 'a godly sorrow' (2 Cor. 7:10).

And then, thirdly, repentance also includes the *will*. This is vital. As Isaiah said, 'Let the wicked forsake his way, and the unrighteous man his thought' (Isa. 55:7). He must forsake it. He is not only to feel sorry, he is not only to see his sin, he must *leave* it. 'Rend your hearts, and not your garments, and turn unto the Lord your God' (Joel 2:13). *Do* something about it. Having seen the sin, the law-work having been done, your mind having been persuaded, having thought it – act upon it! I might have included the text from Joel 2 equally well in the previous section, under emotion. Christian people, the trouble with us is that we are much too healthy; we have never really groaned because of our sinfulness; we have never felt it. We are much too light: that is the trouble in the Church. But this is the scriptural definition of repentance.

Then that brings us to Luke 3, with John the Baptist's preaching: 'Bring forth therefore fruits worthy of repentance, and begin not to say within yourselves, We have Abraham to our father: for I say unto you, That God is able of these stones to raise up children unto Abraham' (Luke 3:8). You have got to do something about it, said John. It is just not enough to feel something while I'm preaching, 'Bring forth fruits worthy of repentance.' And then John went into details. The people came to him in deputations asking him, 'What shall we do? (Luke 3:10, 12, 14). And he gave them very specific answers to their questions, answers which deserve careful consideration. To the people, he said, 'He that hath two coats, let him impart to him that hath none; and he that hath meat, let him do likewise.'

Then publicans also came and asked the same question, 'And he said unto them, Exact no more than that which is appointed you.' Finally soldiers came, 'And he said unto them, Do violence to no man, neither accuse any falsely; and be content with your wages.' The will must be engaged.

You find the same teaching in the parable about the two sons in Matthew 21; there is a turning which is an essential part of repentance. The will comes into operation and it turns us *from* what was wrong *to* what is right. Paul's commission given to him by our Lord on the road to Damascus told him to go and teach the Gentiles, 'to *turn* them from darkness to light' (Acts 26:18). Action is an essential part. And Paul reminds the Thessalonians again, 'How ye turned to God from idols to serve the living and true God' (1 Thess. 1:9).

Now that gives us some estimate of the greatness of this act of repentance: it takes up the whole person. But the fourth principle is: *What are the questions or the matters with which repentance deals?* Here again we will see the greatness of repentance. What are the subjects? The first is *God Himself*. Repentance means a changed view of God. We think again. We have had wrong views of God and we now have another view. Yes, and an entirely different view of men and women.

Then the other subject is the relationship between God and man. We see how that needs to be changed. According to 'the natural man' there is no need to worry about that because God is love. If he believes in God at all, 'God is love,' he says, 'I do a bit of good and everything will be all right.' When men and women repent, they have an entirely new mind on this relationship, and also on life itself and the whole purpose of life and how it should be lived. And a great change takes place in their view of death and of eternity. In other words, repentance not only includes the whole person, it includes that person's whole outlook upon everything that is of value and of concern in this life and in this world.

In the fifth principle we must consider *what exactly repentance leads to in experience*. How can I know that I have repented? First of all, it involves a change in our view of and thoughts concerning God. It is only when we repent that we really see the holiness and the greatness of God. The moment we see it, we have repented. We have this other view. By nature, our view of God is entirely wrong: 'The carnal mind is enmity against God: for it is not subject to the law of God, neither indeed can be' (Rom. 8:7). 'The fool hath said in his heart,

There is no God' (Ps. 14:1). And then there are others who, if they claim to believe in God, have a God of their own conjuring up and of their own imaginations, some projection of themselves and their own ideas. Those who say, 'I believe in God,' have no conception of God. Their view of God is wrong; it is false and they need an entire change.

Once again, is this not also something which has gone sour, which has got lost and gone astray among us? Do we walk in the fear of God? Are we people who give the impression that we know something about the greatness of God? People who come near to God walk softly. We are told in the book of Acts that the believers walked 'in the fear of the Lord, and in the comfort of the Holy Ghost' (Acts 9:31). But somehow or other we seem to have harboured the idea in these last years that the Christian's joy means that there must never be any impression of the fear of God. But we are told by the New Testament to serve Him with 'reverence and godly fear' (Heb. 12:28), because He is great, He is holy. Yes, you can have the joy of the Lord and yet walk in the fear of the Lord at the same time. It is a holy fear. It is not a fear that 'hath torment' (1 John 4:18), it is not a craven fear, but surely the nearer we are to Christ and to God, and the more Christ is formed in us, the greater will be our conception of God and we shall reflect it in our humility. Somehow a sense of God seems to have vanished from us. We are so glib and superficial; we talk about 'being converted' and so on, but we forget that we are brought to a holy God.

So we have lost a reverence for God and, therefore, for the whole of life, and also for the justice of God and the truth of God. But all these things bring us to a knowledge of the mercy of God, of His compassion, His kindness and His love. These things all go together. The Christian, at one and the same time, knows about the justice of God and the love of God. Justice and mercy are met together – that is essential Christianity. It is only the Christian who can hold those two things at the same time.

Indeed, it is this artificial, erroneous dichotomy which we seem to have introduced that is so unscriptural. People are so anxious to emphasise the love of God, that they forget the justice of God which is still there. In Christ they are met together. On the cross of Calvary the justice is fully satisfied and the love streams forth; but at the same time the Christian's love of God is a holy love; the Christian's joy is a holy joy. Everything must be holy. So that is something of the new thoughts and the new idea of God that people, who have repented, have when they come to themselves.

A further change is that far from being self-satisfied as they were, they now have a sense of guilt and of unworthiness. They have a feeling that they have sinned against God. Not only that; they have, as David brings out so amazingly in Psalm 51, and as Paul shows in Romans 7, they have a sense of pollution: 'Behold, I was shapen in iniquity; and in sin did my mother conceive me. Behold, thou desirest truth in the inward parts . . . Wash me . . .' (Ps. 51:5–7). I need to be washed. I am polluted and foul. 'In me,' says Paul, '(that is, in my flesh) dwelleth no good thing' (Rom. 7:18). Is that true of you? Have you realised that? However we may interpret that chapter, it must mean that at some time or other we have felt that.

And that is the question: have you ever felt that pollution? Do you know yourself sufficiently well to know it? Have you ever known that in you dwells no good thing? 'Vile and full of sin I am,' wrote Charles Wesley. The greater the saint the more he or she is aware of that. In other words, their repentance is deeper. They know about the corruption of their heart, the vileness that is in them as the result of the fall and original sin. And then they realise, on top of all that, their own weakness, their own helplessness. Those who think they can live the Sermon on the Mount in their own strength are people who are just ignorant, that is the only thing to say about them because the first statement in that sermon is, 'Blessed are the poor in spirit' (Matt. 5:3), the people who realise they cannot do anything.

What else changes? Well, their views on life and living. They now have a sense of the hatefulness of sin. They are not only aware of their sinful acts and their sinful nature, they hate sin as sin. They have a profound hatred of it as something opposed to God that should never have entered into this world. But, on the other hand, they have a sense of the beauty of holiness, the beauty and the perfection of righteousness. They see the beauty and the glory of God's holy law. These things are no longer abhorrent to them. They acknowledge that the law of God is perfect and pure and holy and just and righteous. It is no longer grievous to them. They do not talk about the Christian life being a narrow life. In a sense, they almost want it to be narrower. They are not trying to live as near as they can to the world; they hate all that and desire to be holy.

What, then, is the result of all this? Let me summarise it. Repentance must result in a sense of grief and of sorrow because of sin. It includes self-loathing – a hatred of one's sinful nature. Do we hate ourselves, I wonder? 'Oh wretched man that I am!' says Paul in

Romans 7:24 – that is it. It also leads to a sense of fear because we have sinned against this holy God, who is righteous and just and who is the Lord of the universe and the Judge eternal.

Our self-loathing in the light of God's justice and holiness leads to a longing for deliverance, and that, in turn, leads to our doing everything we can in order to make deliverance possible. People who repent do their utmost to save themselves. They may mislead themselves for a while in doing that, but it is a good sign, a sign that they are trying to do everything they can to set themselves free.

And then that goes on to confession of sin to God and a consuming desire to please Him. It means not only that they are poor in spirit and mourn, but that they cry out to God to have mercy upon them. 'Have mercy upon me O God' (Ps. 51:1). Our Lord has put it perfectly in His parable of the Pharisee and the tax collector: 'God have mercy upon me a sinner.' That is the position of those who have repented. They do not, they cannot say more than that at that point. They are broken-hearted; they realise it all; they can but cast themselves upon the mercy of God. They cannot plead anything else, but they plead that. That, in a sense, is a definition of repentance.

Now just to complete this, let us consider briefly the differences between remorse and repentance, because they are not the same thing. In remorse, you can have a sorrow because of failure and you can be very annoyed with yourself because you have done something that you know to be wrong and that you should not do. Indeed, remorse can go further; it can even include a fear of the consequences. Let us never forget that remorse can go as far as that. But that is not what Paul calls 'godly sorrow'. Let me remind you of what that is. Paul writes:

> Now I rejoice, not that ye were made sorry, but that ye sorrowed to repentance. [You can be made sorry without sorrowing to repentance.] For ye were made sorry after a godly manner, that ye might receive damage by us in nothing. For godly sorrow [this is the thing] worketh repentance to salvation not to be repented of . . . For behold this selfsame thing, that ye sorrowed after a godly sort, what carefulness it wrought in you; yea, what clearing of yourselves; yea, what indignation; yea, what fear; yea, what vehement desire; yea, what zeal; yea, what revenge!
>
> 2 Corinthians 7:9–11

You see the passion, the feeling, the emotion. They have seen it with their minds, they feel it and have done something about it.

So what are the differences between repentance and remorse? Well, true repentance, differing from remorse, includes these elements. It gives us a sense of having offended against God and having grieved Him and hurt Him. It gives us, I repeat, a sense of pollution and of utter unworthiness. It makes us say

> I hate the sins that made Thee mourn
> That drove Thee from my breast.
> > William Cowper

It gives us a longing and a determination to be rid of sin. This vehement desire, this activity, this zeal, this revenge that Paul is talking about, this is godly sorrow.

We can again sum it up in one of the Beatitudes. This is the ultimate test of true repentance and the thing that differentiates it most of all from remorse – repentance gives us a hunger and thirst after righteousness. It makes us desire to be like Christ and more and more like Him, to be righteous and holy and clean. We do not simply feel sorrow because we have fallen again and because we are suffering afterwards and have let ourselves down – not at all. Remorse is negative – repentance is positive.

> Oh for a heart to praise my God,
> > A heart from sin set free;
> A heart that always feels Thy blood
> > So freely shed for me.
> > > Charles Wesley

That is repentance.

14

Saving Faith

Having looked at the great biblical doctrine of repentance, we are now ready to look at the corresponding doctrine of *faith*. This particular subject is one of which we read right through the Bible. I suppose that there is more said about faith in the Bible than about anything else because faith is that by which all the blessings of salvation ultimately come to us. We are saved by faith, we are sanctified by faith, we walk by faith. 'This is the victory that overcometh the world, even our faith' (1 John 5:4), and so on.

All these blessings come to us through the medium of faith, so that clearly this is a matter about which we should be quite certain in our minds. Furthermore, as you read the history of the Church throughout the centuries you will find that there has been much disputation about faith and obviously so, because, since it is so central, the enemy, the devil, is more likely to attack here than in connection with any other article of the truth, and he has done so. Indeed, the great Protestant Reformation was, in a sense, nothing but a rediscovery and a redefinition of this great doctrine of faith.

However, it behoves us to touch only upon the great central principles in connection with this doctrine. We could spend a great deal of time on it, but we have much ground to cover and, therefore, we shall consider the most salient features. Faith is the instrument or the channel by which all salvation that is in Christ Jesus enters into us and is appropriated. It is the thing that links us to the fulness that dwells in our Lord and Saviour Jesus Christ. That is faith in its essence.

Now as you read the Bible, you will find that the word 'faith' is used to cover a number of different terms and has several connotations. We are confining ourselves in this study to one only and that is *saving* faith, but I will pause very briefly to show you two other uses of the word 'faith'.

In 1 Corinthians 12, you will find a list of the spiritual gifts – gifts of miracles, gifts of healing, and so on, and among them is the gift of faith. Now faith there obviously does not mean saving faith, because the Apostle's whole argument in that chapter is that every Christian does not have every one of these gifts of the Spirit; some have one gift, some have another.

So then, it cannot be saving faith because every Christian has that. No, in 1 Corinthians 12 faith refers to the special ability which God, through the Holy Spirit, gives to certain people to live a life of entire dependence directly upon Him – the kind of gift that George Müller or Hudson Taylor had in order that they might exercise their particular ministries. George Müller, indeed, is often known as 'the man who believed God'. In other words, he had, in an exceptional way, the spiritual gift of faith.

One other use of this word 'faith' is found in the list of the fruit of the Spirit given in Galatians 5:22–23. The Authorized Version has: 'the fruit of the Spirit is love, joy, peace, longsuffering, gentleness, goodness, faith . . .' But that is not a good translation because faith there really means faithfulness. It cannot mean saving faith because that is not one of the fruits of the Spirit. You will generally find that the context will make the meaning quite plain, if you just pay attention to it.

So, to return to saving faith: What is faith? Now, first, we must answer that question generally, and here I would start with a negative. We must stress the fact that it is not something natural. People often put it like this to us. They say, 'Faith is a natural faculty that every person has. You are always exercising faith in your life, you couldn't live for a day without doing so.' Then these are the illustrations they use. 'You go by train from London to Brighton and immediately you're exercising faith – in the engine, in the engine driver and in the rails, the sleepers, the bolts and nuts, and so on.' Or they say, 'A man goes into an aeroplane – well, he's exercising faith.'

Now I entirely dissent from that argument and I think it is very important that we should disagree with it. To start with, I do not call that faith at all, because to sit in that train and go from London to Brighton is not an exercise of faith. We are just doing something based upon the law of mathematical probability. That is a vital distinction. What we are saying to ourselves, either consciously or unconsciously, is this: the chances are that this train will go from here to Brighton without an accident. I know that there are occasional railway accidents but they do not happen every day. The law of mathematical probability tells me that probably this train will take me, without an accident, to Brighton. Now that is not faith at all.

Or, to put it another way: as we sit in the train, we are acting on the general experience of men and women who travel in trains. We see others doing the same thing and we know that they do it every day. Experience teaches us that on the whole it is safe to go on a journey in a train. You could say that we are acting upon an argument which is based upon general observation of certain facts.

But that, I say, is not at all faith in the biblical sense, and it is very important to realise this because sometimes the appeal is made like this: 'As you trust the train and the engine driver, why don't you trust the Lord Jesus Christ? You simply have to apply that faculty which you're using every day to this matter of your salvation and you'll be saved – why don't you do it?' Well, the answer is that you cannot do it, and that is why you see that there must be an essential difference between the two.

No, the faith described in the Bible is something unique. You see it to perfection in Abraham and the birth of Isaac. Charles Wesley echoes this story in his hymn. He says,

> Faith in Thy power Thou seest I have
> For Thou this faith hast wrought.

Faith is not a natural faculty that he has always possessed. It is God who has wrought it.

> Dead souls Thou callest from their grave
> And speakest worlds from nought.

Then again,

> In hope against all human hope
> Self desperate I believe.

You do not go into a train like that, do you? You are not hoping against hope that you will arrive in Brighton. Of course not! Quite the reverse. But when Abraham believed God, he *was* hoping against hope. He was not working on the law of mathematical probability.

He was ninety-nine and Sarah was ninety. All human experience was against it. The law of mathematical probability was dead against it. Observations of life, reason, all were against it. Abraham hoped against hope, but he became the father of the faithful. Now that is the biblical faith. How wrong it is, therefore, to think of faith, and to describe it, and to ask people to exercise it, as if it were some kind of natural faculty which we all have. We do not have it. Charles Wesley puts it perfectly when he tells us that it is something that is 'wrought by God'.

That brings me to my second point. What is the origin of faith? And the answer is, it is the gift of God. Again, you see the importance of taking doctrines in the right order. How important it is that we should have studied regeneration and so on before coming to faith. This again is the gift of God.

But here we come to a controversial point. Take the statement in Ephesians 2:8: 'For by grace are ye saved through faith; and *that* not of yourselves: it is the gift of God.' Now the whole question is: what does the 'that' mean? What does it refer to? There are those who would have us believe that it is a reference to the salvation. But surely it cannot be that. If it were, then Paul is just repeating himself. He has already said, 'By grace are ye saved', and he goes on to say that in the entire paragraph, so if he just repeats it again here, what is the purpose? No. By 'that' he is referring to faith, not salvation. 'By grace are ye saved through faith; and that' – the faith as well – 'not of yourselves: it is the gift of God: not of works, lest any man should boast.'

Yes, faith is the gift of God, and this, of course, can be proved quite easily by the previous doctrines that we have already considered. Think again of 1 Corinthians 2 and all that we have seen about the natural man to whom the things of God are 'foolishness' (v. 14), and Romans 8 where the carnal mind is described as being 'enmity against God' (v. 7). Such a person cannot exercise faith, as we have seen. In other words, the seed of faith is placed in us in regeneration and will be called into activity by the effectual call.

Or, to prove the same point from a different angle, let us look at it like this: faith, ultimately, is governed by what we have called our disposition. It is our fundamental disposition that determines whether we have faith or not. The author of the epistle to the Hebrews talks about 'an evil heart of unbelief' (Heb. 3:12). That is it. Faith is not an intellectual matter only, as we shall see. It is our disposition. If we have an evil heart, then we will be unbelievers. Whether we have faith or not is determined by our fundamental disposition.

Or, again, the Lord Himself says, 'How can ye believe which receive honour one of another, and seek not the honour that cometh from God only?' (John 5:44). 'You people cannot believe,' says our Lord in effect, 'your whole disposition is wrong. You are seeking honour one from another, and while you do that you will never have faith and you will never believe. How can you believe?' And then He repeats it, 'Why do ye not believe me?' (John 8:46). The same thing again: it was their disposition that was wrong. In other words, this is ultimately a moral question. It is something that concerns one's whole moral being, so that we must cease to think of faith as a kind of natural faculty that can be turned in the direction of God. No, it is the gift of God.

So how, exactly, does it come into being? What brings it forth? Here is another very important point, and the answer is that it is brought forth by the Scripture, by the word of God. It is by the truth that it is brought into being. Now there are innumerable proofs of that. Take, for instance, the great commission that our Lord gave to His disciples after His resurrection, just as He was bidding them farewell: 'Go ye therefore,' He said, 'and teach all nations' (Matt. 28:19). Disciple them, if you like, it is the same thing. Give them the information, preach the word to them, hold the truth before them.

Take, too, the commission given to Paul on the road to Damascus. Our Lord told him that He had called him, He was going to send him to the people and to the Gentiles. What for? 'To open their eyes' (Acts 26:18). He was to teach them. He was to show them their bondage to Satan and the terrible fate that was awaiting them.

But perhaps the classic passage on this is Romans 10, verses 10–17, where Paul writes of the preaching of the gospel and how it is that people believe. And here is the conclusion: 'So then faith cometh by hearing, and hearing by the word of God.' That is the way in which faith comes into being and into operation. It is called forth by the word of God, by the truth, by the gospel, by the message preached. And so Paul exhorts Timothy, 'Preach the word' (2 Tim. 4:2). James 1:18 reminds us in the same way: 'Of his own will begat he us with the word of truth.' And it is the same everywhere, right through the Scriptures, it is always by the word.

That, then, enables us now to go on to ask another very important question: What are the elements in faith, or in what does it consist? We are now ceasing to look at faith in general and are beginning to analyse it in particular. The first thing, obviously, as these quotations have established, is that it includes *belief*. You cannot have faith without believing, the very word means that. It means an assent to truth, an assent to the word of God that is being put before us. Yes, but notice that in Hebrews 11 belief is not a vague, general, cursory assent. In verse 13 the word *persuaded* is used – a very important word because it brings out the point. These people, the writer tells us, 'all died in faith, not having received the promises, but having seen them afar off, and were persuaded of them.' They were convinced of these things. So when we say that faith means belief, it does not only mean an awareness of or an assent to truth, but a firm conviction, we are convinced, we are persuaded.

Yes, but faith does not stop at that, and this is a most important point because there are some people who would define faith as just giving an assent to the truth. Clearly all this is of the most vital importance in the whole matter of evangelism. When people go to an enquiry room they are sometimes given certain information and asked, 'Do you believe that?' 'Yes,' they reply and they are told, 'All right, you're saved.' Assent to truth is regarded by some as being the whole of faith – but it is not. Faith also includes an element of confidence, a readiness to commit oneself to it. Look again at Hebrews 11:13: 'These all died in faith, not having received the promises, but having seen them afar off and were persuaded of them' – then – 'and they embraced them, and confessed that they were strangers and pilgrims on the earth.' In faith there is inevitably an element of trust and often problems arise in the spiritual life because people have stopped at the element of belief, and have not realised the vital importance of trust. But it is a part of faith.

Indeed we must go one step further. Faith also includes an element of commitment. You not only believe these things and trust them, you commit yourself – they 'confessed that they were strangers and pilgrims on the earth.' Or as Romans 10 puts it, they *call upon* God. They believe it so much, they trust it so much, that they call upon God: 'For whosoever shall call upon the name of the Lord shall be saved. How then shall they call on him in whom they have not believed?' (Rom. 10:13–14). Belief leads to the calling upon God, the trusting in God, the committing of oneself entirely to Him.

Now it is very important to draw this distinction because there is such a thing as intellectual assent only to truth. And that is not faith. It is sometimes also called historical faith. Alas, I have known people who have been in this position. To be quite honest, I am not sure that I myself have not once been in the position of mistaking historical faith for true faith. Historical faith means that, perhaps because you were brought up in a religious atmosphere and were always taught the Bible, when you were young you went to Sunday School or to some classes, perhaps because of all that, you accepted Christianity intellectually. Not only that, you may see that it all hangs together. You may see that it is the only reasonable explanation of life, and so on. And you accept it all intellectually, as a system of truth. But it is not faith if it stops at that, because it is possible for people to do all that and not trust themselves or commit themselves to it all. There have been men and women, alas, who have been experts on the Bible but whose lives have shown very clearly that they have never trusted in Christ. They have a 'form of godliness' while 'denying the power thereof' (2 Tim. 3:5). The history of the Church, alas, is strewn with illustrations of this very thing; people who have accepted it all intellectually, but whose hearts have never been engaged, who have never been moved. They have never committed themselves. So we must be very careful that what we call faith is not merely that kind of historical faith.

Now, there is an old illustration, and I repeat it because I do not know a better one. It is a story which is told to show the difference between intellectual assent to a proposition and faith, and it tells of a man who could walk back and forth across a whirlpool on a plank. Not only did he walk across himself, he then got a wheelbarrow and wheeled that back and forth also. Now there was a little boy standing by the side of the river and the man asked him, 'Do you think I can go over and come back safely without falling in?'

'Yes,' said the little boy.

'Well,' replied the man, 'jump inside.'

'Oh no!' said the boy.

Now that's it! It is a simple story but it does illustrate the truth up to a point. In faith there is something beyond intellectual agreement. There is trust, commitment. Faith is not merely a matter of belief.

What, then, is it in me that comes into operation in my faith? This again is a most important question because of the problem of historical faith, and also because of what the Bible itself, as we have seen, describes as temporary faith. The seed drops down and it springs up at once but it soon dies because it has no roots. In the same way, there are people who hear the word and believe it with joy, but they have no root and they wither away later on. And there are also the people who are described in Hebrews 6 – those with temporary faith. So it is very important to ask what it is in us that is involved in faith. And the answer, as I have been showing, is that it is the whole person, the mind, the heart and the will. So faith is not some sort of intellectual belief you carry with you in a bag, not something that you manipulate and bring in and put back when you like, but it is something that grips the whole of you.

There are two great texts on this. The first is again Romans 6:17: 'Ye were the servants of sin, but ye have obeyed from the heart that form of doctrine which was delivered you.' The mind, therefore, comes first, and it must. If it is truth that calls forth faith, it must be addressed primarily to the mind. Now the Roman Catholics dispute that. They say that ordinary Christians do not understand the faith and the truth that they believe; the Church alone can do that. So, they say, all that people must do to become Christians is trust themselves to the Church. Their mind as such is not involved. You see, therefore, the importance of definitions. Over against the Roman Catholics, we must assert that the mind is involved.

Yes, but there was also a man called Sandeman who wrought great havoc in the Church towards the end of the eighteenth century and the beginning of the nineteenth. He still has some followers, but, sadly, there are many more unconscious Sandemanians. He taught that faith only touches a person's intellect, nothing else at all, and he misused Romans 10:9. He said that all we have to say is, 'Yes, I believe those things,' and then all is well. Your mere statement saves you: 'If thou shalt confess with thy mouth the Lord Jesus . . . thou shalt be saved.' That was his teaching, and he persuaded many people that it was right. But the result was that they did not worry about their feelings at all, or about their heart, or their will. It was merely a matter of intellect. And many were held and led into bondage by that teaching. So over against Sandeman we say, yes, faith is something that involves the mind and the intellect, but it does not stop at that. It must also involve the heart.

Here I turn to the apostle Peter: 'Unto you therefore which believe he is precious' (1 Pet. 2:7). Notice the *therefore*. You cannot believe in Him without being moved by Him. There is no value in what you call belief unless it leads to love. If you do not love the Lord Jesus Christ, you have nothing but an intellectual assent, a proposition concerning Him. 'It follows, as the night follows the day,' says Peter in effect, 'that if you really believe in Him, he is precious to you and you love Him.' Your affections must be engaged.

You may be surprised that I say this. There are so many people who glory in the fact that there is not much emotion in their evangelism.

But there should be emotion in evangelism. It should not only be emotion, but if there is no emotion, there is something wrong. Your heart should be moved and you should not come without tears of repentance and of joy. If you are not moved by your belief, it is not faith. We must always denounce *emotionalism* but God forbid that we should ever leave out emotion.

And, in turn, the will is engaged. Faith without works is dead. And there is no doubt about that. It is no use your saying that you believe in the Lord Jesus Christ if you are still living a worldly life – that is what it comes to. I am not interested in what experiences people may give, if they are still worldly people, there is no point in their claiming to have faith and to have belief. 'As the body without the spirit is dead, so faith without works is dead also' (Jas. 2:26). 'Ye that love the Lord,' says the psalmist, 'hate evil' (Ps. 97:10). You cannot love the Lord without hating evil. It is bound to happen. You leave it, you turn away from it. Look at David in Psalms 51 and 139. Look at it everywhere in the Bible.

Consider, too, these people in the eleventh chapter of Hebrews. When Abraham heard God's word to him, he believed and left his country though he did not know where he was going. Faith acts. The will is always involved. And if your will has not been involved, it is pointless to say, 'Ah yes, I believe that, I have accepted it.' In other words, the thing that needs to be emphasised today is that faith is not a sort of *believism*. That is a danger because in believism the heart is not involved and the will is not engaged. But in faith, I repeat, the whole person is engaged. Christ saves the whole man or woman and no part is left out. So you see that corresponding to the belief and the trust and the commitment is the intellect and the heart and the will.

That, then, is our essential definition of faith. But there are certain problems left, and we must deal with them because they are so often raised in discussions and people so frequently ask questions about them.

First, what is *the relationship between faith and reason*? The best answer I can give is that faith is not a matter of reason. Some people teach that it is. They say that if only men and women would use their minds, they would be bound to become Christians; they can reason themselves into Christianity. But that is thoroughly unscriptural. They cannot because the natural man or woman's reason is also fallen. Not only that, there are supernatural and miraculous elements in faith to which reason cannot attain. So true faith is not entirely a matter of reason. Indeed, I would quote to you the statement of the great Blaise

Pascal, perhaps the greatest mathematician that the world has ever known and who had an evangelical conversion. He said that the supreme achievement of reason is to teach us that there is an end to reason.

So what about faith and reason? Well, faith is not mere reason, but on the other hand, neither is it contrary to reason. It is not unreasonable; it is not irrational. That is the charge that is brought against us.

'Ah,' people say, 'but what you're teaching is a kind of irrationality. You say that faith isn't a matter of reason. Well then, is it opposed to reason?'

No, it is not. It is not reason, neither is it contrary to reason. What is it then? It is *supra-reason*. It means that our reason brings us to the point when we realise that reason is not enough, and at that point we have nothing to do but submit ourselves to the revelation. And that is faith. Faith is accepting this revelation.

More and more I like to think of it like this. Faith means that I deliberately shut myself down to this book, the Bible. I refuse to philosophise. I refuse to ask certain questions. People are always asking them. They want to understand the doctrine of the Trinity. You cannot. You will never understand it. Your mind and reason cannot grasp it. It is too great. It is too divine. It is too eternal. So, you accept it; and you stop asking questions. One of the best signs of the real birth of faith in people is that they stop asking certain questions. Think of faith more like that, if it will help you. You come to the Bible as a little child and you accept it, and then you begin to find that it is most reasonable. Reason could not bring you into it, but once you are in it, you will find that it all hangs together; it is a great composite whole. There is the one message running right through. The parts are all there. They all fit together like a perfect mosaic. It is the most reasonable thing in the world, and yet reason will never bring you into it.

Faith brings you into the Bible and then you see the great reasonableness of it all. For Christ is not only the power of God, He is the wisdom of God (1 Cor. 1:24), and when you are in it, you see that this alone is wisdom and that everything else would be unfair and unreasonable. If faith were a matter of reason, then only people with great intellects could be Christians. On the other hand, faith is not unreasonable, because if that were so, no one with an intellect could be a Christian either. But because it is what it is, it puts us all on the same level. We accept this revelation, and then we proceed to understand. That is the relationship between faith and reason.

What about the relationship between faith and knowledge? Yes, again, that is a most important point. Let me put it like this. There must be an element of knowledge in faith because faith comes into being as the result of the operation of truth. If the first element in faith is belief, and if it is belief of the truth, we must know what we believe. So Peter exhorts the Christians in this way: 'Sanctify the Lord God in your hearts: and be ready always to give an answer to every man that asketh you a reason of the hope that is in you with meekness and fear' (1 Pet. 3:15).

But there is a great difference between *apprehending* and *comprehending*. Comprehending means that you can span a thing, that your mind can fully understand, while apprehending means being aware with the mind. Now the element of knowledge in faith is not the element of comprehension but it must of necessity be apprehension. When people come to me and I ask them if they are Christians, if they reply, 'Well, I believe, I have faith,' then I have the right to ask them, 'What do you believe?' You always have the right to ask Christians, or those who claim to be Christians, what they believe, and the Christian should be able to answer the question. As Romans 10:14 puts it, 'How shall they believe in him of whom they have not heard? and how shall they hear without a preacher?' And Paul goes on to work out how faith comes by 'hearing, and hearing by the word of God' (v. 17). So there is this element of knowledge and of understanding in faith – it is apprehension rather than comprehension.

And that is why all the epistles go on to appeal to us to grow in knowledge. All the writers' efforts were directed at making the people *understand* more and more, not simply feel more and be entertained more, but grow in an understanding of the truth so that they should know more today than they did a year ago. They are not still living in that old experience, but have more understanding.

'Well then,' someone may ask, 'what is it that we are to understand? What is it that we are to know? Are you telling us that we are not Christians unless we understand the entire gamut of the Christian faith and unless we are experts in every single detail and every doctrine? Are you saying that a person who can't really give a comprehensive account of the whole of Christian theology is not a Christian?' No, as we have just seen, I am not! But I am saying that there are certain truths which are absolutely essential and vital to the integrity of the gospel, to the very being of faith. Then there are other truths which, though not essential to the integrity of the gospel, are essential to its symmetry and perfection.

Let me explain what that means. There is a certain irreducible minimum and we must contend for that. But there are other doctrines and other aspects of the faith which are not absolutely essential to salvation but are essential to a complete, fully orbed, symmetrical conception of salvation, to a balanced, organised faith and the expression of it. In other words, there are certain doctrines that we *must* believe and there are others about which we are doubtful and about which there may be legitimate disagreement.

What, then, are these things that are essential? Well, we must believe in God. We must believe about the character of God. If we do not believe that God is holy, we are not Christians. If we do not believe that God is just and righteous, we are not Christians. In addition to believing in the love of God, we must believe in the other attributes that we considered in an earlier lecture.[1] The biblical revelation about this holy, righteous God who is the Judge of the universe – that is essential.

It is equally essential that we should believe in our sinful and lost condition. I am not prepared to argue about that – that is absolute. If we do not know what a sinner is, that we are sinners and have repented, we are not Christians, we cannot be, and there is no value in our saying that we believe in the Lord Jesus Christ. For what is it to believe in the Lord Jesus Christ unless it is to see that He is the Saviour and the Redeemer and the only one. But what do I need to be saved from? It is the guilt of my sin in the presence of this holy God. So I must be clear about the doctrine of sin and my lost estate and my helplessness, and then about the person and the work of Christ.

Paul himself gives these essentials in the opening verses of 1 Corinthians 15: 'For I delivered unto you first of all that which I also received' – What? – 'how that Christ died for our sins according to the scriptures' (v. 3). That is the first thing – the person and what He has done; the priestly work, the mediatorial work, the atonement. I do not argue about this. I know I am described as narrow, but if people do not see that they are saved only by the blood of Christ, well then, think what you like of me, I cannot see that such people can be Christians. It is essential. 'I determined not to know anything among you, save Jesus Christ, and him crucified' says Paul to the Corinthians (1 Cor. 2:2). Paul 'placarded' His death to the Galatians. It was always at the centre. This is not a matter to be argued about. This

---

1. See Volume 1, *God the Father, God the Son.*

does not belong to the symmetry of faith but to the integrity of faith, as do also some aspects of this great doctrine of the person and work of the Holy Spirit that we are engaged upon at the present time. If you do not believe in regeneration, if you do not see its utter absolute necessity, then I do not see that you have any right to regard yourself as a Christian. If you do not see that you are so lost that nothing but receiving new life from God can reconcile you and take you to heaven, then your are lacking at a vital point, a point that is integral and belongs to the very integrity of faith.

Those, then, are absolute necessities. And I would say that you have a right to insist upon the presence of those doctrines before you are prepared to tell a person, 'Yes, you have got faith.' Faith is not a vague feeling; it is not a vague desire to have certain blessings from Christ. Faith is a belief of this gospel, this word of God, this message, this truth that the apostles were preaching, the truth they write about. It is an acceptance, and an assent to that. It is a persuasion which moves me and makes me do something – that is faith. And I must know what I believe and whom I believe and what I believe concerning Him. Those are the irreducible minimums, the bare essentials, the things that belong to the very integrity of faith.

15
Assurance

The subject at which we have now arrived is not only dealt with very frequently in the Scripture but, from our practical standpoint, is again of very great importance. I refer to the relationship between faith and assurance, or, as it is sometimes known, the assurance of faith. This is not only a practical question, it is one that has often perplexed people and is often the cause of considerable unhappiness. We are looking at it because it is one of the doctrines but, as I constantly remind you, we do not consider them merely to interest ourselves with intellectual problems. The intent behind this series is that our practical knowledge of God may be deepened and increased. So we are really dealing with something that is experiential as well as a doctrine that is taught in the Scripture.

Now there are some people who would say that assurance is impossible to the Christian in this life. That, for instance, is the teaching of the Roman Catholic Church, which regards this doctrine of assurance as one of the most pernicious and objectionable teachings of Protestantism. The whole Roman Catholic teaching is – and it follows, I think, from what we have seen of the Roman Catholic view of faith and of many other doctrines – that Christians cannot have assurance in this life; all they can do is to trust themselves to mother Church. But that is not assurance, because they are kept, as it were, permanently dependent upon the Church and upon the sacraments. But this idea that Christians can have some inward assurance is to them utterly abhorrent and a most dangerous heresy.

But that view is not only held by the Roman Catholics. The theological movement associated with the name of Professor Karl Barth of Switzerland, undoubtedly one of the most powerful theologians of the twentieth century, at this point happens to agree with the Roman Catholic Church. Barth, again, thoroughly abominates and denounces this idea of assurance of salvation and he is quite consistent with his own system of theology in doing so. I think it is good that we bear this in mind, because one often finds good evangelical people applauding Barthianism and certain Barthian preachers without realising that it is an essential part of their position to deny the possibility of assurance of salvation. Barth dislikes experience altogether and his whole view is that you really can be certain of none of these things, and, moreover, that all our attempts at expression of our faith are, of necessity, wrong and fallacious.

Now, over against all that, the Protestant fathers – I mean by that Luther and Calvin and their companions – went to the other extreme and said that assurance of faith is an essential part of faith. Undoubtedly they took up that position partly as a reaction to the Roman Catholic Church. They were so anxious to liberate people from the thraldom and tyranny of the Church that they went so far as to say that without this assurance and certainty, a person's so-called faith was of no value at all.

And, again, this is not confined to the Protestant fathers. John Wesley, especially in his early days, taught exactly the same thing. He, having had his experience in Aldersgate Street, taught quite definitely for a number of years that faith must give the kind of assurance that he himself had received; that alone was true faith. Later on he modified that teaching.

It is interesting, here, to notice that the attitude of these different teachers towards assurance cuts right across their various other differences. John Wesley, the Arminian, taught that this assurance was essential. But there were other Methodists in that eighteenth century who were not Arminian and had the Reformed view, but they, at first, were equally insistent that assurance was an essential part of faith. For instance, this was true of the Methodist fathers in Wales who would only admit people into Church membership who had assurance of salvation. They sometimes went so far as to make aspiring church members say when assurance happened and how they received it, who the preacher was and what his text was!

That shows the extreme reaction that often occurs, especially when the period before it has been vague and indefinite and moral rather than spiritual. But there is no doubt that the prevailing Reformed teaching about this question is that which is taught, for instance, in the *Westminster Confession of Faith*. This says that assurance is not an essential part of faith, that you can have faith without assurance, but that at the same time assurance is not only possible but is desirable and one should never rest until one has it. That has been the teaching most commonly held by evangelical people ever since the Protestant Reformation.

If, then, that is so, if it is right that you can have faith without assurance (though assurance is desirable), then we are entitled to say that in and of itself doubt is not incompatible with faith. You see, doubt must be put over against the assurance, not over against the faith. Men and women who have faith may be grievously assailed by doubts. Peter, for instance, having walked on the water towards our Lord, suddenly began to look at the boisterous waves; then he began to sink, and our Lord said to him, 'O thou of little faith, wherefore didst thou doubt?' (Matt. 14:31). Our Lord did not say that Peter had lost his faith because he doubted, so doubt is not incompatible with faith, but it generally means that there is weak faith or a little faith and that may be due to many causes.

It may be due to sin. If Christian people fall into sin they will have a sense of condemnation and that in turn will probably lead to doubt. It does not mean they have lost their faith, but they may very well be in a condition of doubt until the sin has been confessed and relinquished and all is clear again. The faith remains but it is weak and uncertain and they are the victims of doubt for the time being.

However, doubt can also be due to a misunderstanding of the real nature of faith. People sometimes do not realise that faith is something active, something that must be applied. Take our Lord's question to the disciples in the boat. He was lying asleep and they thought that they were about to sink. But He turned to them and said, in effect, 'Where is your faith? You've got it but you're not applying it' (Matt. 8:26). Now if people do not realise that faith has to be applied, that it involves an activity, for the time being they may very well be the victims of doubt. And in the same way, we must understand that faith has to appropriate, faith has to lay hold on truth, and that again is a form of activity. If we remain in a purely passive state, waiting for something to happen, then the probability is that the doubt will be more prominent than the faith; but if we realise that faith appropriates – lays hold upon – we will get rid of our doubts and then our faith will become strong.

Then the next statement would be that, according to the Scripture, you can clearly have faith without assurance. My authority for this is that Peter says: 'Wherefore the rather, brethren, give diligence to make your calling and election sure' (2 Pet. 1:10). You and I cannot determine our calling nor our election, but we can make them sure, and the whole point of that passage is to exhort people to give this diligence. 'Add to your faith virtue,' he says; 'and to virtue knowledge; and to knowledge temperance; and to temperance patience; and to patience godliness; and to godliness brotherly kindness; and the brotherly kindness charity' (vv. 5–7). And Peter impresses this upon us. You will have your entry into the everlasting kingdom of our Father if you belong to God's people. Yes, but if you want an *abundant* entry – that is his expression in verse 11 – if you want to go in with this blessed assurance, then you must make your calling and election sure. Obviously, then, the implication is that you can have your faith but without the assurance, hence Peter's exhortation to us to have the assurance.

Or again: 'These things,' says John, 'have I written unto you that believe on the name of the Son of God; that ye may know that ye have eternal life' (1 John 5:13). The Revised Version translation of that verse is very much better than the Authorised [King James] Version: 'These things have I written unto you that ye may know that ye have eternal life, even unto you that believe on the name of the Son of God.' That puts the emphasis on the fact that John is not addressing unbelievers. The letter was not written to people outside, in the world, but to members of churches. They are believers, yes, but John writes in order that they may *know* that they have eternal life. He wants them also to have assurance. It is obvious, therefore, that you can have faith without assurance, otherwise this letter need never have been written.

Then the fourth statement is a very interesting point, I think. Obviously, in connection with any sort of faith, however weak, however feeble, however immature, however small it may be, there must be a certain amount of knowledge and, therefore, of confidence, of assurance.

'But that is to contradict what you've just been saying,' says someone.

Well, on the surface it sounds like it, but let me explain. We agreed in the last lecture that faith must, of necessity and by definition, believe something. You cannot have faith in a vacuum. Faith means that, at any rate, you believe with your mind and give intellectual assent to the truth that is taught in the word. You cannot believe without knowing what you believe. So, in believing these things about God and about our Lord and about salvation, there is a sense in which you must have a modicum of assurance and of comfort and of confidence, and yet I do not call that this true assurance of faith.

What, then, is the difference? We can put it like this. What I have just been describing is what I would call an *objective* assurance and there is a difference between an objective and a subjective assurance. Again, the classic illustration of this is John Wesley himself. Before the incident in Aldersgate Street when he felt that 'strange warming' of his heart, John Wesley believed the truth and he knew it was true – that was an objective assurance. But what he did not have until that night was the subjective assurance – the thing inside.

Now I remember this being put to me once very graphically by an old preacher who was lying on a sick bed. He was unhappy and I asked him what was troubling him.

'Well,' he said, 'I am absolutely certain, with the whole of my being, of the truth I have always preached.'

'So, what is wrong?' I asked.

'Well,' he said, 'although I am certain of it, I'm not happy about its registration *here*' – pointing to his heart.

That's it. He had an absolute objective assurance, but he was not clear, he was not happy, in the realm of his subjective assurance. And that is a helpful way of looking at it because there are many people, I find, in that very position. They say that they have no doubt at all about the truth itself and yet they very rightly say, 'Yes, but I'm not happy about myself inside, my own assurance.'

True assurance, of course, includes both – the objective and the subjective.

So that brings us to the next great question: What are the grounds of assurance? I mean now the complete assurance – subjective as well as objective, internal as well as external. The first of these grounds is *the teaching of the word of God*. John says, 'He that believeth on the Son of God hath the witness in himself' – then notice – 'he that believeth not God hath made him [God] a liar, because he believeth not the record that God gave of his Son. And this is the record, that God hath given to us eternal life, and this life is in his Son' (1 John 5:10–11). So the first ground of my assurance is that it is stated here in the word. You will find the same teaching in John 3:33: 'He that hath received his testimony [the testimony of the truth] hath set to his seal that God is true.' So in believing we are putting our seal upon the truth and saying, 'God is true; what God says is true. I put my seal on it.' It is another way of stating that if I do not believe, I am virtually saying that I do not believe God or that God is a liar.

So then, what has God said? What is his testimony? Let me remind you of some of the passages. Take John 3:36, for instance: 'He that believeth on the Son hath everlasting life.' Not shall have – 'he *hath*'. 'And he that believeth not the Son shall not see life; but the wrath of God abideth on him.' Or John 5:24: 'Verily, verily, I say unto you, He that heareth my word, and believeth on him that sent me, hath' – not will have – 'hath everlasting life, and shall not come into condemnation, but is passed from death unto life.' That again is quite categorical. Then go on to John 6:47: 'Verily, verily, I say unto you, He that believeth on me hath' – hath now – 'everlasting life.' Take a verse from Acts: 'To him give all the prophets witness,' said Peter, 'that through his name whosoever believeth in him shall receive remission of sin' (Acts 10:43). The moment you believe in Him you receive remission of sins. And again, Paul, preaching in Antioch of Pisidia, said, 'And by him all that believe are justified from all things, from which ye could not be justified by the law of Moses' (Acts 13:39).

Those, then, are the first grounds. Here I have these statements of Scripture which I have already accepted as the word of God. They make categorical statements about those who believe these things. They say that if they believe them they already have eternal life. So I face these statements; I say, 'Therefore I have eternal life, the Scriptures say so, and if I do not believe that, I am making God to be a liar.'

But that is only the first ground of assurance; and I do want to emphasise this. There are, alas, certain people who would say that that is the only ground, that no more is necessary and they refuse to go beyond that. Now I regard that viewpoint as extremely dangerous. Later on we shall consider false assurance, false grounds of assurance, and I am not sure but that that is not one of them – to stop at that point. Oh yes, you start with that, you must start with it, and it must be there, but there is a kind of teaching which goes to people and says to them, 'This is what the Scripture says, do you agree with that?' If they reply, 'Yes,' then the teaching says, 'Very well, you are all right.' And they are just left at that. But the Scripture does not leave us at that. That chapter from 1 John which I have been quoting does not leave us at that. It tells us that there were once people who were members of the Church who have now gone out because they did not really belong. Yet there was a time when they said that they believed all these things, and no doubt they were perfectly happy. 'But they were not of us,' says John; 'for if they had been of us, they would no doubt have continued with us: but they went out, that they might be made manifest that they were not all of us' (1 John 2:19).

So, then, we have a second ground of assurance – what we may very well call *the test of life*. The Scripture tells me that if I believe, I have eternal life. So are there certain tests that I can apply to myself to make sure that I really have got eternal life? Here they are, again in this first epistle of John. The first is believing that Jesus is the Christ: 'Whosoever believeth that Jesus is the Christ is born of God' (1 John 5:1). That is evidence that you are born of God (I shall define that a little more closely later).

John's second great test is loving the brethren: 'We know that we have passed from death unto life, because we love the brethren' (1 John 3:14). That is good, is it not? Because I prefer to be together with other Christians rather than in a cinema, I love the brethren and all is well with me. But wait a minute, let us be careful! John defines what he means by loving the brethren. It does include what we have just stated, but that is not enough. John goes on: 'Hereby perceive we the love of God, because he laid down his life for us: and we ought to lay down our lives for the brethren' (1 John 3:16). That is a part of loving the brethren. 'But whoso hath this world's good, and seeth his brother have need, and shutteth up his bowels of compassion from him, how dwelleth the love of God in him? My little children, let us not love in word, neither in tongue; but in deed and in truth' (vv. 17–18). Yes, it means enjoying their company and their society but it must include this practical side also if the need arise. Love is practical, always, it does things. So let us be careful that we apply the Scripture to ourselves truly and thoroughly.

Then the third test that John has is *keeping His commandments*. He puts it like this: 'Hereby we do know that we know him, if we keep his commandments' (1 John 2:3). John keeps on repeating this, and in the fifth chapter he says, 'For this is the love of God, that we keep his commandments: and his commandments are not grievous' (v. 3). So as you read your Bible and you see it telling you not to do some things and to do others – does that go against the grain? Do you find it grievous? And are you putting those things into practice? That is a test of whether we have life or not.

And then the last test that I have eternal life is: *having the Spirit*.

'Hereby,' John says in the last verse of the third chapter, 'Hereby we know that he abideth in us, by the Spirit which he hath given us.' That raises a very big question does it not? How do we know whether or not we have received the Spirit? It is important from the experiential standpoint in this way: the Scriptures teach us that the gift of the Holy Spirit is the seal which we have of the inheritance into which we shall enter. Paul says, 'In whom ye also trusted, after that he heard the word of truth, the gospel of your salvation: in who also after that ye believed, ye were sealed with that holy Spirit of promise, which is the earnest of our inheritance until the redemption of the purchased possession, unto the praise of his glory' (Eph. 1:13–14). How do I know that I am going into the glorious inheritance? Well, my answer is: the Holy Spirit within me is the seal upon the document that I am an heir. And, in the same way, in 2 Corinthians 1:22, Paul calls the Spirit, 'the earnest'. Now the earnest is a guarantee, something that is put into your hand in order to say, 'I have given you that as a foretaste; you will get the rest, but I give you this as an earnest – the seal.'

But, further, how can I know exactly whether God has given me the gift of the Spirit? Here are some of the answers you will find in Scripture. The very fact that we believe truly that Jesus is the Christ, the very fact that we believe the doctrine concerning Him – which I elaborated upon in the last lecture in dealing with the person of Christ and the doctrine of the Atonement and so on – truly to believe that is a proof that we have received the Spirit. 'The carnal mind is enmity against God' (Rom. 8:7); 'If any man have not the Spirit of Christ, he is none of his' (Rom. 8:9). The whole argument of Romans 8 proves that. The 'natural man', the 'carnal man' cannot believe, he does not want to.

And, again, in 1 Corinthians we find the same argument: 'the natural man receiveth not the things of the Spirit of God' (v. 14). The 'princes of this world' did not recognise Christ, for had they recognised Him 'they would not have crucified the Lord of glory' (v. 8). And why did they not recognise Him? Because they did not have the Spirit. But God has given unto us, 'Not the spirit of the world, but the spirit which is of God; that we might know the things that are freely given to us of God' (v. 12). 'We have the mind of Christ' (v. 16). So if you really believe these things you can be certain you have got the Spirit because, again as Paul puts it to the Corinthians: 'No man can say that Jesus is Lord, but by the Holy Ghost' (1 Cor. 12:3). You cannot say this otherwise. So there is our first proof that God has given me the Spirit: my belief.

Secondly, if I desire more of this knowledge it is good evidence that I have the Spirit. 'For as many as are led by the Spirit of God,' says Paul in Romans 8:14, 'they are the sons of God.' So if you want to be led by the Spirit; if you have come to the end of your own resources; if you are distrustful of your own human understanding and of all philosophy; if you say, 'I want to be enlightened, I want to be led by the Spirit in every sense,' it is again evidence that you have the Spirit. It is only those in whom the Spirit dwells who want to be led by Him and submit to His leading.

Thirdly, the work of the Spirit within us is a proof that He is in us. What is that? Well first and foremost, revealing sin; that is always the first work of the Spirit. He brings to light the hidden things of darkness, the sins about which we are not at first conscious. As He becomes more powerful within, we become more sensitive to sin and we now regard as sin things which we used to overlook. This is a great evidence of the work of the Spirit. And He also produces a hatred of sin and a desire to be free from it.

Then the fourth evidence is the fruit of the Spirit. Go back to the great list in Galatians 5: 'The fruit of the Spirit is love, joy, peace, longsuffering, gentleness, goodness, faith [faithfulness], meekness, temperance' (vv. 22–23).

And then the fifth is the Spirit of adoption: 'Ye have received the Spirit of adoption, whereby we cry, Abba, Father' (Rom. 8:15).

I trust that this classification is clear to you. We have just been considering our reasons for saying that the Spirit is within us, which is one of the proofs that we have eternal life. This *test of life* is our second ground, or basis, for assurance in our Christian life, and the four proofs under the heading 'test of life' are all found in John's first epistle.

And the third major ground of assurance of faith is *the witness of the Holy Spirit with our spirit*: 'The Spirit itself beareth witness with our spirit, that we are the children of God' (Rom. 8:16). Now this is crucial and at this point I must express a criticism of the Revised Standard Version. You will find that the RSV links verses 15 and 16 together and instead of saying, 'But ye have received the Spirit of adoption, whereby we cry, Abba, Father. The Spirit itself beareth witness with our spirit, that we are the children of God', it has: 'When we cry Abba, Father, it is the Spirit himself bearing witness with our spirit that we are children of God.' Instead of two things, it makes it one; that is, He bears witness by making me cry, Abba, Father.

But the Authorised [King James] Version does not say that and is undoubtedly right. These two things are separate and distinct. The Spirit of adoption is something that is in our spirits. Indeed, Paul has been saying that: 'For as many as are led by the Spirit of God, they are the sons of God. For ye have not received the spirit of bondage again to fear; but ye have received the Spirit of adoption, whereby we cry, Abba, Father' (vv. 14–15). But the witness of the Holy Spirit with our spirit is something different, something additional – a witness. You notice that Paul does not say here, 'that is borne through our spirit'; but 'the Spirit beareth witness with our spirit'. Our spirits cry, 'Abba, Father.' Yes, and we must not say that that is the Spirit bearing witness in me. My spirit cries, 'Abba, Father.' Yes, but on top of that, the Holy Spirit bears witness *with* my spirit; He does not bear witness *to* it. My spirit does one thing and the Holy Spirit does something alongside.

As I have said, this is very important. This is, to me, one of the higher reaches of the Christian life. It is something that is very difficult to describe, and yet our Lord talked a lot about it. You will find the record in John 14, when He begins to introduce His teaching concerning the Holy Spirit. You will find that He says there that He and the Father will come to us and that they will take up their abode in us (v. 23). That is what I am talking about. That is what the Spirit does. When the Holy Spirit, this other Comforter, has come, the effect will be that the Father and the Son will come to us and will take up their abode in us. Indeed our Lord uses another word which is very striking. In connection with this selfsame teaching, He says, 'He that hath my commandments, and keepeth them, he it is that loveth me: and he that loveth me shall be loved of my Father, and I will love him' – notice – 'and will manifest myself to him' (v. 21). He will manifest Himself in a spiritual manner to this person and that is something that is done by the Holy Spirit, about whom He is speaking.

Then there are statements in the first chapters of the book of Revelation about the 'hidden manna' and the 'white stone' that are given to the believer, and about the hidden name – the new name. Nobody else understands it; they do not know anything about these things, but believers do; that is the Spirit witnessing with their spirit. Indeed, Paul has already said it in Romans 5 when he says, 'The love of God is shed abroad in our hearts by the Holy Ghost which is given unto us' (v. 5). So what is this? It is something that is difficult to put into words, but it is an operation of the Holy Spirit within us which is definite and distinct and by means of which He gives us a realisation and a consciousness of the living Lord. Christ manifests Himself to us and we know Him with a kind of inner intuition, over and above all that we believe about Him by faith. He is made real to us. I am very fond of quoting Hudson Taylor's prayer about this:

> Lord Jesus, make Thyself to me
> A living bright reality.
> More present to faith's vision keen
> Than any outward object seen,
> More dear, more intimately nigh
> Than e'en the sweetest earthly tie.

That is it. It is something to which God's people have testified from the very beginning.

Now this is the ultimate, the final ground of assurance. It is a certain knowledge because He is real to us, because He has manifested Himself to us according to His promise. And it is interesting to notice the saints who testify to this. Again, it cuts across all the different schools of theology. Luther had an experience of that; Jonathan Edwards had it; Whitefield had it; so did Wesley, Finney and Moody. In many respects they did not belong to the same schools theologically, but they all together witnessed to this experience which the Holy Spirit had given them when He testified with their spirits, and they felt it to be overwhelming.

Moody was walking down a street in New York City when it happened to him. He had to hold up his hands and pray God to stop; he was afraid he would be crushed and killed physically because of the glory and the grandeur and the transcendence of the experience. That is the ultimate ground of assurance though the feelings accompanying it may vary tremendously. Again, in the case of Finney it came as wave after wave upon him, and he was drenched with perspiration. Read the accounts of these men and what they have to tell you. For John Wesley it was not so overwhelming, but was a 'strange warming' of his heart. And so we could go on.

How, then, is one to obtain this assurance? Here are the rules taught in Scripture: first make certain of your belief. If you have not got assurance, make certain that you are really not relying upon yourself in any respect for salvation. Be sure that you see all your righteousness as filthy rags and know that if you lived a thousand years you would never fit yourself to stand before God. Make certain that you are relying only upon the finished work of Christ upon the cross, that you are solely dependent upon His righteousness. Apply the word of Scripture to yourself, get to know it, read it. Take these scriptures that I have been quoting; stand on them; apply them to yourself. Say, 'I have been crucified with Christ, I have died with Christ. The Scripture says it; I believe it and I stand on it.' Live the life. Yield yourself to be led of the Spirit. Seek His face. If you ask Him to fulfil His promise and to manifest Himself to you, He has pledged to do it.

Finally, let me say just a word on the difference between true and false assurance. False assurance is generally due to bad teaching, to false evangelism, to pushing people to decisions or trying to bring them to the birth before the process of the Holy Spirit is worked out. Our Lord talked about the people who would come to Him and say, 'Lord, Lord, have we not prophesied in thy name? . . . and in thy name done many wonderful works?' And yet He will say to them, 'I never knew you: depart from me, ye that work iniquity' (Matt. 7:22–23). They thought they were all right. They had an assurance, but it was false. The three parables in Matthew 25 teach exactly the same thing: the foolish virgins, the man who hid his talent and the people who asked when they had not done this, that and the other to Him. They thought that they had always pleased Him. But He said, 'You did not do it to these my brethren and therefore you have not done it unto me. You are not saved, you do not belong to me.' False assurance.

What, then, can assure us that our assurance is a true one? The characteristics of a true assurance are these: first and last and always – humility. Christians who have true assurance do not say that this is a jolly good life, nor that they are having a great kick out of it. No, no, there is always a humility about God's children because they know what they are and that they owe it all to Him. If your assurance does not make you humble, I beseech you, examine the grounds again. Go back to the Scripture. True assurance always produces humility. It also always has a practical effect on character and living. It leads to the kind of life depicted in the first epistle of John.

Another very good test is this: if you find yourself examining yourself, it is a sign of a true assurance. People who have a false assurance do not like self-examination; obviously not, because it is going to make them unhappy, it is going to shake them and they do not want that. But people who have true assurance are so concerned about being absolutely right that they examine themselves. Paul says, 'I keep under my body . . . lest that by any means, when I have preached to others, I

myself might be a castaway' (1 Cor. 9:27). He examined himself constantly and in 2 Corinthians 13:5 he exhorts the Corinthians, 'Examine
yourselves, whether ye be in the faith; prove your own selves.' And the
Christian is glad to do so. In 1 Peter 4 we are told, 'Judgment must
begin at the house of God . . . And if the righteous scarcely be saved,
where shall the ungodly and the sinner appear' (vv. 17–18).

Now true Christians walk in reverence and godly fear. There is no
carnal joviality about them, they are humble people who walk in the
light of these truths. And, above all, those who have true assurance
are always striving after a yet nearer conformity to Christ. 'That I
may know him,' says Paul, 'and the power of his resurrection, and the
fellowship of his sufferings, being made conformable unto his death
. . . I count not myself to have apprehended: but this one thing I do,
forgetting those things which are behind . . . I press toward the mark'
(Phil. 3:10, 13–14). And the Christian is always doing that. People
with the true assurance always have an increasing desire to be more
like Him. Yes, says John, 'Every man that hath this hope in him
purifieth himself, even as he is pure' (1 John 3:3).

Finally, listen to Whitefield describing how this amazing assurance,
this direct testimony of the Spirit, was given to him. He had been
seeking this assurance for a long time, and then he fell ill. He writes:

This fit of sickness continued upon me for seven weeks and a glorious
visitation it was, the blessed Spirit was all this time purifying my soul. All
my former gross and notorious and even my heart-sins also were now set
home upon me, of which I wrote down some remembrance immediately
and confessed them before God morning and evening. Though weak, I
often spent two hours in my evening retirement and prayed over my Greek
Testament and Bishop Hall's most excellent contemplations, every hour
that my health would permit. About the end of seven weeks and after I had
been groaning under an unspeakable pressure both of body and mind for
above a twelvemonth, God was pleased to set me free in the following
manner. One day, perceiving an uncommon drought and a disagreeable
clamminess in my mouth and using things to allay my thirst but in vain, it
was suggested to me that when Jesus Christ cried out, 'I thirst,' His sufferings were near at an end. Upon which I cast myself down on the bed crying
out, 'I thirst, I thirst.' Soon after this I found an health in myself that I was
delivered from the burden that had so heavily oppressed me. The spirit of
mourning was taken from me and I knew what it was truly to rejoice in
God my Saviour and for some time could not avoid singing Psalms wherever
I was. But my joy gradually became more settled and, blessed be God, has
abode and increased in my soul saving a few casual intermissions ever since.

Or consider a man who belonged to the Salvation Army talking about the same thing. Here, again, is a man who believed the truth. He had an objective assurance but he had not got the subjective assurance and he was seeking it. He writes:

> I awoke that morning hungering and thirsting just to live this life of fellow-ship with God, never again to sin in thought or word or deed against Him; with an unmeasurable desire to be a holy man acceptable unto God. With that desire, I opened my Bible and, while reading some of the words of Jesus, He gave such a blessing as I never had dreamed a man could have this side of heaven. It was an unutterable revelation. It was a heaven of love that came into my heart. My soul melted like wax before fire. I sobbed and sobbed. I loathed myself that I had ever sinned against Him or doubted Him or lived for myself and not for His glory. Every ambition for self was now gone, the pure flame of love burned it like a blazing fire would burn a moth. I walked out of the Boston Commons before breakfast weeping for joy and praising God. Oh how I loved Him! In that hour I knew Jesus. [He had been a believer for years, remember.] And I loved Him till it seemed my heart would break with love. I was filled with love for all His creatures. I heard the little sparrows chattering – I loved them. I saw a little worm wriggling across my path – I stepped over it, I didn't want to hurt any living thing. I loved the dogs, I loved the horses, I loved the little urchins in the street, I loved the strangers who hurried past me, I loved the heathen, I loved the whole world. God did all that for me, blessed be His holy name. Oh, how I had longed to be pure. Oh, how I had hungered and thirsted for God, the living God, and He gave me the desire of my heart, He satisfied me. I weigh my words – He satisfies me. He has become my teacher, my guide, my counsellor, my all in all.

'I,' said our Lord – He was about to leave the earth and has said that He would send the Spirit – 'I will manifest myself unto him' (John 14:21). And He does it through the Holy Spirit. And when men and women have this 'spiritual manifestation of the Son of God', as the saintly John Fletcher of Madeley called it, they have an absolute certainty and assurance that nothing can change. And, if we have not got that, we can have it. It is for us. Over and above the world; over and above our spirits and the tests we can apply to those spirits, there is this witness of the Spirit with our spirit. It is the heritage of all God's children who feel the need of it, who long to have it, who desire it, who seek for it.

Has He manifested Himself to you? Offer up to Him Hudson Taylor's little prayer, and He has pledged to answer it in His own way and in His own time. You notice the difference between the two men I have quoted. There are still others, each with a different experience. But do not worry about that; do not worry about the exact character of the feelings. When the Spirit comes you will know. Do not believe a teaching which tells you, 'Just believe it has happened whether you've got feelings or not.' These men had feelings! And when you and I have this spiritual manifestation of the Son of God, we will not have to persuade ourselves that we have it; we will know. It is unmistakable, and it is for us.

16
Justification by Faith

This is the fiftieth lecture that I have been privileged to give you on this great and glorious and, to me at any rate, enthralling theme, and I am very happy to think that on this occasion we come to a consideration of the great and vital doctrine of justification by faith only, the biblical doctrine of justification. There is no better test that we who are Christians can apply to ourselves to know the quality of life that we really have in Christ, than this one: What is our reaction to the mere mention of the word 'justification'? It is a test that all Christians should apply to themselves, especially at the present time, because if there has been one word that has stood out more prominently, especially in the history of Protestantism, than any other, it has been this great word *justification*. It was the rediscovery of the doctrine of justification by faith only that transformed the life of the mighty Martin Luther. This it was that brought into being the Protestant Reformation. This led to everything that has been so glorious in the annals of the Protestant cause ever since. But, for some peculiar reason, we do not seem to react to these great words as we used to. Something has gone wrong even with our Protestantism. I do not mean by that anti-Catholicism – that is a very different thing – I mean a positive Protestantism. There should be a thrill at the very word, especially when one realises its history.

But the great question is: What was the Protestant Reformation about? What did Martin Luther rediscover? What did he find when he went back to the Scriptures? And you see, therefore, that it is something which is vital and about which we should be absolutely clear. So another good way of testing ourselves is to picture ourselves seated at a table with an examination paper in front of us and here is the question:

'Give an account of the doctrine of justification by faith only.' Do you
know what it is that makes you a Protestant, what it is the marks you
off from the Roman Catholics? That is the test.

So, let us look at this doctrine together, and perhaps the best
approach is historical. Why was Martin Luther in trouble before his
conversion? What was wrong with him before this truth suddenly
dawned upon him? And what is wrong with all who are vague and
indefinite and uncertain about the whole question of justification by
faith? Now it was not that Luther had not heard of the term 'justification', because he had. What was wrong with him was that he had the
wrong view of it. In other words, he had the typical Roman Catholic
view of justification by faith. Roman Catholics claim to teach that
doctrine, but they never say 'justification by faith *only*'. They regard
that as the Protestant heresy.

First, then, let us look at this Roman Catholic error and in its
essence it is this: the Roman Catholic Church confuses justification
with sanctification. And that had been the trouble with Martin Luther
before his conversion. The Roman Catholic view of justification is,
first of all, that it means and includes forgiveness of sins and they are
all right at that point. But they add that the sin inherent in us is taken
out of us for Christ's sake. And they do not even stop at that. They go
on to say that in justification there is a positive infusion of grace into
us and that, of course, comes by means of baptism. They say that in
the act of baptism, grace is actually infused into the person who is
baptised and that is a part of justification. Forgiveness, removal of sin
– yes – but also the infusion at baptism of a positive righteousness,
and not merely a positive righteousness, but the life of God as well.

And then Roman Catholics go on to say that justification is progressive. Of course, they are quite consistent there. If there is this
infusion of grace, that is going to grow and develop, the justification
must be progressive. Furthermore, typically, they have to go further
and they even say it can be lost if we become guilty of what they call
'mortal sin'. But then, if we do lose it, they say that we can regain it by
going through the sacrament of penance and the process of regaining
it will be completed in purgatory.

Now that is the characteristic Roman Catholic view and that was
the view that was held by Martin Luther before his conversion. But
then, you remember, the story of his life goes on to tell us that suddenly he saw a statement in the Scripture. He had read it many times
before but he had never truly seen it. This is what he saw: 'The just

shall live by faith' (Rom. 1:17) – and these words absolutely changed everything for him. His whole life was revolutionised; he became an entirely different man. He suddenly saw that all his past ideas on justification had been quite unscriptural, utterly false, and the moment he saw this, he experienced a great liberation of his soul. He began to preach this truth and so began the great and mighty work of reformation.

Exactly what, then, did Luther see? It was that justification is a judicial act of God in which He declares that He regards those of us who believe in the Lord Jesus Christ, as righteous on the grounds of the work and merit of Christ. God imputes and ascribes Christ's righteousness to us, and we rest on that by faith. That is what Luther saw. As a result, in a moment, he knew that he was right with God. Luther's problem had been that of Job: 'How should a man be just with God?' (Job 9:2). How can a man stand in the presence of God? That was the problem that oppressed the mind and heart of Luther. There he was, a monk in his cell, asking, 'How can I put myself right with God?' He fasted, he prayed, he sweated, he did good deeds, and yet the whole time he was more and more aware of the blackness and darkness of his own heart and of the utter unutterable righteousness and holiness of God. And he was trying to fit himself, to make himself just, along that Roman Catholic way, and he could not, but there he saw it suddenly. God declares him righteous, and he is righteous, because God says so, because God puts to his account the righteousness of the Lord Jesus Christ.

That is the historical background in which we should rejoice more and more. The crux of the matter is this: the great mistake we all tend to fall in, as Luther had done, with regard to justification, is that we tend to think that justification means that we are made righteous or good or upright or holy. But that is quite wrong. In justification we are not *made* righteous, we are *declared* to be righteous – the thing is quite different. To say that in justification you are made righteous is to confuse it with sanctification. Justification is something legal or *forensic*. It is God, as the Judge, who is responsible for administering His own law, saying to us that as regards the law He is satisfied with us because of the righteousness of Christ. Justification is a declaratory act. It does not do anything to us; it says something about us. It has no reference to my actual state or condition inside; it has reference to my standing, to my position, to my appearing in the presence of God. Now that is the biblical doctrine of justification. That is what Luther

discovered; that is what he began to preach and, in a sense, he spent
the rest of his life in preaching it. It is the great central doctrine of all
Protestantism and in every great revival you will find that this always
comes to the forefront. It was what Whitefield used to preach, as did
John Wesley.

So, then, it behoves us to establish this contention. How can we
prove that this is really the biblical teaching with regard to justification, as over against, in particular, that Roman Catholic error? (And
you will have observed, I think, that it is not an error that is confined
to Roman Catholicism.) Let me give you, therefore, the biblical evidence that justification is forensic and declarative. Take it first of all in
the Old Testament. We read in Exodus 23:7: 'Keep thee far from a
false matter; and the innocent and righteous slay thou not: for I will
not justify the wicked.' That is what God says, that is the commandment given to the Children of Israel and it means: I will not let off the
wicked, I will not say that such persons are guiltless.

But take also Deuteronomy 25:1: 'If there be a controversy
between men, and they come unto judgment, that the judges may
judge them, then they shall justify the righteous, and condemn the
wicked.' You notice, again, the context in which the word 'justify' is
used. Here is a controversy between two men and they come to judgment. The judges who judge the case are told: 'They shall justify the
righteous, and condemn the wicked.' Obviously that is a purely legal
matter. These judges are not going to change the nature of the two
disputants but are going to make a declaration; they will pronounce
judgment, they will say that one is right and that the other is wrong.
And the act of declaring that one is right is referred to as 'justify the
righteous'. It is a legal action.

Then take another verse: 'He that justifieth the wicked and he that
condemneth the just, even they both are abomination to the Lord'
(Prov. 17:15). In that most important proverb justification is put over
against condemnation; again, it is a legal matter. In neither case are
you changing the person. God would never forbid us to make a man
a better man, and if justification is the same as sanctification, then
God could never say, 'He that justifieth the wicked is an abomination
to the Lord,' because that is a good thing to do! No, the condemnation is of those who say that a bad man is a good man, that a man
who is guilty is not guilty. Again the term is forensic.

But take an illustration of the use of this word in the New Testament: 'And all the people that heard him [the Lord Jesus Christ], and

the publicans, justified God' (Luke 7:29). Now that can only mean one thing: they said that God was right and true. They did not change the nature or the being of God, but made a declaration about Him. They justified God. And then, of course, when you come to the scriptures with direct teaching about justification, you find that that is the sense which it carries everywhere. Read, for instance, Acts 13:39: 'And by him all that believe are justified from all things, from which we could not be justified by the law of Moses.'

Then in that great classic passage on this whole matter, in Romans 3:20–28, this meaning of 'justification' is repeated constantly: 'Therefore, by the deeds of the law there shall no flesh be justified in his sight: for by the law is the knowledge of sin. But now the righteousness of God without the law is manifested, being witnessed by the law and the prophets: even the righteousness of God which is by faith of Jesus Christ . . .' And then that tremendous conclusion in verse 28: 'Therefore we conclude that a man is justified by faith without the deeds of the law.' Again, there are most important statements in chapter 4:5–7, especially the fifth verse: 'But to him that worketh not, but believeth on him that justifieth the ungodly, his faith is counted for righteousness.' God does not justify a man because he is good: this is a statement about the ungodly. They are not changed, they are not made godly before God justifies them; He justifies the ungodly – and there are other statements in those verses.

Then you have the same teaching in Romans 5:1: 'Therefore being justified by faith, we have peace with God . . .' and again in the ninth verse. There is also a great statement of this in Romans 8:30–34: 'Moreover whom he did predestinate, them he also called: and whom he called, them he also justified: and whom he justified, them he also glorified.' And then this: 'What shall we then say to these things? If God be for us, who can be against us? . . . Who shall lay any thing to the charge of God's elect?' And the answer is: 'It is God that justifieth. Who is he that condemneth? It is Christ that died, yea rather, that is risen again, who is even at the right hand of God, who also maketh intercession for us.' Again, you see, justification is opposed to condemnation, and nobody can bring an accusation because it is God who declares people just.

The whole time justification is legal and forensic, and as you go on with the Scriptures you will find this in other places: 'But ye are washed, but ye are sanctified, but ye are justified in the name of the Lord Jesus, and by the Spirit of our God' (1 Cor. 6:11). And in

Galatians 2:16 there is a statement which is parallel to those in
Romans: 'Knowing that a man is not justified by the works of the law,
but by the faith of Jesus Christ, even we have believed in Jesus Christ,
that we might be justified by the faith of Christ, and not by the works
of the law: for by the works of the law shall no flesh be justified.'
Galatians is the great epistle that gave Martin Luther his liberty. His
famous commentary on the epistle to the Galatians is a book that you
should read and the more you go on with it, the more you will enjoy
it. Do not be put off by his polemic against the Roman Catholics. He
had to do that because you must show what is wrong as well as what
is right. People do not like that today, but Luther had to do it, and I
think we must do it in our age and generation. So buy Luther on the
epistle to the Galatians and follow through his mighty exposition of
great verses like chapters 2:16 and 3:11.

Now in all the instances that I have given, God makes a legal declaration, that all the demands of the law upon us, as a condition of life,
are fully satisfied with regard to all who believe on the Lord Jesus
Christ. We are no longer in a state of condemnation: 'Therefore being
justified by faith, we have peace with God through our Lord Jesus
Christ' (Rom. 5:1). 'There is therefore now no condemnation to them
which are in Christ Jesus' (Rom. 8:11). Why? Because God has
declared it. He is the lawgiver and he says that Christ has satisfied the
law. 'For Christ is the end of the law for righteousness to every one
that believeth' (Rom. 10:4). God makes this declaration and that is
the whole meaning of justification by faith only.

But we do not leave it quite at that because we must point out that
there are two aspects to this great declaration. There are two elements
to justification. And this is most important. The first is what we may
describe as negative. The negative element of justification is that
which reminds us that God declares that our sins are forgiven. That
is our first need, of course. The law condemns us all. 'By the law is the
knowledge of sin' (Rom. 3:20), and the law says, 'There is none righteous, no, not one' (Rom. 3:10). The whole world is 'guilty before
God' (Rom. 3:19). I need to be forgiven. Something must be done
about my guilt. Now in justification the first step is that I am assured
that by the work of Christ my sins are covered and are therefore forgiven; they are blotted out.

But (and this is the point) justification does not stop at forgiveness.
Justification and forgiveness are not identical. There are, however,
many people – and I must say, to be accurate, that there are even

evangelical people – who identify justification and forgiveness; and they do that because their doctrine of the atonement is wrong, as we saw in an earlier lecture.[1] They do not realise that, as part of the atonement, Christ rendered a positive obedience to the law before He obeyed it passively in His death upon the cross. In other words, there is a second, positive, element in justification. This means that, in addition to having our sins forgiven, we have imputed to us, or put to our account or to our reckoning, the positive righteousness of the Lord Jesus Christ Himself. He kept the law, He honoured it, and therefore He is righteous face to face with the demands of the law. And God puts that righteousness of Christ to my account.

Now that is important in this way. There are many people who foolishly think that justification only means that my sinfulness is forgiven and I am restored to the condition of Adam before he fell. If this is the case, then it is up to me now, by my own righteous living, to justify myself. Those who believe that say, 'God, for Christ's sake, forgives your sins and because you're forgiven, you're going to live a godly life. And if you do so, God will put that down to your account.'

But that is quite wrong! I have nothing at all to do in my justification. It is entirely the act of God. He attributes to me, He puts to my account, He imputes to me, the positive righteousness of the Lord Jesus Christ. I am not simply restored to the condition that Adam was in before he fell; I am much beyond that. Adam did not have the positive righteousness of Christ. I, as a Christian, have it; God has put it to my account. Count Zinzendorf's hymn puts it perfectly:

> Jesus, Thy robe of righteousness
> My beauty is, my glorious dress.

We are covered with the positive righteousness of Christ.

> O let the dead now hear Thy voice,
> Bid, Lord, Thy banished ones rejoice;
> Their beauty this, their glorious dress,
> Jesus, the Lord our righteousness.

You see, that goes entirely beyond forgiveness. It is not negative, it is

1. See Volume 1, *God the Father, God the Son.*

positive. We are clothed with the spotless robe of His perfect righteousness.

That, then, is the contention, and we can prove it by these very Scriptures that we have already considered. It is there perfectly in Romans 3:20–22: 'Therefore by the deeds of the law there shall no flesh be justified in his sight: for by the law is the knowledge of sin. But now the righteousness of God without the law is manifested, being witnessed by the law and the prophets; even the righteousness of God which is by faith of Jesus Christ unto all and upon all them that believe.' It is a righteousness that God gives us and it is positive. Or you have it again in Romans 4:6: 'Even as David also describeth the blessedness of the man, unto whom God imputeth righteousness without works.' He is not talking about forgiveness. David saw it, he was a prophet at this point and the Holy Spirit revealed it to him. And it is also to be found in Paul's great argument which runs through the second half of that most important fifth chapter of Romans.

> For if by one man's offence death reigned by one; much more they which receive abundance of grace and of the gift of righteousness shall reign in life by one, Jesus Christ. Therefore as by the offence of one judgment came upon all men to condemnation; even so by the righteousness of one the free gift came upon all men unto justification of life. For as by one man's disobedience many were made sinners, so by the obedience of one shall many be made righteous. (vv. 17–19)

Here we see not only Christ's passive obedience, but His active obedience as well, His keeping of the law and the contrast with Adam who broke the law and who therefore fell.

We have already considered Romans 10:4: 'For Christ is the end of the law for righteousness to every one that believeth.' There is also 1 Corinthians 1:30: 'But of him are ye in Christ Jesus, who of God is made unto us wisdom, and righteousness, and sanctification, and redemption.' And 2 Corinthians 5:21: 'For he [God] hath made him to be sin for us, who knew no sin; that we might be made the righteousness of God in him' – not merely forgiveness, but positive righteousness in the presence of God. And finally, we read in Philippians 3:9: 'And be found in him, not having mine own righteousness, which is of the law, but that which is through the faith of Christ, the righteousness which is of God by faith.'

All that is enough to show you that this is the essential teaching with regard to righteousness. Let me make if still more certain by showing, very briefly, the essential differences between justification and sanctification. Look at it like this: justification is an act of God the Father, as we have seen; sanctification is essentially the work of God the Holy Spirit. There is this division of work, you remember, in the blessed Persons of the Holy Trinity.[1] It is the Father who declares righteous and just. It is the Holy Spirit who sanctifies.

Secondly, justification takes place outside us, as in a tribunal; sanctification takes place within us, in our inner life. I stand in the court when I am justified and the judge pronounces that I am free, it is a statement about me, outside me. But sanctification is something that is worked and takes place within.

Thirdly, justification removes the guilt of sin; sanctification removes the pollution of sin and renews us in the image of God.

And therefore, lastly, by definition justification is a once-and-for-all act. It is never to be repeated because it cannot be repeated and never needs to be repeated. It is not a process but a declaration that we are declared just once and for ever, by God. Sanctification, on the other hand, is a continuous process. We continue to grow in grace and in the knowledge of the Lord until beyond the veil we are perfect.

So there is nothing quite so erroneous and confusing and unscriptural as to mistake the essential difference between justification and sanctification. As we have seen, it is the whole trouble with Roman Catholic teaching and all Catholic piety. It was the thing that held Luther in bondage, and once he saw it, and knew that he was free and just with God, he began to glory and to rejoice – and this is the essence of the Protestant position. Furthermore, of course, it led, in turn, as we saw in the last lecture, to Luther's assurance of salvation. But if you once confuse sanctification with justification, you will be doubtful as to whether you are justified or not. If you once bring in your state and condition and your sin which you may commit, then you are querying your justification. But if you realise that justification is forensic, external and declaratory, you know that you are justified whatever may be true about you.

How, then, does justification happen? The answer is, of course, that it is entirely God's act. It is something that He and He alone does. The Bible is very careful to put it negatively by saying 'not of works' (Eph. 2:9). Paul repeats that in Romans 4:5, 'But to him that worketh

---

1. See Volume 1, *God the Father, God the Son*.

not, but believeth on him that justifieth the ungodly, his faith is counted for righteousness.' We do nothing at all about our justification. It is God's declaration about us; we know it and we receive it by faith.

Now here we come to a crucial point. What do we mean when we say that we are justified by faith only? What is the relationship between faith and justification? This is important because some people think it means that we are justified on account of our faith. But that is the very essence of heresy and must be condemned root and branch. If I am justified on account of my faith, or because I exercise faith, then my salvation is definitely by works and God justifies me because of this work that I have done which I call faith. But the Scripture does not say that I am justified on account of my faith or because I am exercising faith, it says that I am justified *by* faith, which means that faith is the instrument – and nothing but the instrument – by which I am enabled to receive the righteousness which God gives me.

I wonder whether you realise the significance of this? There are people who say that the difference the coming of the Lord Jesus Christ and His death upon the cross has made is that, until then, God judged men and women according to the law. But they say that now the law has been put on one side; it is no longer in existence and God no longer asks us to keep it. All He asks us now is to believe on the Lord Jesus Christ, and if we do that He will declare us just. But that is a complete travesty of the Apostle's teaching! The Bible never says that anywhere, because, if that were true, what would really save us in the end is *our* believing on the Lord Jesus Christ.

The biblical teaching is that faith, our faith, is not the grounds of our justification. The grounds of our justification is the righteousness of the Lord Jesus Christ imputed to us. Christ, and not my faith, is my righteousness. It is not my believing in Him that saves me. It is He who saves me. So you see the subtle danger of regarding my faith as the grounds of salvation?

'Well, where does faith come in?' you ask.

Faith is but the channel, the instrument, by which this righteousness of Christ comes on to me. And as we saw when we considered faith, God does it like this. He gives us the new birth; He gives us this power and faculty of faith and then He enables us to exercise it. Through this exercise of faith we receive the righteousness that God imputes to us. It is all of God. 'For by grace are ye saved through faith; and that not of yourselves: it is the gift of God' (Eph. 2:8). If we had not been given the gift of faith, we could not receive the right-eousness of Christ, but we are justified by the righteousness of Christ, not by our faith.

'But wait a minute,' says someone. 'Aren't you, in saying all that, forgetting what James has to say about faith in chapter 2:14–26? Doesn't he there contradict what Paul teaches in Romans 4? Paul says, "by faith only"; James says, "by works". What about that?'

Well, surely, the answer is that neither Paul nor James, at that point, is concerned with the question of justification as such; they are both simply dealing with the character of faith. They are arguing against different types of people. Paul is dealing with people who believed that they could justify themselves by their works, by the lives and their actions. And to them he has to say, 'No, justification is by faith only, and it was Abraham's faith that saved him.'

But James is speaking about people who, like certain people today, were saying, 'As long as I say I believe in the Lord Jesus Christ and I'm saved, it doesn't really matter what I do. If I say I'm a Christian and a believer, well, I can go and do what I like my sins will be forgiven.'

'Not at all!' says James. Then he proceeds to show that saving faith, faith worthy of the name faith, is a faith that includes obedience, it includes action: 'As the body without the spirit is dead, so faith with-out works is dead also' (Jas. 2:26). It is no use talking about faith and about being justified by faith,' says James in effect, 'if you haven't got true faith. And the way you test whether or not your faith is true is by asking whether it leads to certain things in your life.'

Now Paul is saying exactly the same thing. Paul's faith was not a kind of dead faith. it was very active; it proved itself and showed itself. Indeed, in Romans 6, Paul is making exactly the same point as James: 'What then? shall we sin, because we are not under the law but under grace?' (v. 15). The whole of that chapter is really parallel with James 2. Paul and James are looking at two different problems and are correcting two particular types of error.

But as we have said, the great thing for us to realise is that our faith does not constitute our righteousness. God does not look at me and say that because I believe, He will count that as righteousness. Not at all! What He says is this: 'I will give to you the righteousness of my Son, who kept the law perfectly for you, and who died for your sins. He is absolutely righteous before the law and He has represented you before the law. He has fulfilled its every iota and therefore I will give you His righteousness.' He calls upon me to believe in Him, and He has given me, by the gift of faith, the power to believe. So I look to Christ, not to myself, not to my faith, my righteousness is entirely in the Lord Jesus Christ. God has made Him 'wisdom, and righteousness, and sanctification, and redemption' (1 Cor. 1:30). So I do not lean on anything in myself, not even on my faith. My faith makes me lean entirely on the Lord Jesus Christ. And, knowing that God has imputed His righteousness to me, I know that all is well between me and God. I believe His declaration. My faith accepts it. He has put to my account the perfect, spotless, seamless robe of righteousness of His dear Son. That is the biblical and the Protestant doctrine of justification by faith only.

17

Adoption

In the last lecture we saw how that great doctrine which was the great battle cry of the Reformation – justification by faith – is still, in many senses, the most vital and important doctrine for us to grasp and to understand. We now come to a consideration of some of the things to which justification leads, and among them is the biblical *doctrine of adoption*.

Now we must not stay with this, but I do beg of you again to consider the order of these doctrines, and to notice that the doctrine of adoption comes at this particular point. Here again we have a most glorious subject which is most encouraging and comforting to the believer. And yet, once more, for some inexplicable reason, it is a doctrine about which we very rarely hear. How often have you heard addresses or sermons on it? Why is it that, even as evangelical people, we neglect, and indeed seem to be unaware of, some of these most comforting and encouraging doctrines which are to be found in the Scriptures?

So, then, let us approach this doctrine by first of all considering the Scriptures in which the term is mentioned. Turn first to Romans 9:4, where we read these words: 'Who are Israelites; to whom pertaineth the adoption, and the glory, and the covenants, and the giving of the law, and the service of God, and the promises.' The Apostle is there referring to his kinsmen according to the flesh – the Jews, the Israelites – and I will show you later why I put that particular quotation before the next which comes from Romans 8:15: 'For ye have not received the spirit of bondage again to fear,' says the Apostle, 'but ye have received the Spirit of adoption, whereby we cry, Abba, Father.' In verse 23 of that same chapter Paul uses the term again, when he is talking about this day that is to come. He says that 'the whole creation groaneth and travaileth in pain together until now. And not only they, but ourselves also, which have the firstfruits of the Spirit, even we ourselves groan within ourselves, waiting for the adoption, to wit, the redemption of our body.' Then the next time we find the term is in Galatians 4:4–5. Paul is talking about how 'when the fulness of the time was come, God sent forth his Son, made of a woman, made under the law' – for this reason – 'to redeem them that were under the law, that we might receive the adoption of sons.' And there is another reference to it in Ephesians 1:5: 'Having predestinated us unto the adoption of children by Jesus Christ to himself, according to the good pleasure of his will.'

There, then, are our Scriptures, and it is our business now to discover what exactly they mean and what this term 'adoption' represents. So, as we come to a definition, we had best perhaps, first of all, look at it from the standpoint of the etymology – the root meaning of the word – and it is this: *the placing* of a son. But in ancient languages it also came to mean something which it still means with us, namely, the transfer from one family to another and the placing of the one who has been so transferred as a son or daughter in the new, the second family.

Now if that is the primary, fundamental meaning of the term, that, at once, brings us to a consideration of the meaning of the term 'son' and especially the meaning of the term as used in Scripture. As you go through the Bible you will find that 'son' is used in the following ways: in the singular it invariably refers to the Lord Jesus Christ and to Him alone. He is *the* Son. Sometimes He is even referred to without the indefinite article as *Son*. He stands alone, in that sense, as *the* Son of God.

The term is also used in the plural of angels, and one gathers from the way in which it is so used and from the context that this is because the angels are God's favoured creatures, and because, in the matter of intelligence and in certain other respects, they are like God Himself. The term is applied to angels in that way in Job chapters 1 and 6.

Then, in the third place, there is a very interesting use of this term 'sons' in Psalm 82:6 where it is applied to human magistrates: 'I have said, Ye are gods; and all of you are children of the most High.' That is a very important statement because you will recall that in John 10:34 our Lord Himself quoted it when certain people objected to the fact that He was claiming to be the Son of God. Clearly it means that

magistrates are sons of God in the sense that authority has been dele-
gated to them from God and that, therefore, in the exercise of their
magisterial functions, they are doing something that God Himself
does.

The fourth use of this term refers to men and women as subjects of
divine adoption; and here we must divide it up into general and special
adoption. In the statement in Romans 9:4 Paul is referring to the
nation of Israel. He says in verses 2–4: 'I have great heaviness and
continual sorrow in my heart' for 'I could wish that myself were
accursed from Christ for my brethren, my kinsmen according to the
flesh: Who are Israelites; to whom pertaineth the adoption . . .' In a
sense, that is a reference to Exodus 4:22 where God addresses the
nation of Israel and tells them that He is adopting them as His son.
Adoption is a term, therefore, that can be used in general of the nation
of Israel. They were God's particular people. That is why, in speaking
through Amos, God said to them, 'You only have I known of all the
families [the nations] of the earth.' Of course, He knew about all the
other nations but He had a special interest in Israel. As a nation, they
were the son of God. But the special use of this term is spiritual, and
that is our primary concern – God adopting certain people to become
His sons in a spiritual manner.

Now there are two points which I must take up here. I do so not
because they are essential to a positive exposition, but because they
are so frequently raised as arguments. They cause such confusion,
that it becomes essential that we should consider them. There are
those, for instance, who say that Scripture teaches us that all men and
women are the children of God. Such people believe in what they call
the universal fatherhood of God and the universal brotherhood of all
men and they claim that the Scriptures which support their contention
are the following: first of all, a statement in Acts 17:25–29, where the
apostle Paul, speaking in Athens, uses the phrase, 'For we are also his
offspring.' Now that is a very important statement. Paul is telling the
Athenians about this God whom they ignorantly worship – they
called him 'the unknown god' – and this is what he says:

> God that made the world and all things therein, seeing that he is Lord of
> heaven and earth, dwelleth not in temples made with hands; neither is
> worshipped with men's hands, as though he needed any thing, seeing he
> giveth to all life, and breath, and all things; and hath made of one blood
> all nations of men for to dwell on all the face of the earth, and hath

determined the times before appointed, and the bounds of their habitation; that they should seek the Lord, if haply they might feel after him, and find him, though he be not far from every one of us: For in him we live, and move, and have our being; as certain also of your own poets have said, For we are also his offspring. Forasmuch then as we are the offspring of God, we ought not to think that the Godhead is like unto gold, or silver . . .'

The second Scripture which these people quote is Hebrews 12:9 where the writer is exhorting us to be obedient and not to grumble at the chastisement of God. He says that we have all subjected ourselves to our earthly parents, and then he argues, 'Shall we not much rather be in subjection unto the Father of spirits [which means the father of all spirits] and live?' And again, in James 1:17, we find a reference to God as 'the Father of lights, with whom is no variableness, neither shadow or turning.' So what do we say to this contention that God is the Father of all men and that all men and women are therefore the children of God?

Our first answer is that these very scriptures clearly refer to the relationship of God to all people in creation and in providence only. They are very similar to 1 Timothy 4:10 where we are told that God is 'the Saviour of all men, specially of those that believe.' It is the same kind of distinction. God is the creator of all humanity. In that sense He is the Father of the spirits of all people, but it has nothing to do with redemption and with the special relationship of God to men and women in terms of adopting them as children.

That is a distinction which you find everywhere in Scripture. We have already seen that in the Old Testament God regards Israel as His son in a special way. It is because of this that He says, 'You only have I known of all the families of the earth' (Amos 3:2). But you get this distinction especially in the New Testament. For instance, in John 1:12 we read, 'But as many as received him, to them gave he power to become the sons of God, even to them that believe on his name.' Obviously, therefore, the people who are given this power or right or authority to become sons of God are in an entirely different category from others who do not believe. These are those who believe in his name, and the adoption only happens to them, not to the others.

Take also Romans 8:15: 'For ye have not received the spirit of bondage again to fear; but ye have received the Spirit of adoption, whereby we cry, Abba, Father.' Who is Paul writing to? Only to Christians, only to believers. He is not writing a general letter to the world, but a special letter to those who believe on the Lord Jesus Christ, who are in Christ, and who have the Spirit of Christ.

Our Lord put it like this to the unbelieving Jews who had said that they were all children of God: 'If God were your Father,' He said, 'ye would love me' (John 8:42). But then He was more specific and said, 'Ye are of your father the devil, and the lusts of your father ye will do' (v. 44). Surely that one verse alone is more than enough to demonstrate the case that not all men and women are the children of God in this special sense. Our Lord Himself draws that sharp distinction. And the apostle Paul in the epistle to the Ephesians says that we were all 'by nature the children of wrath, even as others' (Eph. 2:3). And it is only those who have been quickened with Christ who have become the children of God.

I could adduce many other Scriptures which show exactly the same thing, but those are enough. Indeed, any one of them is enough. There is a sharp distinction between the children of God and the children of this world. 'The whole world,' says John in the first epistle, 'lieth in wickedness' but, 'we are of God' (1 John 5:19). It is a distinction that is found everywhere, so we must reject this notion of the universal fatherhood of God and the universal brotherhood of man.

The second point is the whole question of the relationship of our sonship to our Lord's Sonship. This, again, is very important. In becoming the children of God we do not become identical with the Lord Jesus Christ. He is the God-man, very God of very God and perfect man, perfect God, perfect man. We are not made gods. When we become children of God we do not become God in the sense that our Lord was. Our Lord Himself was very careful to emphasise that distinction. Take, for instance, what He said in giving His disciples the model prayer. He said, 'After this manner therefore pray ye' (Matt. 6:9). He did not include Himself. That is how you and I are to pray, and we say, 'Our Father'. He is not included with us, He did not pray that particular prayer.

But after His resurrection, our Lord made a still more specific statement. He said to one of the women, 'Go to my brethren, and say unto them, I ascend unto my Father, and your Father' and to my God, and your God' (John 20:17). Why did He divide it up in that way? The reason is, obviously, that He was anxious to preserve this distinction. He did not say, 'I ascend unto our God and unto our Father.' No, He is the only begotten, He is the Son of God by generation; we are sons of God by adoption. And that is a most essential distinction.

This enables us to go a step further in our exact definition of what is meant by the adoption. We can describe it, therefore, as that judicial act of God by which He confers or bestows upon us the status or the standing of children. That is its real meaning. And I am anxious to stress the fact that it is a distinct and a special movement, or division, of the work of the Holy Spirit in the application of redemption. It must be differentiated from all the other acts and yet we must not separate it. It is a distinct step but it is not an entirely separate step, as I have been emphasising. There is a sense in which these things, as it were, happen all together – regeneration and faith and justification, and so on. The same applies to this great act of adoption, and yet, for the sake of clear thinking, we must differentiate in our minds between these things. Adoption is not the same as justification; it is not even a part of justification, but is quite separate. In justification, you remember, we found that God declares us to be righteous; it is a declaratory, a forensic act. He declares that our sins are forgiven and that He accepts the righteousness of Christ which He has put upon us. So justification is not adoption. In the same way, we must be clear that adoption and regeneration are not synonymous. In regeneration we are given the new nature; we become partakers of the divine nature. We become new creations, new creatures. But that is not adoption.

In a sense, adoption is a combination of justification and regeneration. It is the new creature in a new relationship to God – as a child of God. Adoption is more than justification, it is more than regeneration, but it includes them both. Here is the man or woman with the new nature, declared to be just and free from the law and its condemnation, and to be positively righteous. Yes, but, in addition to all that, now declared to be a child of God. In a sense, again, it is a judicial act and another proclamation. But it proclaims something new, something different. By adoption, then, we become the children of God and are introduced into and given the privileges that belong to members of God's family.

Now once more, unfortunately, I must turn aside and say something negative, which I shall put in the form of a question. Does this adoption apply to all Christians or only to some? Is there a distinction between being children of God and sons of God? I have to deal with this subject because there are two groups which teach that all Christians are children of God but that only some are sons of God. What is their attempt at a justification for that statement? Their main evidence, they say, is Matthew 5:9: 'Blessed are the peacemakers: for they shall be called sons of God.' Now they get that in the Revised Version. In the Authorised [King James] Version the translation is 'children of God'. Now, they say, our Lord was preaching there to those who were believers and were therefore children of God – shown by the fact that He taught them to say, 'Our Father'. Yes, but it is only the people who act as peacemakers who become sons of God. That is the argument.

Then they say that in verse 45 of that same Sermon on the Mount, our Lord exhorted us not only to love those who love us but also to love our enemies: 'I say unto you, Love your enemies, bless them that curse you, do good to them that hate you, and pray for them which despitefully use you, and persecute you; that ye may be sons of your Father which is in heaven.' Again, that is the Revised Version, while the Authorised Version reads, 'That ye may be the children of your Father which is in heaven.' We do not dispute that they are quite right in translating it as 'sons', but they say that while all Christians are children, it is only those who love their enemies who become sons.

Then their next piece of evidence is in Luke 20:36 where our Lord is dealing with a question about the resurrection. The problem put to Him was about what would happen to a woman who had married a whole series of brothers. In the Revised Version the passage ends by saying that in the resurrection they are as the sons of God: 'being sons of the resurrection'. Now that, say the proponents of this view, only applies to certain people. Furthermore, they try to argue that in Galatians 3 and 4, where Paul reminds the Galatians that whereas they were children under the law, they are now, as the result of the work of Christ and the giving of the Spirit, sons of God (see, for example, Gal. 4:6–7). There again, they say, we find that same distinction. The Old Testament saints were only children of God; the New Testament saints, some of them who realise this, can become sons of God. And on the basis of this argument they say that not only is it true that not all Christians are sons of God, but it is only those who behave in this particular way who do become sons of God.

In other words, they say that by grace we are all children, but that becoming sons is not a matter of grace, but of application – making an effort, loving your enemies, being peacemakers and so on – and that if we only do these things we will then become sons of God. This is not of grace but of effort and of activity on the part of the believer. And they even go so far as to say that Christians who are merely children will not take part in the first resurrection but only the sons, and that it is only the sons who will spend their eternity in the immediate presence of the Lord – the children will not have that privilege. Children will be in the new heavens and the new earth, but they will not be in our Lord's immediate presence.

You may be astonished to hear that there is such a teaching, but there is, and it is put forward by Christian people. But it is just another instance of the way in which, if we become overinterested in words and in mechanics, we can end by wresting the Scriptures from their true meaning, and doing them grave injustice, because, surely, this is an utterly artificial and, indeed, false distinction. I can demonstrate that from the very eighth chapter of Romans, which they are also so fond of quoting. I suggest to you that the very use of the terms in verses 15, 16 and 17 falsifies their entire argument: 'For ye have not received the spirit of bondage again to fear; but ye have received the Spirit of adoption, whereby we cry, Abba, Father. The Spirit itself beareth witness with our spirit, that we are sons of God' – that is the Revised Version. Then it goes on – 'and if *children*, then heirs; heirs of God, and joint-heirs with Christ.' Surely it is obvious that the Apostle is there using the two terms interchangeably.

But take again Paul's words in Galatians 3:26: 'For in Christ Jesus,' he says, 'we are all sons of God through faith.' That is the Revised Version. Who are the *we*? All Christians. And in Galatians 4:4–7, he is again speaking, not of some special Christians, but of all Christians, even of these Galatian Christians who are going into error in certain respects. They are 'the sons of God,' Paul says; not only some of them, all of them. And in the same way in Ephesians 1, he is referring again to all believers, all Christians. All who are saved and redeemed by the blood of Christ are redeemed unto the adoption of children.

And perhaps the most significant thing of all is that the word that is rightly translated 'sons' – and not 'children', because there are two different words in the Greek – that word is never applied to believers in any of the writings of the apostle John. In his Gospel and in his epistles the apostle John always refers to believers as *children*. He never uses the precise term 'sons', but obviously the whole time he is describing us in the position of sons and of those who have been adopted into sonship. Now it is quite inconceivable that the apostle John would have done that if there is this vital distinction between sons and children. According to that argument, the apostle John had never realised that Christians are sons of God, he simply regarded them as children of God and, therefore, in his teaching he was depriving them of this special position which they claim the apostle Paul teaches with respect to them. So I conclude that taking the writings of Paul himself, this is an utterly artificial, false and meaningless distinction which is pernicious in its implications and teaching. And when you look at it from the standpoint of the whole of Scripture, and especially the writings of John, it is seen to be completely and entirely untenable.

So let me come to something more important and more interesting. What are the proofs that any one of us can have that we have been adopted? Well, you can find the scriptural proof. 'For ye are all the children of God by faith in Christ Jesus' (Gal. 3:26). Also in 1 Peter 1:3–6 you find it again: we have been begotten again 'unto a lively hope by the resurrection of Jesus Christ from the dead, to an inheritance incorruptible, and undefiled, and that fadeth not away, reserved in heaven for you' – for us who believe in Him. We are the inheritance, that is the children. It is for all of us who believe in Christ.

Then the second way of assurance is that we are given 'the Spirit of adoption, whereby we cry, Abba, Father' (Rom. 8:15); 'we receive the adoption of sons' (Gal. 4:5). You can be assured of the fact that you have received the adoption because you know that the Holy Spirit is dwelling within you. We saw the evidence for that earlier, so you can work it out. Especially we have His testimony with our spirits that we are the children of God. If we have that testimony of the Spirit with our spirit, it is an absolute proof that we have received the adoption.

And then last of all I would put the fact that we are led by the Spirit. That is Paul's argument: 'For as many as are led by the Spirit of God, they are the sons of God' (Rom. 8:14). Paul does not say 'As many as are actively acting as peacemakers or who are loving their enemies . . .' No! 'As many as are led by the Spirit of God'; those who subject themselves to His leading and who rejoice in being led by Him, they are the sons of God.

There, then, are the proofs. Now, finally, let us consider the *results of our adoption*. First, if we have the Spirit of adoption, we have lost 'the spirit of bondage again to fear' (Rom. 8:15). Positively, in the second place, we have been given a spirit of liberty. In other words, we are no longer afraid of the law and its condemnation; we are no longer afraid of death; we are enjoying something of the glorious liberty of the children of God. Again, thirdly, I would remind you that we receive this spirit of adoption through the indwelling Spirit.

But then, in addition, there are these results: because we have been adopted into God's family, we are entitled to bear His name. We can say that we are the children of God. We are members of the household of God. We belong to God's family. God's name is upon us. He has said, 'I will be your God, and ye shall be my people' (Lev. 26:12). We are His people. You remember that Peter applies to Christians what God had said to the nation of Israel of old (1 Pet. 2:9–10).

What else? Well, the fifth benefit is that we enjoy the present protection and consolation which God alone can give, and the provision that He makes for His children. 'Even the very hairs of your head are all numbered' (Luke 12:7); nothing can happen to us apart from Him. Think of those gracious and glorious promises which are given to the children and which we prove to be true in experience: protection, consolations and the perfect provision for our every need. He has said, 'I will never leave thee, nor forsake thee' (Heb. 13:5) – come what may.

The next benefit, at first, is not so pleasurable – fatherly chastisements. That is the whole argument of the first half of Hebrews 12: 'For whom the Lord loveth, he chasteneth, and scourgeth every son whom he receiveth' (v. 6). The argument is that if we are not receiving chastisement, then, we are not sons, but bastards. If we are children of God, He will chastise us for our good: 'Now no chastisement for the present seemeth to be joyous, but grievous: nevertheless afterwards it yieldeth the peaceable fruit of righteousness unto them which are exercised thereby' (v. 11). So that this is a very definite result of our adoption. If we are children of God, He is determined to bring us to glory and if we will not listen to His leading and teaching, He will chastise us because He loves us and because we are His sons. Because He has set His love and affection upon us, He is going to bring us through. So He chastises His children, but not those who are not children.

The next is this: *heirship*. 'And if children, then heirs, heirs of God, and joint-heirs with Christ' (Rom. 8:17). What a wonderful argument! It is because we have been adopted into the family of God and are declared to be children, that we are the heirs of God and joint heirs with Christ. The inheritance is certain.

The last point is the certainty and the security of it all. Yes, says Peter, you have been called to this 'inheritance incorruptible, and undefiled, and that fadeth not away, reserved in heaven for you' (1 Pet. 1:4), and therefore secure. Paul has said the same thing in

Romans 8:38–39: 'I am persuaded, that neither death nor life . . . shall be able to separate us from the love of God, which is in Christ Jesus our Lord.' If God has adopted you into His family, if you are a child of God, your destiny is secure, it is certain.

> Things future, nor things that are now,
> Nor all things below nor above,
> Can make Him His purpose forego,
> Or sever my soul from His love.
> Augustus Toplady

It is a guarantee. If God has taken me into the family I am not only a child, I am an heir, and nothing, and no one can ever rob me of the inheritance.

As I said at the beginning, this is a most consoling, comforting and encouraging doctrine. Is it not a tragedy that it is neglected, that men and women stop at forgiveness, or even at sanctification, and fail to realise that this is the thing that ever reminds us, directly, of our relationship to God and of the wonderful inheritance, the indescribable glory for which we are destined? We are saved unto this adoption of children. Not merely forgiven; not merely declared righteous; not merely with this new nature. Above, beyond, in addition to that we are declared to be the children of God – sons of God, heirs of God, joint heirs with the only begotten Son of God.

18

Sanctification – the Different Views

I would like to remind you again at this point that it is most important in these lectures on doctrine that we should see the relationship of these different aspects of the truth to one another. We shall need to emphasise this considerably in this lecture because in connection with the doctrine that we are now considering, it is one of the most important points of all. We have, in other words, come to the doctrine of sanctification. The position we have reached is this: we have a new nature; we are born again; we are in union with Christ; we are declared to be just; we are adopted into the family. Yes, but what about the problem of sin? We have not suddenly been made perfect. There is still the problem of sin in the life of the believer and the doctrine of sanctification deals with what God does about this.

This doctrine is highly controversial because there are a number of different views and theories about it, more with respect to exactly *how* sanctification takes place, than with respect to *what* it is. The questions are about how it happens, and its extent. There has been considerable controversy, especially for the last two hundred years, and the prime cause was none other than the great John Wesley. John Wesley propounded a theory with regard to sanctification and holiness which he regarded as absolutely vital; he taught it himself, and taught his preachers to preach it. It led to great discussion, and, I am afraid, to acrimonious debate between equally good and equally evangelical Christian people.

Those who are interested in theology and in the history of this matter should read the great debate that went on between, on the one hand, John Wesley and his coadjutor and helper, the saintly John Fletcher of Madeley, and on the other hand, people such as George

Whitefield, Augustus Toplady and others. That is important, not only historically, but for all who take their Christian faith seriously. The debate began then and it has continued more or less ever since, because John Wesley is, in some ways, the father of the various popular views with regard to sanctification that have been propounded since. The views, for instance, of the Salvation Army come directly from John Wesley. William Booth was a Methodist and he took over Methodist teaching, introducing certain modifications. And the various other holiness movements that came into being both in the nineteenth and in the twentieth centuries, all stem from the teaching of John Wesley.

Now, I am well aware of the fact that there are certain Christian people who, when they hear or read something like that, say at once, 'What does it matter what one believes about it?' They may ask, 'Do you believe that John Wesley was as much a Christian as George Whitefield?' To which my reply is – yes. Indeed, I would even use the reply that was given by George Whitefield on one famous occasion. One of Whitefield's very strong and aggressive supporters went to him one afternoon and said, 'Mr Whitefield, do you think that we shall see Mr Wesley in heaven?' To which Mr Whitefield replied, 'Probably not, he will be in such a high and exalted position that you and I won't see him there.' That is the right way to approach this matter.

Now of course, our salvation is not determined by our view of sanctification, whatever that view may be. But that is no reason for saying that it does not matter what we believe about it. It is always the business of Christians, believers, to study the Scriptures and to arrive at what they regard as the most scriptural understanding of the truth of a doctrine. If you do not do that and if you say that it does not matter at all, that you cannot be bothered, and that these things do not count, then what you are really saying is that truth does not matter. That is often maintained. There are people who say, 'Of course we don't agree with such and such a man's theology, but what does his theology matter, as long as he is able to gather a crowd and to bring people to Christ?'

Now such people are really saying that truth does not matter at all, they are only interested in results. The moment you say that, you are opening the door wide to every conceivable cult. Not only that, you are putting yourself in the dangerous position that if a very plausible teaching should suddenly be presented to you, you will probably believe it because you will have no standards whereby to evaluate it. The various heresies and cults that are popular succeed only because Christians have not taken the trouble to learn their own case. The people who come to our doors selling their books and bringing their theories, know their case, they have been drilled and trained in it and they know exactly what they believe. Shame on us Christian people, if we do not know our own doctrines. If we take up the attitude, 'Why bother if people disagree?' then it will lead inevitably to those results. However, the view of sanctification that I hope to propound to you very definitely does say that though people may be in very serious error in their views of sanctification, ultimately this does not prevent their being sanctified – that will develop as we go on with the argument.

So, then, as we approach this whole problem, let us start again with a definition. What does sanctification mean? Now if you go through your Bible and pick out the terms in the Old Testament and in the New, you will find quite a number, and I will summarise the meaning very briefly. The authorities are not quite agreed about the meaning of the word used in the Old Testament. Some say that it means 'to shine', like a bright light, a shining, while others say that it means 'to cut', 'to separate'. I am very ready to put both meanings together because I think the two aspects do come into the whole question of sanctification. There is a cutting off. There is a separation. Yes, but true sanctification also involves a shining – the sort of thing that was seen on Moses' face after he had been up on the mountain with God. There is a sort of brightness about holiness, something of the *shekinah* glory itself. So both those ideas are there in the Old Testament. When you come to the New Testament, the various words all mean – in the main – the idea of separating.

There are two main meanings to sanctification. The first is: to set apart for God and for His service. This is a great meaning of sanctification in both the Old and New Testaments. It is very interesting to observe that it applies not only to men and women but even to inanimate objects. The mountain on which God gave Moses the Ten Commandments is referred to as the 'holy mount' or the sanctified mount. It had been set apart for this specific purpose, so it became a holy mount. The temple building is referred to as holy, and in it there was the holy place and the holiest of all. The vessels in the temple, the instruments and these things are all again described as being sanctified, set apart, made holy (Ex. 28:29 etc.).

There is a double meaning to the idea of being set apart. The first is separation *from* everything that is profane or unclean or impure. Those vessels were never to be used in an ordinary way again. Once they had been sanctified, they had been set apart from ordinary use. But, secondly, it also means, positively, that anything that is sanctified is devoted entirely *to* God, presented to God, offered to God, that He may use it for His own service. Now in that connection it is very interesting to observe that the term 'to sanctify' is actually used about the Lord Jesus Christ Himself. You will find it twice in John's Gospel. The first is in John 10:36. Our Lord was arguing with the Jews who were asking Him about His identity and He said, 'Say ye of him, whom the Father hath sanctified, and sent into the world, Thou blasphemest; because I said, I am the Son of God?' The Father has sanctified me, He says. This means, 'set apart for His own service'. And in John 17:19, He says, 'For their sakes I sanctify myself, that they also might be sanctified through the truth.' And there can be no doubt that there it means that He was setting Himself at the disposal of God, that God may do, in Him and with Him and through Him on the cross, that work which was essential before our sins could be dealt with and we could be forgiven. So in the double sense of separating from and devoting entirely to God, the term is used of inanimate objects and even of the Lord Jesus Christ Himself.

You will also find that the term 'to sanctify' is very frequently used in that sense about believers. Let me give you some examples. On the road to Damascus, the risen Lord gave the apostle Paul his great commission – you will find the account in Acts 26 especially in verse 18. The Lord told Paul to go to the Gentiles, 'To open their eyes, and to turn them from darkness to light, and from the power of Satan unto God, that they may receive forgiveness of sins, and inheritance among them which are sanctified by faith that is in me.' Now that I suggest is this generic use of sanctification, meaning that people are set apart for God.

Or take again 1 Corinthians 6:11 which is a most interesting and important verse. We believe, do we not, that sanctification, in our logical order, should follow justification. And yet this is what you read: 'And such were some of you: but ye are washed, but ye are sanctified, but ye are justified in the name of the Lord Jesus, and by the Spirit of our God'. Notice that here sanctification comes before justification, so what does it mean? It is that the Corinthian Christians were taken out of the world, out of the sinful Corinthian society, and set apart for

God – washed and sanctified. They had become the people of God, set apart for Him and for His service.

Then you have the same use of it in Hebrews 10:10: 'By the which will we are sanctified through the offering of the body of Jesus Christ once for all.' That means – and it can have no other meaning in that verse and in its connection – set apart. Or take again the fourteenth verse, in that chapter: 'For by one offering he hath perfected for ever' – it is the same idea – 'them that are sanctified.' By His death upon the cross He has perfected those who are sanctified, and the word there can only mean set apart for God as God's people.

Take another illustration from Peter: 'Elect,' he says, 'according to the foreknowledge of God the Father, through sanctification of the Spirit, unto obedience and sprinkling of the blood of Jesus Christ' (1 Pet. 1:2). Now there again, sanctify obviously means set apart, taken out of the world, put for God and at God's disposal. And in the same way in 1 Peter 2:9, you find this: 'Ye are . . . a royal priesthood, an holy nation, a peculiar people,' and so on. In other words, Peter there applies to the Church, to Christian people, the very term that was used in Exodus 19 of the nation of Israel. The Children of Israel were God's holy nation, a sanctified nation; He had set them apart for Himself. It is equally true of Christian men and women. In that sense we are, all of us, already sanctified, once and for ever, as the author of the epistle to the Hebrews puts it, by the work of the Lord Jesus Christ upon the cross.

But sanctification has a second meaning which is not so much a positional as an inward meaning. It does not so much make a statement about us as set apart for God as add that, because of that, something happens within us to make us worthy of our new position. This is an ethical meaning – 'to make holy'. Being set apart for God does not *make* us holy; we are *regarded* as holy. But the second meaning describes how we are made holy. It means, therefore, a certain work of purification and cleansing which goes on within us, which makes us conform more and more to the Lord Jesus Christ and which changes us into His image from glory to glory. And that is the meaning which people generally have in mind when they talk about sanctification. It is the common use of the word. If people ask you, 'What do you believe about sanctification? How do you believe one is sanctified?' that is what they probably mean. They are referring to this inward cleansing, this inward purification, this being made conformable to the image of God's dear Son.

So then, I suggest to you that this will do as a good definition of sanctification: it is 'that gracious and continuous operation of the Holy Spirit by which He delivers the justified sinner from the pollution of sin, renews his whole nature in the image of God and enables him to perform good works.' Let me make that clear: 'It is that gracious and continuous operation of the Holy Spirit by which He delivers the justified sinner' – the one who is already justified – 'from the pollution of sin' – not from the guilt any longer, that has happened. Justification has taken care of that. He is declared just and righteous, the guilt has been dealt with. Now we are concerned more about the power and the pollution of sin – 'renews his whole nature in the image of God and enables him to perform good works.'

As we saw when we were dealing with justification, a convenient way of putting it, perhaps, would be this: in justification righteousness is imputed to us, put to our account. God, you remember, justifies the ungodly. He does not wait until people are fully sanctified before He justifies them. That, we saw, was the Roman Catholic error. No, God looks at men and women in their sins, and, applying to them the righteousness of Christ, declares them to be just. That is *imputed* righteousness. But in sanctification, we are discussing *imparted* righteousness. Not the righteousness that is put to my account, but the righteousness that is created within me and produced within me. Now that is a great distinction. The Church Fathers used to talk a lot about the difference between imparted and imputed righteousness, and it is a measure of our degradation that these terms are not as familiar to us as they were to them. They were great terms of the seventeenth, eighteenth and even the nineteenth centuries. What has gone wrong with us in this century? Why have we lost these great terms and their great meanings?

So sanctification is really God's way of dealing with the problem of sin after our regeneration and justification. But there is just one other thing I must deal with before I leave the question of definition. We must always be careful to define sanctification not only in terms of our moral state and condition but of our moral state and condition in relationship to God. That is absolutely vital. People can be highly moral but that does not mean that they are sanctified. The word must always carry with it this conception of our relationship to God, our standing in His presence. So sanctification is not morality and purity in and of itself. It is all that in its relationship to God. There is, therefore, an essential difference between the best moral person that the world may put forward and the Christian who is being sanctified.

So let us leave definition at that point and come on to the next step. The great questions is: How does it take place, this process of purging us and purifying us from the pollution of sin and of making us increasingly conformable to the image of Jesus Christ? And here we come to the heart of the different views and schools of thought, which can be divided into three main groups. There are, first of all, those I would describe as *perfectionist* views, views that in some shape or form teach the possibility of some kind of perfection for the Christian in this world. I do not apologise for that sort of language because I am being strictly accurate. The moment you begin to study these people you find that, though they have different ideas as to what constitutes perfection, they are all concerned about perfection in this world.

Now we cannot go into all the details and the ramifications of the different schools of thought to be found in this first group, but let me try to summarise. There are some who teach that sin is entirely eradicated from the Christian. It is like going to your garden and seeing a weed. You do not merely cut off the top, you get your fork, you push it down and take out the whole weed – roots and all. But when the teach that, these people go on to say that by sanctification they mean that we are living as perfectly as we are capable of living at any given moment. We may, they say, be capable of much more in a year or in ten years' time, but perfection is that you are living as perfectly as you can at this moment. They have a kind of sliding scale of perfection. That was the teaching, for instance, of the famous Charles G. Finney and his great associate, Ezra Mayhem – of the so-called Oberlin School in the United States. That was what they taught and they have many followers.

But John Wesley did not put it quite like that. John Wesley said that Christian perfection means that Christian men and women are not wilfully committing any known sin at any given moment. John Wesley granted that they may be committing sins that they are not aware of, but he very carefully (let us be fair to his teaching) defines it as not being guilty *wilfully* of any known sin. It is a moment by moment state, says Wesley; you may sin the next moment but you are perfect at this moment. And it only applies to known sins. From Wesley's definition and standpoint, if you are sinning ignorantly, it does not matter, that will be revealed to you later, and the moment you see and understand, then you must forsake that sin also, and then you are perfect in that respect. So sanctification means some kind of perfection, but not an absolute perfection.

Others talk about sanctification in terms of having a clean heart, the heart has been entirely cleansed from sin, but again they, too, would say known sin and wilful sin. Others put it in yet another way. Here again I am referring to John Wesley who was very fond of describing it as 'perfect love'. He said that Christian people may be guilty of sins of ignorance, things they are not aware of. They are still frail and ignorant in many respects. So, 'How do you call such people perfect?' he was asked. And his response was that if they can say that they love God with all their heart and mind and soul and strength, then though they are not actually perfect in life and in practice, they are perfect in love. They are loving God perfectly as far as they can at that moment; with the whole of their being they want to love God and are loving Him. That is perfect love, said Wesley. It may be greater later but at the moment it is perfect. As we have seen, he was very much concerned to emphasise this moment by moment aspect of perfection and sanctification.

Now it is a characteristic of all those perfectionist views that sanctification is something that is to be received and can be received in a moment. It is something that is done to us by God through the Holy Spirit and all we have to do is to desire it, to believe that it is possible, and to exercise faith. We have only to believe that if we ask God for it, He will give it to us. So we can receive it in a moment, in a flash. They are very fond of putting it like this: 'As you received your justification, so you should receive your sanctification.' It is an experience, something that can happen in a moment, completely.

The second group advocates or tells us that men and women are sanctified by means of what is called *the principle of counter-action*. This was the view which became popular in the seventies of the nineteenth century, and it is still popular. Now the people who hold this view do not believe in eradication of sin. They are very clear and explicit about that, and they regard the teaching of eradication as dangerous. So does the Christian just struggle throughout life in defeat? Oh no, they say, there is a new principle. Their great text, the very basis of their teaching, is Romans 8:2: 'The law of the Spirit of life in Christ Jesus hath made me free from the law of sin and death.' 'Yes,' they say, 'sin remains in the believer, but if he looks to Christ, abides in Him and relies upon Him by faith, Christ will keep him from sinning. There is this power of sin within the Christian, yes, but the power of Christ more than counteracts it' – that is where the counteraction comes in. And large numbers of illustrations are used.

Many of these illustrations came from the Reverend Evan Hopkins. His two favourites were these: first, the poker. There is a poker – it is cold, black and rigid. Yes, but put that poker into a fire and what happens to it? It becomes red, becomes hot and malleable. Take it out of the fire and it again becomes cold, black and rigid. That is the teaching of this school with regard to sanctification. As long as you abide in Christ, you remain, as it were, red, hot and malleable; you are kept free from sin. But if you do not abide in Christ you revert to exactly the state in which you were before.

The other illustration is the one about the lifebelt. They say that the law of gravity causes heavy bodies to sink in water. There is a man in the water and he cannot swim, so he sinks. Ah yes, but now introduce the law of counter-action. Put a lifebelt, inflated with air, round that man and what happens? Well, it counteracts the law that makes him sink, it keeps him afloat. But if the man shuffles out of the lifebelt, the old law comes in and down he goes! He must abide. He must keep on looking and trusting. So, again, whether it be the whole condition or a particular sin, all that a Christian has to do is just confess it and acknowledge it. He has to look to Christ, abide and trust in Him, and rely upon Him, and Christ will keep him victorious. Now, like the perfectionist views, this teaching again says that normally this starts as an experience and then continues as a process. In other words, sanctification is something that is to be received, and can be received in a moment, and all you do then is to abide in that experience.

Then the third and last teaching says that sanctification is a process which starts from the very moment of our regeneration, continues progressively throughout our lives and will only be perfect beyond death. The big thing that differentiates this view from the others is that it does not describe sanctification as an experience which can be received subsequent to justification; it emphasises the fact that the moment we are regenerate, sanctification has started and it goes on and is only complete and entire when our bodies shall ultimately be glorified and delivered from corruption. As Paul says, in Romans 8:23 where he is talking about the whole creation groaning and travailing together in pain until now, 'And not only they, but ourselves also, which have the firstfruits of the Spirit, even we ourselves groan within ourselves, waiting for the adoption, to wit, the redemption of our body.' It is only when the body is finally redeemed that our sanctification will be perfect.

The book I strongly recommend you to read as an exposition of this teaching is *Holiness* by Bishop Ryle. This book was largely written in order to deal with the various other ideas and theories that I have put before you. Now, as I said at the beginning, let me say again as I close, it is our duty to examine these things, but it is not our duty to examine them in a party spirit, or solely with the idea of defending our own view and criticising another. As I have often said, I am a great debtor to John Wesley. I am even a debtor to John Wesley on his holiness teaching. I do not accept it all, obviously, and there are points at which I would say that it is definitely wrong, but I spend a good deal of my time reading works and books on sanctification and holiness, by and about people who belong to my first group – the perfectionists. And I am glad to testify to the glory of God that whereas I do not believe and have to reject what is perhaps their main emphasis, I read them and they warm my heart, and they encourage and promote the process of sanctification within me, and I thank God for them.

So let us read these books, which are all of them expositions of Scripture, and let us go to the Bible. Let us try to examine them as dispassionately as we can and try to arrive at the truth concerning this matter. If we do it together in that way, our souls will be blessed and enriched, and we will thank God that we have given time to the study of the doctrine of sanctification.

19

Sanctification – God's Work and Ours

We have considered the three main views of the doctrine of sanctification and we must keep them in mind as we now seek to approach the subject in a more direct and expository manner. Certain principles are taught quite plainly in the Scripture, and we must test those three views and theories by these principles.

The first great principle found everywhere in the Bible, in the Old Testament as well as in the New, is that sanctification is God's will for us. There is the great statement in 1 Thessalonians 4:3, where we are told explicitly, 'For this is the will of God, even your sanctification.' That is the starting point and it is fundamental. God's purpose in doing everything that He did in the Old Testament is ultimately our sanctification. His purpose when He 'sent forth his Son, made of a woman, made under the law' (Gal. 4:4) was still our sanctification. When Christ went to the death of the cross, the object was our perfection, as it was in the giving of the Holy Spirit. Indeed, everything God has done about us and our salvation has as its end and object our sanctification.

Now it is absolutely vital that we should grasp that principle. If you want further proof you will find it in John 17:17. Our Lord is about to leave His own, and He is praying to the Father for them, and what does He pray? 'Sanctify them through thy truth: thy word is truth.' Indeed, He goes further and says in verse 19, 'And for their sakes I sanctify myself, that they also might be sanctified through the truth.' Now when our Lord says there, 'I sanctify myself,' He is saying to His Father, in effect, 'I am putting myself at your disposal; I am separating myself unto this final work that you have for me to do.' That is nothing but the death upon the cross. He does that in order that we may be sanctified; it is the object which is behind everything. Again, the apostle Paul says to Titus, 'Who gave himself for us, that he might redeem us from all iniquity, and purify unto himself a peculiar people, zealous of good works' (Tit. 2:14). That is why He died for us on the cross, for that, and for nothing less. There is a hymn which puts it well:

> He died that we might be forgiven;

yes, but it does not stop at that:

> He died to make us good.
>   Cecil Frances Alexander

The tendency is to forget the second part, and, as I shall show you in a moment, to associate the death upon the cross only with forgiveness. But the Bible never does that.

So the first principle to grasp is that sanctification is the end of the whole process of salvation. If that is true, then we must recognise that there are certain dangers which must be avoided at all costs. Let me note them. The first great danger is that of isolating these various doctrines and of separating them from one another in a false way. We have often emphasised the fact that nothing is so clear, as you work through the Bible and look at its doctrines, as the way in which they all belong together. They all form one piece. They are not disjointed, dismembered teachings that hang loosely together. There is a vital connection between them all and we have seen that all along.

Now it is right to distinguish them, but there is all the difference in the world between distinguishing between things and separating them. For the purposes of thought, and, indeed, in accordance with the Scripture, we must distinguish justification from sanctification. But that is a very different thing from separating them. And we must never do that because, according to this teaching, they are part of the same process, they are part of God's one great movement of salvation. Therefore we must never suggest that you can have one without the other; that you can be justified without being sanctified, or only later become sanctified. That is totally unscriptural.

Take, for example, that great statement of Paul's in Romans, '. . . whom he called, them he also justified; and whom he justified, them he also glorified' (Rom. 8:30). The Apostle is saying there that this whole process of salvation is one, and that when God starts this work in a man or woman, there is a sense in which the whole work is already complete; they go straight from justification to glorification. So it is very wrong to draw these divisions and distinctions which mean separation. Or take another statement by the Apostle, in 1 Corinthians 1:30: 'But of him are ye in Christ Jesus, who of God is made unto us wisdom, and righteousness, and sanctification, and redemption.' It is the Lord who is made all these things to us, and therefore we must not separate them for this good reason – you cannot divide the Lord Jesus Christ! You are either in Christ or else you are not. If you are a Christian, you are joined to Christ, and all the benefits of Christ are yours.

We saw that very clearly when we were dealing with the doctrine of the union of the believer with Christ, the great doctrine of Romans chapters 5 and 6. Paul says: You were crucified with Him, you died with Him, you were buried with Him, you have risen again with Him, and you are *already* seated in the heavenly places with Him. If we are in Christ, He is made unto us not justification only but sanctification also, and redemption. He is the all and in all, and therefore I suggest that the people who separate justification and sanctification, and say that the two have no essential inherent connection, are guilty of dividing Christ, and we have the right to ask, 'Is Christ divided? (1 Cor. 1:13). That, then, is our first deduction: God's will, God's purpose in the whole of salvation, in everything He has done in His Son and by the Spirit, is our sanctification.

The second danger, therefore, is the danger of thinking in terms of seeking pardon and forgiveness only, and then of imagining that later on we ought to seek our sanctification. 'Ah yes,' people say, 'so and so sought salvation. He believed on the Lord Jesus Christ, and his sins were forgiven, but he has not gone on to sanctification yet. He has remained at that first stage of justification and forgiveness.' And they now believe it to be their duty to try to get him to go on to sanctification and to receive that as he received justification.

But, surely, that is utterly false reasoning. People cannot seek forgiveness only, for this good reason: Why do they seek forgiveness? Why should anybody desire it? Well, there can be only one answer to that question. Some people, of course, when they seek forgiveness, are only seeking a feeling of comfort within themselves, but that is not seeking true forgiveness. To seek forgiveness must mean that they have seen something of the holiness of God and the holiness of God's law; they have already seen themselves as sinners. They must have hated this thing which has separated them from God, and, therefore, if they are truly seeking forgiveness, they must be anxious to be delivered from that which has made them miserable and made them sin against God, and which has put them into such a dangerous position. Surely that is the basis for seeking forgiveness. I see no meaning in the term 'forgiveness' if it does not mean that. No, no, if you are concerned about forgiveness, you know something about yourself as a hell-deserving sinner.

In dealing with repentance we had to go into the meaning of forgiveness in detail, and we pointed out how in true repentance the whole person is involved; the mind understands this truth, the heart feels it. We emphasised, in passing, that, until comparatively recently, repentance was associated with weakness and with people being broken down and sometimes crying out in agony as they failed to find peace. That is the biblical repentance and throughout the centuries that has been the Church's teaching about repentance. If men and women are not aware of all these things, there is no true content to their use of the term forgiveness. But if forgiveness includes all that, it is already the beginning of sanctification. The moment we see something of the sinfulness of sin, and long to be separated from it, and to be nearer to God, and to enjoy God, that in itself is sanctification, that is to be separated unto God.

Then, in the third place, there is obviously, therefore, a very real danger of a false evangelism which is concerned only about giving people some kind of temporary relief and release, and does not press upon them the vital importance of sanctification. An evangelism which stops at forgiveness is not biblical evangelism because the heart of all preaching is that the essence of sin is to be separated from God, and if we preach reconciliation truly, we must be preaching sanctification.

So as our basic conception we must know that we are not our own, that we have been bought with a price. That is Paul's argument. He teaches sanctification in terms of the death upon the cross: 'Know ye not that . . . ye are not your own? For ye are bought with a price' (1 Cor. 6:19–20). In preaching sanctification the Apostle does not only preach the Holy Spirit, he is always preaching the cross at the same time. These things are linked together. In his early evangelism among the Thessalonians, for instance, the effect was that these people 'turned to God from idols to serve the living and true God' (1 Thess. 1:9). To serve God is sanctification and so that was Paul's first

message in Thessalonica. So the end of all evangelism should be to
reconcile men and women to God, and to separate them unto Him.
Again, we need to remember that old concept of doing a thorough
'law work' in presenting Christ as Saviour. These things must always
go together and sanctification is a part of the message of evangelism.

Let me put it, finally, like this. The whole trouble with regard to
sanctification arises from our fatal tendency to start with ourselves
instead of with God. We think of ourselves and our problems, our
sins and our needs, and we have those things in our mind when we
begin to talk about sanctification. But there is the whole error. The
apostle Peter, in preaching sanctification, adopts the exact opposite
procedure. This is how he puts it: 'Wherefore gird up the loins of your
mind, be sober, and hope to the end for the grace that is to be brought
unto you at the revelation of Jesus Christ; as *obedient children*' – it is
your relationship to God that determines it – '. . . as he which hath
called you is holy, so be ye holy in all manner of conversation;
because it is written, Be ye holy' – why? – 'for I am holy' (1 Pet. 1:13–
16).

Now the idea has somehow gained currency that meetings and con-
ventions in which holiness is preached are clinics where people should
go because they are being bothered by some particular sin. They have
a sin which they cannot get rid of, so they are encouraged to go to this
'clinic' which will deliver them of their problem. But that is not how
the Bible puts it. There is one reason, and one reason only, why we
should all be sanctified and holy, and it is this: not that we may be
happy, nor that we may get rid of our problems, but because God is
holy, because we are God's people and because Christ has died for us,
and purchased us. We do not belong to ourselves. We have no right
to live a sinful life.

That, then, is the way in which we should start facing this subject
of sanctification. Salvation is God's work from beginning to end, and
therefore there can be no gaps, no hiatus. It is something that is
started by God, continued by God and perfected by God Himself. The
moment, therefore, that we are regenerate and united to the Lord
Jesus Christ, the process of sanctification has already started. The
moment I receive the divine nature, the moment I am born again,
something has come into me which is going to separate me from sin.
Take that statement of James which is sometimes not properly understood because of our translations. 'Do ye think that the scripture saith
in vain, The spirit that dwelleth in us lusteth to envy?' (Jas. 4:5). Now

the margin of the Revised Version very rightly puts that like this: 'Do you not know that the Spirit that God has given you, that is in you, is lusting even to the point of envy, to wean you from the world and its spirit and to God?' That is it. So the moment I am born again and have received the Holy Spirit, this process of separating me has already started, and I cannot be regenerate without the process of sanctification having already started to work within me. The conflict between the flesh and the Spirit has already begun and that is the fight to separate me from the world and unto God, in every part and in every step.

That, then, brings us to the second great principle: What is the agent in sanctification? If that is the process, if that is God's will, if that is what all salvation is tending unto, how does it take place? How does sanctification proceed within us? Now here again we must be careful. We have seen, in looking at a number of these doctrines, that in some of them God alone acts. In regeneration, for instance, we do nothing, it is entirely the action of God. In justification, likewise, we do nothing at all; justification is entirely the action of God in pronouncing us to be just and righteous. The same applies to our adoption. We have nothing to do with our adoption, it is God's declaration, God's action. But, on the other hand, when we were considering repentance and faith, we pointed out that though these again are started by the Holy Spirit, we have our part to play. We must confess our sins, and forsake them. We believe on the Lord Jesus Christ and we cannot do so without the initial movement of God – it is started by Him – but then we have to express that belief. And it is exactly the same with sanctification.

The classic text to describe our active participation is found in the epistle to the Philippians, chapter 2: 'Work out your own salvation with fear and trembling. For it is God which worketh in you both to will and to do of his good pleasure' (vv. 12–13). Now there the balance is presented to us perfectly. So when we are discussing the agency in sanctification, when we are asking, 'How is this work of sanctification carried on in us?' we must start by saying that it is primarily the action of God; it is God who works in us both to will and to do.

The Scripture is quite clear about this and in a very remarkable manner. Sanctification in the Scripture is attributed to the Father, to the Son and to the Holy Spirit. Let me give you the texts. 1 Thessalonians 5:23 teaches us that it is the Father's work: 'And the very God of peace sanctify you wholly; and I pray God your whole spirit and soul and body be preserved blameless unto the coming of our Lord Jesus Christ.' Then in the same way in Hebrews there is that great statement: 'Now the God of peace, that brought again from the dead our Lord Jesus, that great shepherd of the sheep, through the blood of the everlasting covenant, *make you perfect* in every good work to do his will . . .' (Heb. 13:20–21). It is the God of peace who is going to do this. It is the Father. It is He, who brought the Lord Jesus, His Son, from the dead, who will make us perfect.

But in exactly the same way the Scriptures tell us that sanctification is the work of the Son. And have you noticed how often, in working through these doctrines, we have seen how the same work is attributed to the three blessed Persons? I know of nothing so uplifting as the realisation of that great truth that the three blessed Persons in the Trinity have co-operated in order that a worm such as I might be rescued and redeemed, and made perfect, to stand in the presence of God in the Judgment. Here is a text about the Son: 'Husbands, love your wives, even as Christ also loved the church, and gave himself for it; that he might sanctify and cleanse it with the washing of water by the word' (Eph. 5:25–26). He died in order that He might sanctify the Church. And in the same way, as I have already reminded you, in Titus 2:14 we read that He 'gave himself for us'. Why? Not merely that we might have our sins forgiven, not merely that we might escape hell, not merely that our conscience might be put at rest. No. 'Who gave himself for us, that he might redeem us from all iniquity, and purify unto himself a peculiar people, zealous of good works.'

But, in exactly the same way, sanctification is also the work of the Holy Spirit. Paul writes to the Corinthians, 'But ye are washed, but ye are sanctified, but ye are justified in the name of the Lord Jesus, and *by the Spirit of our God*' (1 Cor. 6:11). And there are various other references to the Spirit's work in separating us: 'God hath from the beginning chosen you to salvation through sanctification of the Spirit and belief of the truth' (2 Thess. 2:13). While, therefore, we can say that sanctification is the work of the three Persons in the Trinity, it is especially, of course, the work of the third Person, the Holy Spirit, because, as we have seen already, it is He who mediates Christ to us; it is He who applies the work of Christ to us; it is He who forms Christ in us; it is He who joins us to Christ.

We can never emphasise too strongly that sanctification is first of all, and primarily, the work of God in us, through and by the Holy

Spirit. Therefore it is thoroughly unscriptural to say that as a believer, as a Christian, you can be without sanctification and decide, yourself, to go in for it! That is impossible. It is God's work; it is His intent, His purpose; it is something He is doing in all whom He has separated unto Himself. Our Lord died for us in order that this might happen and it is inconceivable that it should not happen in any for whom He has paid the price with His own blood. Therefore we start with that, and it must be emphasised. Then we go on to the second part of Paul's statement in Philippians 2:12–13: 'For it is God which worketh in you both to will and to do of his good pleasure.' That is why we are told, 'Work out your own salvation with fear and trembling.' Be careful what you are doing; realise who you are; realise the meaning of the 'fear and trembling'.

Now here, once more, we come to a vital point of difference between justification and sanctification. In justification, as I have reminded you, we do nothing because we cannot. It is the declaratory act of God. But here, we are called to activity. This again, then, is crucial in this whole doctrine of sanctification. Many people find themselves in trouble at this point, especially those at the two extremes. Some people seem to think that once men and women are born again, the activity of God in them ceases. Because God has given them a new nature, they say, they have nothing to do now but to exercise the new nature, and they do that by reading the Scriptures and understanding and applying them. In connection with their sanctification they do everything themselves. Now I have already shown you that that is wrong. Sanctification is God's work in us. The first move, the motive, the force, all is this power of God working in us 'both to will and to do'.

Yes, but in trying to avoid the one extreme, some go right to the other, and the second school says that we have nothing at all to do except look passively to Jesus and abide in Him, and then all the work is done in us and for us. I reminded you of that in the last lecture when I mentioned the illustration of the poker and the man with the lifebelt around him, both of which give the impression that we have nothing to do at all, that the work is done entirely by the Lord, as we look to Him. And the answer to that is Philippians 2:12–13: 'Work out your own salvation . . . for it is God which worketh in you.'

But these friends sometimes tell us that surely in John 15 our Lord teaches the selfsame idea, that we do nothing, but look to Him. John 15 gives us the parable, the picture, of the vine and the branches: 'I

am the vine, and ye are the branches' (v. 5), and this is interpreted as
meaning that the branch does nothing at all, that the work is done
entirely by the tree, and that the branch is just there to show the fruit.
But that, surely, is a profound misunderstanding of our Lord's picture. The branch in a tree is not inactive. It is not like a hollow tube
which is inert and has no life in it. The branch is full of life. Of course,
the branch can do nothing if it does not receive the sap that comes up
from the tree; yes, that is absolutely essential. But, given the sap, the
branch is full of vitality and life. It draws things from the air; it sends
things back into the air. Every leaf of a branch is very active.

So you see the danger of illustrations, how easily they can be misunderstood. But the Scripture itself is perfectly clear about this:
'Work out your own salvation.' You could not do that if God did not
work in you first, but He does work in you in order that you may
work out. God works in my will, He works the will to act, and He
enables the action. It is 'God which worketh in you both to will and
to do of his good pleasure,' but I must do the willing, and the doing.

There are a number of statements in the Scriptures that say exactly
the same thing and surely this is something that ought to be perfectly
clear to all of us. Take Romans 6, for instance, where there is a col-
lection of these phrases. 'Reckon yourselves', says Paul; 'Reckon ye
also yourselves to be dead indeed unto sin, but alive unto God . . .'
(Rom. 6:11). That is something that I have to do; nobody can 'reckon
this' for me. I have to indulge in that activity. The Holy Spirit working
in me leads me to this recognition, but I am exhorted to do the
reckoning. It is an appeal to me; it is a part of sanctification. Then
listen to Paul putting this negatively: 'Let not sin therefore reign in
your mortal body' (v. 12). *You* must not let sin reign in *you*. It is an
exhortation to *you*. Paul also puts this positively as he goes on to say,
'Neither yield ye your members as instruments of unrighteousness
unto sin: but yield yourselves unto God . . . and your members as
instruments of righteousness unto God' (v. 13). We must yield the
members of our body; it is a positive thing that we must do.

Again, Paul says, in Romans 8: '. . . If ye through the Spirit do
mortify the deeds of the body, ye shall live' (v. 13). We must mortify
the deeds of the body; yes, you will notice, through the Spirit. Without the Spirit we cannot do it. That was the error of monasticism and
that is the error of all morality. But having received the Spirit, and
with the Spirit working in us, then through the Spirit, we must mortify the deeds of our body. Or listen to Paul again in Colossians 3:5:

'Mortify therefore your members which are upon the earth.' We must do that. There are other phrases: 'Stand fast' (1 Cor. 16:15); 'Fight' (1 Tim. 6:12) – Paul even exhorts us to fight! That is not a very passive thing, is it? Then he says, to Timothy specifically, 'Flee also youthful lusts' (2 Tim. 2:22) – He is calling upon Timothy to flee, not to wait to be delivered, he must do something. And in 1 Timothy 6:11 Paul says, 'But thou, O man of God, flee these things; and follow after righteousness.' Timothy had to seek after it, to strive after it. We are told to put off the old man and put on the new (Eph. 4:22, 24).

But I sometimes think that the most important text of all is 2 Corinthians 7:1: 'Having therefore these promises, dearly beloved, *let us cleanse ourselves* from all filthiness of the flesh and spirit, perfecting holiness in the fear of God.' Is there any possible alternative exposition of that statement? All these terms point in the same direction. Indeed, as I have said earlier, if what I am saying is not true, then none of these New Testament epistles need ever have been written. If all we have to do to be sanctified is to 'let go and let God', to surrender ourselves and look to Jesus, then the apostles have wasted a great deal of ink and of time and energy in arguing with us about doctrine, in saying, 'Therefore, in the light of that, now then, apply it; do this, don't do that, cleanse yourselves.' Why should they have said all that is we need only surrender, wait, look and abide?

No, let us be careful lest we wrest the Scriptures, if not to our destruction, at any rate to our confusion. The Scriptures plainly teach us that God is working in us because He has saved us; but He is working in us in order that we may work it out, and those are the ways in which we do it. What we really have to do is this reckoning, this understanding, this application, this mortifying, and so on – this cleansing. But there is the great balance in the Scripture – primarily, initially, vitally, all-importantly, sanctification is the work of God by the Spirit. As 'new born babes', as 'dearly beloved', as 'children of God', we are exhorted to be holy because the One at work in us is holy, and His whole purpose in redemption is that we might indeed be His children, worthy of the name.

20

The Mighty Process of the Holy Spirit

We have seen that sanctification is primarily the work of God, but that we also have our part to play and now, having said that, we can come to what is, in many ways, the most interesting aspect of this question of sanctification, and that is the method or the mode in which and by which this takes place within us. Of course, it is at this point that the controversy between the various schools to which I have referred has been most acute. Perhaps the most convenient way to look at this subject is to ask three questions.

First, is sanctification something that is to be received? Now, there are many who hold the view that it is, and they often put it like this: 'As you have received your justification, so receive your sanctification;' and they use different illustrations. There was a teacher, famous in the early part of this century, who used to say, 'You have a purse in your hand and there are two golden sovereigns inside. First you pick out a golden sovereign, that's your justification. Then,' he said, 'you can go on and pick out the other golden sovereign, that's your sanctification. And the tragedy is that so many Christians only pick out the first sovereign and don't pick out the second.'

Others put it like this: I am standing with a coin on both my palms, and I say to you, 'Come along and take.' So many simply take the one from the right hand, which is justification, but the preaching of sanctification is that as you have taken the first coin, so you take the second. You have received your justification by faith, now receive your sanctification by faith in the same way.

Thus it is taught that sanctification can be accepted like that, in one act. Now obviously those who say this must have certain Scriptures which appear, at any rate to them, to justify that kind of teaching, and the verse which they are very fond of quoting is in Acts, where our Lord is giving His commission to His great servant, Paul, on the road to Damascus. Our Lord tells Paul that He wants him to go and preach to the people and to the Gentiles, 'To open their eyes, and to turn them from darkness to light, and from the power of Satan unto God, that they may receive forgiveness of sins, and inheritance among them which are sanctified by faith that is in me' (Acts 26:18). 'There you are,' they say; 'sanctified by faith!'

And that seems to them to be the end of all controversy and discussion. But surely when you look at that verse, if you have borne in mind our earlier point about the twofold meaning of sanctification, then you must come to the conclusion that 'sanctified' is obviously used in the first sense of being set apart. It is not the inward process of cleansing and purification, but the setting apart. You remember that we saw that the mountain on which God gave the Ten Commandments to Moses is called the 'holy mount'. Also, Peter, in his first epistle, introduces himself by saying that he is writing to those who are 'Elect according to the foreknowledge of God the Father, through sanctification of the Spirit, unto obedience and sprinkling of the blood of Jesus Christ' (1 Pet. 1:2). There sanctification comes before belief. And, as we saw, when Paul writes to the Corinthians and says, 'And such were some of you: but ye are washed, but ye are sanctified, but ye are justified . . .' (1 Cor. 6:11) he puts sanctification before justification.

Now in all those instances it means 'set apart'. And surely that is what it means in Acts 26. Paul is told to preach to the Gentiles and to tell them that if they believe on the Lord Jesus Christ, they shall have their inheritance with all others who have been set apart by the Holy Spirit for God, by faith in Jesus Christ. Now I think the more you read that twenty-sixth chapter of Acts, you will come to the conclusion that the meaning of that term, 'sanctified by faith', is that Gentiles have been set apart for the inheritance. But even if you do not agree with that, I would still say that obviously everything in the Christian life, ultimately, is by faith. 'We walk by faith, not by sight' (2 Cor. 5:7). So, in a very general sense, everything is by faith, but in Acts 26 in particular, I suggest that sanctification means this 'setting apart'.

The people who hold this view are also fond of quoting the first epistle of John, especially chapter 1 verse 7, where we are told that the blood of Jesus Christ cleanses us from all sin, and chapter 3 verses 8 and 9. We cannot stay with this, but what we really have there is a picture of the Christian walking in the light in fellowship with God. Yes, but the Christian is worried by this, and says, 'I like this idea of walking with God in the light, but what if I should fall into sin? What happens to me then?'

'Well,' says John in effect, 'what happens is that the fellowship is in a sense broken, but if you confess your sins, He is faithful and just to forgive you your sins and to cleanse you from all unrighteousness. While we are walking with Him in the light, the blood of Jesus Christ His Son cleanses us from all sin. So you needn't be troubled.' The problem which is being considered in 1 John is the problem of the defilement which we undergo as we are walking in fellowship with God and with His Son, Jesus Christ. And John is concerned to show us how that defilement is removed, so we need not be downcast and feel that we have sinned against the light and that we cannot go on any further.

Indeed, I always feel that the first verse of chapter 2 clinches this in a very definite manner: 'My little children,' John says, 'these things write I unto you, that ye sin not. And', he goes on, 'if any man sin, we have an advocate with the Father, Jesus Christ the righteous; and he is the propitiation for our sins; and not for ours only, but also for the sins of the whole world.' In other words, John says that he is writing in order to teach them not to sin. He is not telling them that they can receive something and never sin again. No, no, he is exhorting them not to sin, but if they do sin, he says, there is the answer: Jesus Christ the righteous, who is the propitiation.

But perhaps the favourite verse of all the friends who hold this particular view is Romans 8:1–2: 'There is therefore now no condemnation to them which are in Christ Jesus . . . For the law of the Spirit of life in Christ Jesus hath made me free from the law of sin and death.' They interpret that by saying that it is here that the principle of counteraction comes in, that there are two laws. In me there is the law of sin and death, dragging me down, causing me to sin. 'Ah yes,' they say, 'but it's all right, another law has come into being, the law of the Spirit of life in Christ Jesus. And as long as I look to Him, and abide in Him, this new law will keep me from falling to that first law.' You remember the illustrations about the poker and the lifebelt.

That is how Romans 8:2 is interpreted. This, of course, is really crucial. Romans 8:2 is a most important verse and the interpretation I have just described is a very serious misrepresentation of it. So what does this verse really say? Paul writes, 'There is therefore now no condemnation to them which are in Christ Jesus.' Why? 'For' – here is the answer – 'the law of the Spirit of life in Christ Jesus hath made me free from the law of sin and death.' Paul is here recapitulating something that he has already told us several times in the two previous chapters. Here it is, first of all, in the sixth chapter: 'What shall we say then? Shall we continue in sin, that grace may abound? God forbid,' says Paul. 'How shall we, that are dead to sin, live any longer therein?' (Rom. 6:1–2). We are dead unto sin. Now there was a time when we were not. Every man or woman born into this world, as a result of the fall of Adam and as a result of the inheritance of original sin, is under the dominion of sin. Sin rules, governs and controls the natural person. Men and women may not be aware of that, they may not even believe in such a category as sin. Nevertheless they are slaves of sin. They cannot help themselves. Sin is their master. But in those verses, Paul says that we are in Christ and we have died to sin.

That is the first statement, but let me take you to a second, in verse 18 of chapter 6. 'Being then,' says Paul, 'made free from sin, ye became the servants of righteousness.' That means, '*you have been made* free', or, '*you were made* free'. It is something that has happened and that has happened once and for all. Christians, says Paul, are people who have been made free from sin. What does he mean by that? Well, he cannot possibly mean that we are sinless and perfect because we are not and we know we are not. No, he just means the same thing again. We are free from sin in the sense that sin is no longer our master. We are not under the law or the dominion of sin. Paul has already put that in the fourteenth verse when he says, 'sin shall not have dominion over you', and he goes on repeating it in this most interesting and extraordinary manner.

Then again he says it in the twentieth verse: 'For when ye were the servants of sin' – which means the slaves of sin – 'ye were free from righteousness.' Notice Paul's contrasts. When we were servants of sin, we were free from righteousness, but now we are the slaves of righteousness and we are free from sin. This is all going to help us to understand Romans 8:2, but come along to the seventh chapter and to some very important verses: 4, 5 and 6. 'Wherefore, my brethren,' Paul says, 'ye also are become dead to the law by the body of Christ,' and 'are become' there means 'have become'; it is the Greek aorist tense which means 'once and for ever'; it is final.

In his argument Paul has used the illustration of the woman married to her husband. Of course, he says, as long as the husband is

alive, the woman is bound to him, she is under his law. But if the husband dies, she is at liberty to marry another man. If she did that while
the husband was alive she would be an adulteress, but if the husband
is dead, the law no longer applies to her; she is absolutely free, and
she can marry again. Now, says Paul, in exactly the same way, you
also have become 'dead to the law by the body of Christ' (v. 4). Paul is
not talking of some subsequent experience that people get after they
have been justified. No, he says in effect: When you were justified by
the body and the death of Christ and His rising again and His righteousness, you have become dead to the law so that 'ye should be married to another, even to him who is raised from the dead, that we
should bring forth fruit unto God.' Paul is back again to his favourite
doctrine of the union of the believer with Christ. As the woman is in
union with her husband and they have children (that is the fruit) so a
Christian is joined to Christ and they bear fruit together to God's
glory. 'For when we were in the flesh,' he continues, 'the motions of
sins, which were by the law, did work in our members to bring forth
fruit unto death. But now we are delivered from the law, that being
dead wherein we were held; that we should serve in newness of spirit,
and not in the oldness of the letter.' How clear it is when you go back
and follow his argument right through. So let us look at Romans 8:2
in the light of all this.

Paul says, 'For the law of the Spirit of life in Christ Jesus hath made
me free from the law of sin and death.' Now let us be clear about this;
it is still this same aorist tense. 'The law of the Spirit of life in Christ
Jesus has, once and for ever and finally, set me free, liberated me,
from the law of sin and death.' What is 'the law of sin and death'? It is
that law to which Paul has been referring at great length. The 'law of
sin' is sin dominating the life of unbelievers, mastering and controlling them. Every one of us is born under that particular law. But now
Paul tells us that as Christians we are no longer in that position. We
have died with Christ, we have risen with Him and that is 'the law of
the Spirit of life in Christ Jesus', which has come into us, the life of
Christ. Therefore, Paul says, because we have this life with Christ, we
have finished with that dominion of sin under which we formerly
lived.

In other words, the Apostle is still here talking about this great doctrine of his which he started dealing with in the middle of Romans 5,
the doctrine of the union of the believer with the Lord Jesus Christ. If
that is so, how wrong, therefore, how seriously wrong, it is to say that

there are many Christians who are yet to come to the position of Romans 8:2. 'Oh yes,' maintain the proponents of this view, 'they are forgiven and they are justified, but as yet they know nothing about this wonderful thing, the Spirit of life in Christ Jesus setting them free.' They say that this verse is really saying that the law of the Spirit of life in Christ Jesus goes on setting me free from the law of sin and death. But that is not what Paul says, it is an aorist: 'The law of the Spirit of life in Christ Jesus *hath made* me free.' It has happened, he is looking back. An event has taken place, once and for ever, with an absolute finality. The moment I am in Christ, I have finished with the law of sin and death. It is not something I can go on to as second experience. I am not a Christian at all unless this is true of me. That is the Apostle's teaching.

So you see once more how serious it is to separate justification and sanctification, and this verse, of all verses, does not lend any countenance to that. Paul is saying something which is inevitably true of every single Christian. Joined to Christ, the new Husband, means that you have finished with the old. You are no longer under the dominion of sin or of Satan or under the law, but you are under grace. In Romans 8:1–2 Paul is summing it all up once more, and that is why 'There is therefore now no condemnation to them which are in Christ Jesus.'

Having tried to deal with these Scriptures that are so often abused in support of that argument, let me remind you of some other reasons for saying that sanctification is not something that is to be received. We saw last time, did we not, that great emphasis given to our part in sanctification, to what you and I have to do. What, as we have indicated, is the point of the mighty arguments of Paul and the apostles in their letters if sanctification is something that I am to receive? Why the exhortations?

I have already given you many quotations from the apostle Paul, so now let me give you one from the apostle Peter: 'Dearly beloved,' says Peter, 'I beseech you as strangers and pilgrims, abstain from fleshly lusts, which war against the soul' (1 Pet. 2:11). Do you notice what he says? We do not receive our sanctification and are then delivered from these things. No, he tells us to abstain from them and to keep ourselves from them. And the tragedy is that so many people are spending their lives waiting to receive something, and in the meantime they are not abstaining from these fleshly lusts.

Take another statement from Paul: 'Let him that stole steal no more' (Eph. 4:28). That is what he is to do. He is not to wait to receive something, he is commanded to give up stealing. What can be more specific than that? And people who are guilty of foolish talking and jesting and all these other unseemly things are *not to do them* (Eph. 5:4). 'Be not conformed to this world' (Rom. 12:2). You do not wait to receive something; if up to this moment you have been conforming to the world, you must stop.

People have often come to me about this and said, 'You know, I've been trying so hard, but I can't get this experience.' To which the reply is that the Scripture commands you to abstain: 'Cleanse your hands, ye sinners; and purify your hearts, ye double minded' (Jas. 4:8). And I repeat that these injunctions are quite pointless and a sheer waste of ink if sanctification is something that I can receive. If it is, we would surely be told, 'You need not worry about this question of sin, you can receive your sanctification in one act, and all you do then is to maintain it and abide in it. But that is most certainly not the New Testament teaching. No, in every single New Testament epistle there is all this great doctrine and the ethical appeal and exhortation.

So we have dealt with our first question: Is sanctification something that is to be received? Now let us turn to the second: Is sanctification an experience? Again, many teach that it is. And at this point the argument is generally to tell a number of stories. There are large numbers of stories about people who have had marvellous experiences, of people, for instance, who had a bad temper, or something like that. They struggled with it for years and could not get rid of it, and at last they came to some great crisis. So they went into their rooms and there they fought it out with God and had this marvellous experience and never again lost their temper. Similar stories are told about people who have had a great struggle giving up smoking, and alcohol, and so on.

Now, it behoves us to examine these experiences carefully and with real sympathy. Of course, I accept the experiences without any hesitation at all. Thank God, I am able to testify to some such experiences myself in my own life. So what of them? Well here is my answer. First and foremost, there is no evidence at all in the New Testament that that kind of experience means sanctification. It may be a part of sanctification, it may greatly aid sanctification, but it is not sanctification in and of itself. As I have just been pointing out, if that is the way in which all our problems are to be solved, what is the point of the New Testament epistles? Their whole assumption is the opposite of that.

But there is something else which is perhaps more serious. During the course of my ministerial experience I have had to deal with large numbers of people who have come to me and said that they have heard the teaching about the experience of being delivered from all sin and they say, 'I've sought it and I've prayed for it. I read about the man who prayed about his temper, and I have a terrible temper, and I'm always going down with it and I'm ashamed of myself. I've surrendered myself and prayed to the Lord to do for me what he did for that man, but it doesn't happen to me.' There are many in that position with sins of many different types. Now surely we are entitled to say that if that is God's way, then it must happen to all and there would be no cases of failure.

'Ah yes,' say the other people, 'but the trouble is there's an incomplete surrender somewhere.'

But that is not an answer. There are honest souls who have tried to surrender and to make themselves willing and, as far as they know, they are absolutely willing for anything, and yet they cannot get this experience. That is a fact that should surely engage our attention. If an experience is God's way, it is for all and not only for some. Another argument I would suggest is that if it works like that with regard to one sin, why should it not work for every sin? Why, therefore, should we not all be sinless and absolutely perfect? If you can get rid of a temper like that, well, why not immediately arrive at a state of sinless perfection? And yet I am sure that we would not claim to have reached that state. So we must examine this question of the experience very carefully.

So my last statement at this point would be that there are other people who can testify to similar experiences, who can tell you how they suddenly lost that temper of theirs, or this lust and craving for drink, in a flash, who are not Christians at all. It has come about by some other teaching, through one of the cults or something like that. There are many such instances. At the risk of being misunderstood, I would say that one of the most dramatic changes I have ever known in an individual was in the case of a Christian Scientist who found deliverance from the particular thing that got her down. In one meeting she was delivered from a morbid anxiety, and I can testify to that fact, but it had nothing to do with Christianity at all. In biographies you will sometimes come across similar stories of sudden and unexpected deliverance. So deliverance can have psychological causes, quite apart from the further suggestion that it may even be some kind of spiritist manifestation.

So let us consider some principles on this question of experiences. First, God may grant sudden deliverance in this way from certain sins – or He may not. I knew two men who were members of the same church. Both had been terrible drunkards and both became saints in the Church of God. The one man always used to testify that from the night of his conversion the taste for strong drink had been taken right out of his life. It never worried him again. He could pass a public house as easily as he could pass any other building. The other man, who was as great a saint, and who had equally given up drink, often told us that he knew what it was at times to have a most awful struggle as he passed public houses but, thank God, God always enabled him to walk past. Two saints, both delivered from drink. The taste goes in one, it does not go in the other. You see how dangerous it is to generalise from experiences. We must not base our doctrine on experiences but on the teaching of the word of God.

Secondly, sanctification is not just the problem of a particular sin or even of particular sins but is a question of my total relationship to God. I may be delivered from certain sins and yet my sanctification may be very small and immature. Indeed, this other teaching which we have been considering involves us in the position that at one moment I may be sanctified completely and then by one act of sin I lose my sanctification. Then I have to get it back. According to that view, sanctification is something that comes and goes. It is not a process that goes on continuously but is something variable that I keep on losing and then regaining.

But the teaching of the Scripture is that 'We all, with open face, beholding as in a glass the glory of the Lord, are changed into the same image from glory to glory' (2 Cor. 3:18). Sanctification is a growth, a development; it is a going forward. But it seems to me that the main trouble with this teaching about experience is that it confuses two things that are different, and the two things are these various experiences that we do get in the Christian life, and the grace of God and sanctification.

Sanctification is not an experience, it is a condition. It is my relationship to God: I am 'changed into the same image [of Jesus Christ] from glory to glory' (2 Cor. 3:18). Sanctification involves experiences and is helped by them, but in itself it is not an experience. May I, with great daring, venture upon an illustration, though illustrations are always liable to misunderstanding. I suggest to you that the relationship between experiences and sanctification is the relationship between a field in which you have sown oats or barley or wheat, and the rain and sunshine. The farmer has ploughed the earth, he has harrowed it, and sown the seed; he has then rolled it and, as far as he is concerned, he has finished for the time being. Then the seed begins to germinate and to grow and the crop makes its appearance.

Then there is, perhaps, a spell of cold, grey weather. The farmer looks at the field every day and there seems to be no change at all. The crop is not any higher one day than the previous day. Yet the whole time the life is there and it is moving, very slowly perhaps, but it is going on. Suddenly the weather becomes finer and the sun begins to shine. Then there is a most delightful shower of rain followed by another burst of glorious sunshine. And the farmer goes back and looks at his field the next morning and says, 'I can almost see it growing.'

You see the illustration? Sanctification itself is that life, that process of growth and development which starts the moment we are saved, the moment we are justified, the moment we are regenerated. There may be times when it is very small and you cannot see any change but then you get some blessed experience. God manifests Himself and His love to you. Now people foolishly call that experience sanctification. But it is not. It is like the shower of rain or the burst of sunshine. It stimulates and promotes sanctification but it is not sanctification itself. And it is there, I think, that you get this terrible error of confusing these two things that are so essentially different. The experiences are not the process of growth, but they do help and stimulate it.

Now experiences can, of course, be sudden, they can be dramatic. If you like, you can get many second special blessings. I do not hesitate to say that. But sanctification is not a 'second blessing'. People may have undergone a great emotional upheaval when they first believed in Christ; they may have had nothing like that for years. Then they get another experience, a second experience. And the more they experience the Lord the more they are concerned about obeying His word and loving Him in practice, and that promotes our sanctification. But I repeat, the experience is not the sanctification.

We must be clear about all these things. People may suddenly come to a realisation of aspects of truth, and as the result of that realisation, something may happen in their lives. But they must not say that until that point they were not sanctified, because they were, being sanctified from the moment of regeneration. But of course if they realise a truth like this, it promotes their sanctification. They seem to jump on in their sanctification just as that field of wheat seemed to sprout up while you looked at it, but that is not the initiation of sanctification. And thank God that this is the truth because, as we know, feelings are variable, experiences come and go, and if my sanctification is to be equated with, or to be regarded as synonymous with my experiences, then there are times when one would doubt whether one is being sanctified or not.

Then the third question is: Is sanctification something that happens suddenly? Obviously this follows logically from all that we have been considering. The people who believe that it is an experience to be received, believe it is sudden. But if you do not believe that, you will see from all the considerations that I have put before you, that sanctification is clearly not something that happens suddenly. What are the Scripture terms here? 'You are born again,' you are 'babes in Christ', as Paul says to the Corinthians (1 Cor. 3:1). John talks about 'children', 'young men' and 'fathers' (1 John 2). These are the scriptural terms, and they indicate growth, you do not suddenly jump from birth to adulthood. No, you go almost imperceptibly from one stage to another. That is sanctification, according to the Scriptures. You grow in grace and in the knowledge of the Lord.

Now people are very fond of analogies from the Old Testament and quite right, so let me use one. We would all agree that the history of the Children of Israel is a perfect picture of the salvation of a soul. The People of Israel were delivered out of Egypt, once and for ever, and the Egyptians were drowned in the Red Sea. But would you like to tell me that the troubles of the Israelites ended at that point? Not at all; they were even taken right into Canaan, but they had their troubles there in Canaan, they were in the sanctified position, but they still had enemies to fight, they had problems and difficulties. It is like that in the Christian life. But this is God's method everywhere and there is nothing more glorious to contemplate than the uniformity of the principle by which God works in every realm. Does he not work like that in nature? Our Lord used the picture of the farmer sowing the seed into the ground and then going home and sleeping and rising night and day. And he did not know anything about it, apparently, but the seed began to grow and went on growing (Mark 4:26–29). Such, our Lord says, is the kingdom of heaven.

Let us put certain questions here. If sanctification is meant to happen suddenly, why does it not? God could have made us all absolutely sinless and perfect at once if He had desired to do so. There is nothing to stop Him; with God nothing is impossible. He could have made us perfect and entire the moment we believed, but God obviously has not chosen to do that as we know from experience. And the New Testament epistles teach us the same thing. Why do you think that Satan was not destroyed the moment our Lord rose from the grave? Why is he allowed to continue? That is God's method, you see. He could have destroyed Satan at the time of the cross as easily as He will destroy him at the end. But He has not chosen to do so. These things show clearly God's method and God's manner.

Why has God not abolished death altogether? He will do it one day. Why do Christian people have to die? Why has God not abolished it at the beginning? The only answer is that He has not chosen to do so, and it is exactly the same with our sanctification. God's method of sanctification, as we have seen and as I hope to show still more clearly, is this process which starts from the moment of regeneration. And it goes on and on; every experience we get stimulates it, and we are changed from glory into glory. We are advancing and developing. We are to be more sanctified now than we were a year ago and it will go on and on until finally, in glory, we shall be perfect, without spot and without blemish.

21
Sanctification in Romans 6 to 8

Having dealt with the various theories and teachings and certain of the problems, we now come to a positive exposition of the biblical doctrine of sanctification. Our Lord prayed for His disciples, 'Sanctify them through [or in] thy truth: thy word is truth' (John 17:17). Now that is clearly an indication of the method of sanctification as it is taught in the Scripture. The question arises at once: What truth is this? And our Lord answers the question: 'Thy word is truth.' What word? The whole of the word, everything in the Bible ministers to our sanctification. You cannot read truly about God Himself, in His being and His Person, without its promoting your sanctification. The doctrine of God, the doctrine of sin, the law of God, the doctrine of punishment, of judgment and of hell – all that is truth and points in the direction of sanctification; it is the whole truth.

But, while that is perfectly true, it is also true to say that there are certain statements in Scripture and certain sections of it in which this great doctrine concerning sanctification is dealt with in a very explicit and specific manner. And in many ways the most striking illustration of that, what we may well call the *locus classicus* of biblical teaching in respect to sanctification, is undoubtedly chapters 6, 7 and 8 of the epistle to the Romans. Now I want to emphasise that this is not the only place where sanctification is dealt with. It is to be found everywhere, but these chapters deal with it in an explicit manner. And they do so, of course, because Paul, having dealt in the first five chapters with the great doctrine of justification, takes up what he imagines may be a false deduction drawn from that by certain of the members of the church at Rome. Indeed, he did not require much imagination to do this, because many people were drawing that very false deduction from the Apostle's teaching, They charged him with being guilty of *antinomianism* which means that the doctrine of justification says that because you are saved by Christ, it does not matter what you do. And the Apostle writes these chapters in order to refute that terrible suggestion, which he dismisses with a sense of horror and the words, 'God forbid!'

That is the point at which we have arrived and I want now to give you a general analysis of these three chapters in Romans. It can be nothing more than that because there is no time, obviously, to deal fully with chapters 6, 7 and 8 of Romans in one address; so we must be content with this general outline of the teaching. The first thing, therefore, which we must do is to realise exactly what Paul's argument is, and we can put it like this: the Apostle is here out to show the utter impossibility – he puts it as strongly as that – of a Christian's continuing in sin; and he says that it is impossible because of the whole nature and character of Christian salvation. Paul puts it in that question: 'What shall we say then? Shall we continue in sin, that grace may abound? God forbid!' That is it. 'How shall we, that are dead to sin, live any longer therein?' (Rom. 6:1–2). That is the theme. Indeed, we could say that the theme of Romans 6, 7 and 8 is to denounce, with horror, the tendency of people to separate justification from sanctification; to say that if you think you can stop at justification, you are doing something which the Apostle believes is so terrible that he can say nothing about it but, 'God forbid' that anybody should think such a thing or ever draw such a deduction. So you see the vital importance of these great chapters.

The argument as a whole is stated and summarised in chapter 6. Paul then works it out in greater detail in chapters 7 and 8. I do want to emphasise that chapter 8 does not introduce a new principle; the whole argument is stated in chapter 6. What you get in chapters 7 and 8 is simply greater detail. That is a vital matter because as we have seen, there are people who say that as a Christian you can stay in chapters 6 and 7 without going on to chapter 8, and that is really an extremely dangerous error. Let me give you my evidence for making such a categorical statement. The Apostle says something in 8:5–9 which I think will substantiate it:

> They that are after the flesh do mind the things of the flesh; but they that are after the Spirit the things of the Spirit. For to be carnally minded is death; but to be spiritually minded is life and peace. Because the carnal

mind is enmity against God: for it is not subject to the law of God, neither indeed can be. So then they that are in the flesh cannot please God. But ye are not in the flesh, but in the Spirit, if so be that the Spirit of God dwell in you. Now if any man have not the Spirit of Christ, he is none of his.

You see what that means? In chapter 8 Paul is not describing some special Christian who has had some second blessing, but any Christian, every Christian. 'If any man,' he says, 'have not the Spirit of Christ, he is none of his.' If you have not got the Spirit of Christ in you, says Paul, you are just not a Christian at all. And he says of Christian people that they are not carnal; they are not in the flesh; they are in the Spirit. Before conversion they were in the flesh, but the moment they were converted, they were no longer in the flesh but in the Spirit. Is it conceivable that Paul can say of a man who is a Christian, 'To be carnally minded is death . . . because the carnal mind is enmity against God'? That cannot be true of any sort of Christian; from the moment of our rebirth and regeneration we are united with Christ and we are in the Spirit. That is the vital point.

So let me repeat: Romans chapter 8 is a description of *all* Christians and not merely certain Christians who have gone on to some second blessing or some further experience. Paul is not introducing anything new but recapitulating and explaining more fully what he has already said in chapter 6. Now that, to me, is a most vital foundation. From what we have considered in previous lectures, you will see that it is because people have not realised this that they have gone astray in their understanding of sanctification. But surely Romans 8:5–9 ought to settle this question once and for ever. So you must no longer divide Christians up into those who are spiritual Christians and those who are not. All Christians are spiritual, of necessity, by definition; the momeі.t we are born again we are spiritual. We have received the Holy Spirit; we are united to Christ; the nature of God is in us and we are partakers of the divine nature.

Now having put it like that, in general, to give you a summary of the whole teaching, let us look at it in a little more detail. In those three chapters, what is Paul's argument – because it is an argument – on the question of sanctification? To answer that, we must start away back with the doctrine of sin. The Apostle himself has done that in the second half of chapter 5 where he teaches that we were all in Adam and because we were all in Adam, we all fell with him and have all reaped the full consequences of his sin. And the consequences of that sin are that men and women are dominated and controlled by sin, and Satan. In an earlier lecture, we went into the consequences of the fall. We now have this sinful nature. At the fall we lost our alignment with God, so that instead of controlling the body, and the bodily parts, by our spirit which is in tune with God, our whole life is dominated by the body and the sinful principle that controls it.

That is what sin has done. Before the fall, man and woman worked in a perfectly harmonious manner, they had all their instincts, the hunger instinct, the sex instinct and all these things. They were all there, yes, but as the man and the woman were perfect and in the right relationship to God, their instincts did not constitute any problem at all but were subservient to their highest and best interests. But with the fall, that balance was completely upset and men and women became the victims of their own bodies. They became governed by what Paul calls 'the desires of the flesh and of the mind' (Eph. 2:3). They became creatures of lust, dominated by sin and Satan. That is the biblical teaching. They suffered in the whole of their being and are now in a condition of confusion and of riot.

But in Jesus Christ there is salvation. That is what Paul is saying in the second half of that fifth chapter of Romans in that magnificent statement: 'But where sin abounded, grace did much more abound' (v. 20). So, here is the salvation. But what sort of a salvation? Is it merely forgiveness of sins? And the answer is an eternal 'No!' That is exactly what Paul begins to say at the beginning of chapter 6. He imagines some people saying something like this: 'This is rather good, all our sins are covered by Christ. "Where sin abounded, grace did much more abound." It doesn't matter, therefore, how much we sin. Indeed, we might even argue that the more we sin the more grace will abound. I know my sins are forgiven, so it doesn't matter what I do, I'm in Christ, I'm safe, I can live any sort of life.'

'God forbid,' says the Apostle in verse 2. That is what he is denouncing. Why? Because our salvation in Christ is not partial, it is an entire, a complete salvation. And in this great passage in chapters 6, 7 and 8, he sets out to work out that theme and prove it.

So the great text, in my opinion, is Romans 6:14: 'For sin shall not have dominion over you: for ye are not under the law, but under grace.' Observe what Paul says. He does not say that sin ought not to have dominion over you. He says, 'Sin *shall not* have dominion over you' (v. 14). It will not be allowed. Because you are not under law but under grace, sin shall not have dominion over you and he shows us how that comes to pass. Fundamentally, the principle is our union with Christ. We dealt with that doctrine of the union earlier, and that is why it must be taken before we come to sanctification. If you read again the second half of chapter 5, you will see that the argument is that as we were in Adam so we are in Christ. We have reaped all the consequences of what Adam did; we have reaped all the consequences of what Christ has done. That is the parallel.

What does this mean? Well, we are joined to Him in every respect. We are not only joined to the Lord Jesus Christ in some respects, we are joined to Him entirely; you cannot divide Christ. As we have seen, we have been crucified with Him – you will find it all in the sixth chapter – we have died with Him, we have been buried with Him, planted in the likeness of His death and we have risen with Him. Turn also to Ephesians 2:6: 'And hath raised us up together, and made us sit together in heavenly places in Christ Jesus' – at this very moment. Yes, or to put it in terms of 1 Corinthians 1:30, 'But of him are ye in Christ Jesus, who of God is made unto us' – what? – 'wisdom, and righteousness' – but you do not stop there – 'wisdom, and righteousness, and sanctification, and redemption.' Christ is already made all that unto us who are Christians. Can you imagine anything therefore more dangerous or unscriptural than to say that, to some Christians, Christ is only justification? 'He is not sanctification to them yet,' people say, 'they'll go on to that.' But the Scripture says the exact opposite! He is made all these things to us. You cannot divide Christ and we are in Christ, joined to Christ, we have a whole Christ, always. So this is what we must grasp.

What does that lead to? Well, the Apostle's own deductions are these. Because of our union with Christ, and because we have been crucified and have died and been buried and have risen with Him, He says: You are 'dead to the law' (Rom. 7:4). The law cannot touch you. Christ has died, He is the end of the law once and for ever for sin. So the law has nothing more to say to me by way of condemnation. Yes, but it does not stop there. The Apostle tells us that not only are we dead to the law but we are also, and equally, dead to sin. 'God forbid. How shall we, that are dead to sin . . . ?' (Rom. 6:2). Or, 'How shall we that have died to sin . . . ?' It is as definite as that: the tense is aorist, the death has happened once and for all. We are not *dying* to sin, we *are dead*, we *have died* to sin. Paul repeats that many times: 'Knowing this, that our old man is crucified with him, that the body of sin might be destroyed, that henceforth we should not serve sin' (v. 6). Our old self has been crucified, was crucified. It has happened. 'For he that is dead is freed from sin' (v. 7). And that is the Christian. 'Being then made free from sin, ye became the servants of righteousness' (v. 18). But now, 'being made free from sin' – which means, having now therefore been made free from sin – 'and become servants to God, ye have your fruit unto holiness, and the end everlasting life' (v. 22). Then Paul puts it as the form of an appeal: 'Likewise reckon ye also yourselves to be dead indeed unto sin, but alive unto God through Jesus Christ our Lord' (v. 11).

So, then, we are not only dead to the law, we are also dead to sin. As far as we are concerned, Paul says, sin is no more. To prove that, in the next chapter Paul has the great argument of the woman married to her husband who is free the moment her husband dies. Paul argues this in the sixth chapter by saying that a slave is owned by a master, but if another master comes and buys the slave, then he does not belong to the first, but to the second. So not only are we dead to sin, but, more than that, we are risen with Christ. And that means that Christ's life is our life. 'Therefore we are buried with him by baptism into death: that like as Christ was raised up from the dead by the glory of the Father, even so we also should walk in newness of life' (v. 4). In verse 5, it is the same thing, 'For if we have been planted together in the likeness of his death, we shall be also in the likeness of his resurrection.' And then in verse 8: 'Now if we be dead with Christ, we believe that we shall also live with him.' That is really the present tense: we *are* living with Him. This is true of us already. You find this also in verses 11 and 13: 'Likewise reckon ye also yourselves to be dead indeed unto sin, but alive unto God through Jesus Christ our Lord.' And in verse 13 Paul says, 'Yield yourselves unto God, as those that are alive from the dead.' We have risen with Christ and therefore we are in this new life.

And, as I have already indicated, in chapter 7 Paul says, in effect, 'In a sense you were married to the law, but not any longer because the law, as far as you are concerned, is dead.'

> Wherefore, my brethren, ye also are become dead to the law by the body of Christ; that ye should be married to another, even to him who is raised from the dead, that we should bring forth fruit unto God.

We are married to Christ and we ought to bring forth the fruit of a good and a sanctified life.

That, then, is Paul's fundamental statement. As the result of our union with Christ, we are dead to sin and alive unto God. The life of Christ is in us and that is the position of every Christian.

'Well,' says someone, 'does that mean, then, that we are completely sinless and perfect? Has Christ done this to the whole self? Am I entirely finished with sin in every shape and form?'

The answer Paul gives is: 'No. All that I have just been saying is true and true of our spirits. Our spirits are already entirely delivered from sin. I, as a spirit, and as a spiritual being, am dead to sin. I have finished with it once and for ever, but that is not true of my body.' So you see the argument? The result of the fall of Adam was that the entire person has been involved, my spirit and my body. In our Christian salvation at this moment Christ has redeemed my spirit perfectly; that is the 'new self'; but my body still remains under the thraldom of sin. I am dead to sin, I am finished with it, but my body is still under its dominion.

Let me give you the evidence. First of all in chapter 6. Paul says in verse 6: 'Knowing this, that our old man is crucified with him, that [in order that] the body of sin might be destroyed . . .' The old self has been crucified, it is finished with. Yes, in order that this body of sin might be destroyed – but that has not yet happened. But look at verse 12. In verse 11 Paul says in effect, 'You yourself have reckoned yourself dead indeed unto sin but alive unto God.' Then, verse 12: 'Let not sin therefore reign [as it has been doing] in your mortal body that ye should obey it in the lusts thereof.' But go on to verse 13: 'Neither yield ye your members' – that is to say, my instincts and my limbs, my faculties and all I am – 'as instruments of unrighteousness unto sin.' No, rather, Paul tells us 'Yield . . . your members as instruments of righteousness unto God.'

And then there is the final statement in the nineteenth verse, where Paul says, 'I speak after the manner of men because of the infirmity of your flesh: for as ye have yielded your members servants to uncleanness and to iniquity unto iniquity; even so now yield your members servants to righteousness unto holiness.' That is the evidence in chapter 6 to the effect that though my spirit is emancipated and redeemed my body still is not.

So let us turn now to chapter 7. Paul says in verse 16, 'If then I do that which I would not, I consent unto the law that it is good.' Then verse 17: 'Now then it is no more I that do it, but sin that dwelleth in me.' You see, it is not I, I am redeemed, it is sin that dwells in me.

Verse 18 says, 'For I know that in me (that is, in my flesh) dwelleth no good thing' – he does not say that in *me* there is no good thing, not, it is, 'in my flesh dwelleth no good thing.' Then again in verse 20 Paul says: 'Now if I do that I would not, it is not more I that do it, but sin that dwelleth in me' – the same thing, you see. But go on to verse 23: 'But I see another law in my members' – not in me, in my members – warring against the law of my mind, and bringing me into captivity to the law of sin which is in my members.' That is what happens. Unless I understand this doctrine, I will allow myself to be governed by that sin again. But I need not, because the sin is in my members, not in me.

Then in verse 24: 'Oh wretched man that I am! who shall deliver me from the body of this death?' 'Who shall deliver me from this body of death?' It is a logical conclusion, is it not? Paul has been saying in effect, 'This is my position; I am saved and redeemed, yes, but I am still in this body and this body is still under the dominion of sin and is trying to drag me down. Who shall deliver me out of this body? How can I be perfectly emancipated?' That is his question. And indeed he puts it again in the last part of verse 25: 'So then with the mind I myself serve the law of God; but with the flesh the law of sin.' That is the evidence in chapter 7.

Now let me give you the evidence in chapter 8. First of all it is in verse 10, one of the most important verses of all: 'And if Christ be in you, the body' – and he means the body; he does not mean the flesh but the physical frame, the *soma* – 'the body is dead because of sin; but the Spirit is life because of righteousness.' He has just said, 'But ye are not in the flesh, but in the Spirit, if so be that the Spirit of God dwell in you. Now if any man have not the Spirit of Christ, he is none of his. And if Christ be in you' – that is your position as a Christian, what is true of you? It is this – 'the body is dead [dead spiritually] because of sin; but the Spirit is life because of righteousness.' You see the distinction? Then in verse 13, Paul says it again: 'For if ye live after the flesh, ye shall die: but if ye through the Spirit do mortify the deeds of the body, ye shall live.' He does not say you are to mortify *yourself*; he says you are to mortify the deeds of your body, the place in which sin is dwelling; you shall live if you do that.

And then there is the great verse towards the end of the chapter, summing it all up: verse 23. Paul is talking about the whole creation, groaning and travailing in pain together until now. Then: 'And not only they, but ourselves also, which have the firstfruits of the Spirit, even we ourselves groan within ourselves, waiting for the adoption' –

what is that? Here is the answer – 'to wit, the redemption of our body.' You see what he is saying? Here I am as a Christian, my spirit is already redeemed, but my body is not. What I am waiting for is the day which is coming when my body shall be redeemed as well as my spirit. Because of sin and the fall of Adam I have gone down – spirit and body. But Christ has come in. He has already saved my spirit; the body is not yet redeemed and I am waiting for the adoption, the redemption of my body.

'What, then, is our position?' you ask. Does that therefore mean that as Christians we are condemned to a life of hopeless misery and failure in this world? Are we just to go on struggling vainly and being down and out, as it were, in wretchedness and misery? To which the answer is that yes, you are condemned to that if you are relying only upon yourself and your own ability and energy to conform to God's law. Yes, you are condemned to that if you draw a separation between justification and sanctification. Yes, you are condemned if you say that a Christian can have his sins forgiven but nothing more. But the answer of the Scripture a thousand times over is that that is not our position!

Now turn to the meaning of the great statement in Romans 7:7–25 about which people have argued so often. Does it describe a person unredeemed altogether, or one who is redeemed but not yet fully sanctified? The whole point of that passage is just this. Paul has been saying in the first part of the chapter that we are no longer under the law. We are like the woman whose first husband has died, leaving her free to be married to another. We are no longer tied up with the law because Christ has put an end to it through His body. We are now married to Christ and have finished with the law in that sense. 'But,' says someone, 'are you saying then that there is no value in the law of God? Are you saying that the law of God is absolutely useless and that there is no worth in it at all?' 'God forbid!' says Paul. The law itself is all right, but if you think that it can either justify you or sanctify you, you are making a big mistake. If you are relying for ultimate deliverance from sin on your own attempts to carry out that law, then you are indeed doomed.

And then Paul puts it in his typical dramatic way. He says in effect, 'You're leaving me in this sort of position: as a Christian I have now seen the value of the law and I want to keep it; but this body of mine is dragging me down; this sin that remains in my body is making that impossible. And if that is the whole truth, then I am a failure, I am a wretched man. But that is not the position,' says Paul. You notice how he puts it. He makes this statement: 'Oh wretched man that I am! who shall deliver me from this body of death?' And immediately he answers his own question: 'I thank God through Jesus Christ our Lord.' His summary in chapter 6 has already answered the question. I am not condemned to that wretchedness because of my union with Christ; because of my union with Christ, sin shall not have dominion over me. It will not be allowed to and indeed it does not.

So, then, Paul has answered the question, first and foremost, in chapter 6:14, but you notice how he likes to repeat it. Having said it there, he says it again in chapter 7:25: 'I thank God through Jesus Christ my Lord.' He then goes on to say it in a most extraordinary way in chapter 8:10–11: 'If Christ be in you, the body is dead [still] because of sin; but the Spirit is life because of righteousness.' Then, 'But if the Spirit of him that raised up Jesus from the dead dwell in you, he that raised up Christ from the dead shall also quicken your mortal bodies by his Spirit that dwelleth in you.' Now that not only refers to the resurrection of saints at His coming, it also refers to something that is already happening in these mortal bodies; the process is going on already. What a wonderful statement!

Paul then repeats this again in much the same way in verses 15–17. He says, 'For ye have not received the spirit of bondage again to fear.' You must not be cast down; you must not say that this is a weary pilgrimage and all is against you and you are constantly defeated, not at all! 'Ye have not received the spirit of bondage again to fear; but ye have received the Spirit of adoption, whereby we cry, Abba, Father. The Spirit itself beareth witness with our spirit, that we are the children of God; and if children, then heirs; heirs of God, and joint-heirs with Christ.' The ultimate result is certain.

And then, I repeat, Paul finally says it again in verse 23: 'We ourselves groan within ourselves, waiting for the adoption' – it is coming! – 'the redemption of our body.' So we are not doomed to a sense of failure and frustration. We are not struggling vainly and hopelessly and helplessly. This great process is proceeding because we are in Christ. How does this happen? The Lord Jesus Christ is in us. If we are Christians, He is in us and He is working in us by His Holy Spirit, and, as the result of this working, He has already delivered our spirits and He is in the process of delivering even our bodies, and finally they will be perfectly delivered.

How does the process go on? Philippians 2:12–13 gives the answer:

'Work out your own salvation with fear and trembling. For it is God which worketh in you both to will and to do . . .' The Spirit is in us and we are led by Him. He works upon our wills; He creates desires after holiness; He reveals sin to us in all its foulness and ugliness and creates aspirations after purity and the life of God. Not only that. He gives us strength and power, enabling us to do what we now want to do. What else? Well, as Paul tells us in Romans 8:14: 'For as many as are led by the Spirit of God, they are the sons of God.' And that is true, again, of every single Christian.

How does that happen? How does His leading take place within us? And what does He lead us to? Well, He leads us in many ways, but He leads us particularly through the truth. It is He who is the author of the truth and He leads us to it and gives us an understanding of it. And as He does so, we are being sanctified. And the truth, as I have already outlined, is that our spirits are already redeemed, but the problem remains in this body. We are to see that even that eventually will be delivered. And in the meantime, Paul shows us what to do: 'Reckon ye also yourselves to be dead indeed unto sin, but alive unto God . . .' (6:11). He gives us this assurance and certainty of ultimate victory. I no longer feel defeated, I know that I am on the victorious side and that I must just go on. Then he appeals to me. He says, 'Let not sin therefore reign in your mortal body' (6:12). And I feel that is a perfectly fair appeal and I am going to put it into practice. He says: In view of all this, do not yield your members 'as instruments of unrighteousness unto sin', but yield them as 'instruments of righteousness unto God'. 'Quite right,' I say.

And so Paul goes on to make this great appeal to me, to refuse to allow my unredeemed body to dominate me as it used to. I must realise that I am a child of God, destined for glory, and I must not allow my body to influence me. There is a process which goes on and on and on and is not complete while I am still in this life. Sin remains in the body. But, thank God, the day is coming when the process will be complete. I must quote Romans 8:23 once again because it is one of the most glorious verses in Scripture: 'And not only they, but ourselves also . . . groan within ourselves, waiting for the adoption . . .' A day is coming when my very body shall be entirely delivered from sin in every shape and form. He shall change my vile body, that it may be fashioned like unto his glorious body (Phil. 3:21). There is a day coming when this process of redemption started in me by Christ, which has already delivered me as a spiritual being and has made me dead to sin, there is a day when my body shall be equally dead to sin and I shall be perfect and entire, faultless and blameless without spot and blemish, standing face to face with God.

'Beloved,' says John, who agrees entirely with Paul, 'now are we the sons of God' – now – 'and it doth not yet appear what we shall be: but we know that, when he shall appear, we shall be like him; for we shall see him as he is' (1 John 3:2). And we shall be like Him in that not only will our spirits then be like Him and partaking of His nature and reflecting His image, but our bodies also shall be as glorified as His body; we shall be like Him for we shall see Him as He is. That is what is coming and it is coming for certain. What of it, therefore? Well, I am still in this life and in this world, I shall still have to wage this battle against the sin that is in my body. So John puts it like this: 'Every man that hath this hope in himself purifieth himself' – he does it – 'even as he is pure' (1 John 3:3). 'I keep under my body' (1 Cor. 9:27), says Paul: again he does it. He does not just passively look to Christ. I mortify my 'members which are upon the earth' (Col. 3:5). That is the argument. Given all this truth, this power of the Spirit working in me, I am exhorted to do that, I want to do that, and that is sanctification.

So we must, of necessity, reject all talk about eradication of sin, all talk of being delivered entirely from sin in this life. We reject it in the name of the Scripture. We reject equally talk of the principle of coun-teraction, because that does not say enough about me. It does not tell me that I, spiritually, am already delivered and that the problem is only in the flesh and that that is a problem which I have to face. It draws a false distinction between a Christian who may only be in the seventh chapter of Romans with one who is in the eighth chapter. It does not realise that every Christian is in the eighth chapter of Romans because if the Spirit of Christ is not in you, you are none of His.

We see sanctification as a part of a great and glorious plan: Christ the redemption; the believer joined to Christ; and from the moment of rebirth, regeneration and union, this mighty process begins which eventually will lead to a perfected redemption and salvation, includ-ing even the body, which, hitherto and until we die and are raised again, still remains under the dominion of sin. But as I realise this glorious truth I should master it and increasingly conquer it so that there may be development and growth in my sanctification.

22

Baptism and Filling

We must now consider aspects of the biblical teaching concerning the doctrine of the Holy Spirit which, hitherto, we have not been able to deal with; and, it seems to me, the most convenient approach is this: there are certain terms with regard to the relationship of the Holy Spirit to the believer which we have touched on in passing, but were not able to go into, in detail, then, and we will look at these now.

They are most important terms, and, in a sense, because they are important, they are not easy. Indeed, I might even say that they are difficult and that they have often led not only to confusion but to a good deal of discussion and disputation. As I have often pointed out before, you always find that when a doctrine is vital, there are generally difficulties, for the obvious reason that the devil, the adversary of our souls, realising the centrality and the importance of the doctrine, concentrates his attention upon it. We saw that in the case of the atonement and the person of our Lord, so it is not surprising if he does it at this point.

The first term, then, is the term *baptism*, the baptism of the Holy Spirit or the baptism with the Holy Spirit. Now the difficulties, I feel, generally arise because on all sides we are all a little too prone to be dogmatic. The confusion certainly arises because of that. You will find that equally saintly Christians look at these matters and do not say quite the same thing. That is inevitable with certain aspects of truth, but, when that happens, it behoves us not to be over-dogmatic. We should tread carefully, and with reverence and godly fear. Of course, to come people there does not seem to be any difficulty and you hear them speaking so glibly. They say, 'Of course, to me there is no problem; one baptism – many fillings, there it is.' Now to speak like that about such a solemn and sacred subject is almost to deny the total doctrine of the Holy Spirit. It is not a question of how easily and conveniently to our own satisfaction we can classify these terms; the vital questions is: What do these terms represent and what do we know about them experientially?

Let me remind you again that my whole object in going through these biblical doctrines is not simply or primarily to enlarge my own knowledge or yours, certainly not in an intellectual sense. I am concerned about these things for one reason only, and that is that a deep and a real experience of the power of salvation is dependent upon a knowledge of these doctrines – and not a mere intellectual or theoretical knowledge. Anybody who stops at that is courting trouble and asking for disaster. This knowledge is essential on condition that we approach it in the right way, and realise that it is something that will enrich our experience. And that is particularly true over a question like the one we are now considering.

So let us start like this: Where are these terms used, how are they used, and by whom? Well, the term 'baptism' is used by John the Baptist. You will find it, for instance, in Luke 3:16–17 and its parallel passages. We are told about the people who listened to the preaching of John at the Jordan, 'They mused in their hearts of John, whether he were the Christ, or not.' And John, realising what they were thinking, turned upon them and said,

> I indeed baptize you with water; but one mightier than I cometh, the latchet of whose shoes I am not worthy to unloose: he shall baptize you with the Holy Ghost and with fire: whose fan is in his hand, and he will throughly purge his floor, and will gather the wheat into his garner; but the chaff he will burn with fire unquenchable.

John predicted it. But our Lord Himself also used the same expression. In Acts 1:5 you will find, 'For John truly baptized with water; but ye shall be baptised with the Holy Ghost not many days hence.' And He said that ten days before the Day of Pentecost.

Then a number of other terms are used which obviously refer to the same thing, although not all would agree with that statement. For instance, in Romans 6, the Apostle says, 'Know ye not, that so many of us as were baptized into Jesus Christ were baptized into his death?' It is very difficult to think that that is a reference to water baptism, because surely baptism in water does not baptise us into Christ's

death. It is by the Holy Spirit we are baptised into Christ and into His
death.

And then there is that great passage in 1 Corinthians 12:13: 'For
by one Spirit,' says Paul, 'are we all baptized into one body, whether
we be Jews or Gentiles . . .' In Galatians 3:27 you get this: 'For as
many of you as have been baptized into Christ, have put on Christ.'
And in Ephesians 4:5: 'One Lord, one faith, one baptism,' which is
undoubtedly a reference to the baptism by the Holy Spirit, our baptism
into Christ.

That, then, is the actual use of the word *baptise* in connection with
the Holy Spirit. But, it is important for us to bear in mind that certain
other terms are used, which obviously refer to the same thing. The
terms seem to be interchangeable as though more or less synonymous.
We are told, for instance, about the Holy Spirit being poured out.
That is in the prophecy of Joel which was quoted by the apostle Peter
in Acts 2:17. In Acts 8:16 you will find the statement that the Holy
Ghost had not yet 'fallen' upon the Samaritans. Then there is the
question that the Apostle Paul asked the disciples at Ephesus: 'Have
ye received the Holy Ghost since ye believed?' (Acts 19:2). And Peter,
justifying his action in admitting Cornelius and other Gentiles into the
Christian Church, said, 'The Holy Ghost fell on them, as on us at the
beginning' (Acts 11:15). Peter's argument was that he saw very
clearly that the same thing had happened to Cornelius and his household that had happened to him and the other apostles, the hundred
and twenty in the upper room, and to others on the Day of Pentecost
at Jerusalem. When I saw that, he said, 'What was I, that I could with-
stand God?' (Acts 11:15–17). He could not refuse to baptise them, he
said, because the Holy Spirit had fallen upon them.

It seems to me, therefore, that all these terms clearly point to the
same thing and, therefore, we face the question: What is the baptism of
the Holy Spirit? Now there are some, as we have seen, who say that
there is really no difficulty about this at all. They say it is simply a reference to regeneration and nothing else. It is what happens to people
when they are regenerated and incorporated into Christ, as Paul
teaches in 1 Corinthians 12:13: 'By one Spirit are we all baptized into
one body.' You cannot be a Christian without being a member of that
body and you are baptised into that body by the Holy Spirit. Therefore,
they say, this baptism of the Holy Spirit is simply regeneration.

But for myself I simply cannot accept that explanation, and this is
where we come directly to grips with the difficulty. I cannot accept

that because if I were to believe that, I should have to believe that the disciples and the apostles were not regenerate until the Day of Pentecost – a supposition which seems to me to be quite untenable. In the same way, of course, you would have to say that not a single Old Testament saint had eternal life or was a child of God. But we have seen very plain teaching of the Scripture to the effect that they were regenerate and that all of us when we become regenerate become children of Abraham. We have seen, too, that nothing happens to us apart from them and that we are sharers in the same blessing, because there is only one great covenant, this covenant of salvation and redemption.

We would also have to say that the Samaritans, to whom the evangelist Philip had preached, were not regenerate until Peter and John went down to them. As you read the eighth chapter of Acts, you will find that Philip evangelised in Samaria, and many believed and were baptised into the name of the Lord Jesus Christ. But we are told that they did not receive the Holy Spirit until the advent of Peter and John who came down and prayed for them and laid their hands upon them so that they received or were baptised by the Holy Spirit. But it seems to me that the whole chapter denies that supposition. They were regenerate, but they had not received the Holy Spirit. And the same thing, of course, can be argued, in a sense, in the case of the Ethiopian eunuch who was spoken to by Philip. So I cannot accept the idea that baptism is simply a reference to regeneration.

What, then, is it? Well, it is clear that this is what John the Baptist and our Lord had both predicted. This is what Peter calls 'the promise of the Father', a term that is often used. 'Therefore,' says Peter, 'being by the right hand of God exalted, and having received of the Father the promise of the Holy Ghost, he hath shed forth this which ye now see and hear' (Acts 2:33). And the term is used elsewhere 'the promise of my Father' (Luke 24:49). This was something to which the Children of Israel had been taught to look forward, it is the fulfilment of that promise.

What, then, is it? Well, when we were dealing with this doctrine of the Holy Spirit right at the very beginning, I emphasised that what happened on the Day of Pentecost was primarily that the Christian Church was instituted and proclaimed as the body of Christ. There were believers, there were regenerate persons – yes. But they only became the body of Christ at Pentecost when they were baptised into the one body by the Holy Spirit, by the one Spirit. And that is undoubtedly the primary meaning of Pentecost.

But it seems to me that we must not stop at that. If that is what it is in its essence, there is also the subsidiary meaning. It includes also the consciousness of that fact. I say that for this reason: go back again to the question put by the apostle Paul to those people at Ephesus: 'Did ye receive the Holy Ghost when ye believed?' Now the fact that he asked that question implies that it is a question one can answer, that people know when they have received the Holy Spirit – whether they have or whether they have not. But then the Apostle put almost exactly the same question to the Galatians: 'Received ye the Spirit,' he writes, 'by the works of the law, or by the hearing of faith?' (Gal. 3:2). In effect, Paul was saying to the Galatians, 'You've received the Holy Spirit and you know that; now did you receive the Holy Spirit as the result of your works of righteousness, works under the law, or by the hearing of faith?' They knew that they had received the Spirit, otherwise Paul's question was pointless. Indeed the whole teaching about the sealing and the earnest of the Spirit must lead in the same direction. The Apostle also refers to 'ourselves also, which have the firstfruits of the Spirit' (Rom. 8:23); we know that we have received them.

What, therefore, do I mean when I say that this baptism includes the consciousness of being baptised into the body of Christ? It is at this point that the confusion tends to come in, because some friends would confine this only to certain gifts of the Spirit and they say the one and only proof that we have received the Spirit is that we manifest these gifts. They would base that on 1 Corinthians 12, but that very chapter itself teaches that all do not have the same gifts, one person has one gift and one another. So we must never say that unless we have one particular gift we have never been baptised with the Holy Spirit or have never received the Spirit. That very chapter denies that. It asks the question, 'Do all speak with tongues? Do all prophesy? Have all the gifts of healing?' and so on, and the answer is obviously 'No'.

But the danger is to think of the baptism of the Holy Spirit only in terms of gifts rather than in terms of something much more impor-tant, which is this: *the* mark, ultimately, and proof of whether we have received the Spirit or not is surely something that happens in the realm of our spiritual experience. You cannot read the New Testa-ment accounts of the people to whom the Spirit came, these people upon whom He fell, or who received as the Galatian Christians and all these others had done, without realising that the result was that their whole spirit was kindled. The Lord Jesus Christ became real to them in a way that He had never been before. The Lord Jesus Christ manifested Himself to them spiritually, and the result was a great love for Christ, shed abroad in their hearts by the Holy Spirit.

Now this, surely, is something which should cause us to pause for a moment and meditate very deeply and very seriously. This is an experience, as I understand this teaching, which is the birthright of every Christian. 'For the promise,' says the apostle Peter, 'is unto you' – and not only unto you but – 'to your children, and to all that are afar off' (Acts 2:39). It is not confined just to these people on the Day of Pentecost but is offered to and promised to all Christian people. And in its essence it means that we are conscious of the incoming, as it were, of the Spirit of God and are given a sense of the glory of God and the reality of His being, the reality of the Lord Jesus Christ, and we love Him. That is why these New Testament writers can say a thing like this about the Christians: 'Whom having not seen, ye love; in whom, though now ye see him not, yet believing, ye rejoice with joy unspeakable and full of glory' (1 Pet. 1:8). And they did. They rejoiced in Him, they gloried in Him, they accounted it an honour to suffer for His name's sake. For Him they would suffer any persecution; they would even be turned out of their homes and their families. Why? Oh, not simply because they had a head knowledge of certain doctrines or truths. No, but because the Lord Jesus Christ had become so real to them and so dear to them and so lovely in their sight, that He was their all in all.

And that, as you read these accounts, is the invariable result of this baptism of the Holy Spirit. Furthermore, you will find that this is something to which the saints of the centuries have testified. Everybody remembers the story of how this happened to John Wesley in Aldersgate Street in London in 1738, but many people have never heard of it as it happened in a still more striking manner to George Whitefield before that. We have heard of it in the case of Moody, walking down the street in New York City one afternoon, when suddenly he became aware of the glory of God in such an overwhelming manner that he felt that even his strong body was on the point of being crushed, and he held up his hands and asked God to stop. It is true of Finney and Jonathan Edwards and David Brainerd. It is something to which many ordinary Christians, whose names we do not know, have testified and for which they have thanked God: this sense of the glory of God, the reality of the Lord; this love towards Him;

this indescribable experience of these things.

A definition, therefore, which I would put to your consideration is something like this: the baptism of the Holy Spirit is the initial experience of glory and the reality and the love of the Father and of the Son. Yes, you may have many further experiences of that but the first experience, I would suggest, is the baptism of the Holy Spirit. The saintly John Fletcher of Madeley put it like this: 'Every Christian should have his Pentecost.'

'This is life eternal,' our Lord prayed, 'that they might know thee the only true God, and Jesus Christ, whom thou hast sent' (John 17:3). And it is only the Spirit who can enable us to know that. The baptism of the Holy Spirit, then, is the difference between believing these things, accepting the teaching, exercising faith – that is something that we all know, and without the Holy Spirit we cannot even do that, as we have seen – and having a consciousness and experience of these truths in a striking and signal manner. The first experience of that, I am suggesting, is the baptism of the Holy Spirit, or the Holy Spirit falling upon you, or receiving the Spirit. It is this remarkable and unusual experience which is described so frequently in the book of Acts and which, as we see clearly from the epistles, must have been the possession of the members of the early Christian Church.

Now there is no essential difference between the Church today and that early Church, and you cannot read the New Testament account of the early Church without seeing that these were spiritual people, people with a spiritual reality. They were not just formal Church members, there was a living Spirit, and they knew in whom they had believed, and they rejoiced in these things. Without any hesitation you could put the question to them, 'Did you receive the Spirit by the works of the law, or by the hearing of faith? (Gal. 3:2). What if I put that question to you at this moment? Can you answer it? This is the experience which is for you and for your children and for them that are afar off: this blessed knowledge of the reality of God and of our Lord and Saviour Jesus Christ through the Holy Spirit, the spiritual manifestation of the Son of God in the heart of the believer.

Let us then consider briefly the second term which always goes with this term and which, in a sense, is complementary to it. It is the term *filling*. You notice that after that great event on the morning of Pentecost, we are told this: 'And they were all filled with the Holy Ghost, and began to speak with other tongues . . .' That is Acts 2:4, and if you go on to Acts 4:31 you will find that it was repeated: 'And when they had prayed, the place was shaken where they were assembled together; and they were all filled with the Holy Ghost, and they spake the word of God with boldness.' Who were they? The disciples, the apostles, the same people. They were filled on the Day of Pentecost and they were filled just a few days later in exactly the same way. And we also have another instance in Acts 13:9, where the apostle Paul is dealing with Elymas the sorcerer. We are told: 'Then Saul . . . filled with the Holy Ghost, set his eyes on him.'

The other use of the term 'filling' is found in Ephesians 5:18, where we are told, 'Be not drunk with wine, wherein is excess; but be filled with the Spirit.' And then you will find references to it in Acts 6:3–5: 'Wherefore, brethren, look ye out among you seven men of honest report, full of the Holy Ghost and wisdom, whom we may appoint over this business' – the appointment of the deacons in the Church – '. . . And the saying pleased the whole multitude: and they chose Stephen, a man full of faith and of the Holy Ghost.'

So the question which arises is: What does it mean to be *filled* with the Holy Spirit? Clearly, there are two things, at any rate, which obviously go with this term. It is something that happens which gives authority and power and ability for service and witness. The apostles were given it there at the very beginning, and the result was that they began to speak with other tongues, and Peter, filled with the Spirit, preached his sermon. Then again, after they had prayed, they were all filled with the Holy Spirit and spoke the word of God with boldness. And when Paul was confronted by the opposition of that clever man, the magician Elymas, he was filled especially with the Spirit in order to pronounce a judgment, and the judgment fell upon the man. So it is clear that the filling with the Spirit happens for the sake of service; it gives us power and authority for service.

Let me emphasise this. This filling is an absolute necessity for true service. Even our Lord Himself did not enter upon His ministry until the Holy Spirit had descended upon Him. He even told the disciples, whom He had been training for three years, who had been with Him in the inner circle, who had seen His miracles and heard all His words, who had seen Him dead and buried and risen again, even these exceptional men with their exceptional opportunities, He told to stay where they were, not to start upon their ministry, not to attempt to witness to Him, until they had received the power which the Holy Spirit would give them.

This is something, therefore, which is vital to our witness. It was the whole secret of the ministry of the apostle Paul. He did not preach with enticing words of human wisdom, but preached, he said, 'in demonstration of the Spirit and of power' (1 Cor. 2:4). He was filled with the Spirit for his task. Is this not something which causes us all to pause? Whatever the form of our ministry, it is only of value while we are filled with the power of the Spirit. So we should realise the necessity of seeking this filling of the Spirit and of power before we attempt any task, whatever it may be.

Let me put it like this: there is all the difference in the world between being a witness and being an advocate. Men and women can be advocates of these things without the Holy Spirit. I mean that they can have an understanding of the doctrine; they can receive the truth, and can present it, argue for it and defend it. Yes, they are acting as advocates. But primarily, as Christians, we are called upon to be witnesses, to be witnesses of the Lord Jesus Christ as the Son of God and as the Saviour of the world, as our own Saviour, as the Saviour of all who put their faith and trust in Him. And it is only the Holy Spirit who can enable us to do that. You can address people and act as advocates for the truth but you will not convince anybody. If, however, you are filled with the Spirit, and are witnessing to the truth which is true in your life, by the power of the Spirit that is made efficacious. So this filling is essential to all our Christian service.

But also it is equally clear that the infilling of the Spirit is essential to true Christian quality in our life. That is why we are commanded to be filled with the Spirit. It is a command to every single Christian: 'Be not drunk with wine, wherein is excess; but be filled with the Spirit' (Eph. 5:18). We are exhorted to be filled with the Spirit. And this is commanded in order that our graces may grow, in order that the fruit of the Spirit may develop in us and may be evident to all. It is as we are filled with this life that the fruit and the graces of this life will be manifest. Indeed, the filling of the Spirit is essential to a true act of worship. Did you notice how Paul uses that commandment of his in that very connection? He says, 'Be not drunk with wine, wherein is excess; but be filled with the Spirit' – and then he goes on at once – 'speaking to yourselves in psalms and hymns and spiritual songs, singing and making melody in your heart to the Lord; giving thanks always for all things unto God and our Father in the name of our Lord Jesus Christ.'

So the way to test whether we are filled with the Spirit is to ask: Are we full of thankfulness? Are we full of praise? Do we sing to ourselves and to one another in psalms and hymns and spiritual songs? Do we make melody in our hearts? Do we praise God when we are alone? Do we delight in praising Him with others? Do we delight in praising Him in public as well as in private? Are we full of the spirit of praise, of thanksgiving, of worship and adoration? It is an inevitable consequence of being filled with the Spirit. This is something that can happen many times. The baptism, I suggest, is the initial experience, the filling is an experience that can often be repeated.

So there are those two great terms: to be baptised with the Spirit and to be filled with the Spirit. Surely, no subject is more important for us all than just this. What is a revival? It is God pouring out His Spirit. It is this tremendous filling that happens to numbers of people at the same time. You need not wait for a revival to get it, each of us is individually commanded to seek it, and to have it, and indeed to make sure that it is there. But at times of revival God, as it were, fills a number of people together, they almost describe it as the Spirit *falling* upon them. That is a revival, and that is the greatest need of the Church today. And it is only as you and I, as individuals, know the reality of these things, and know their power and their glory, and are concerned about being always filled with the Spirit, that we shall not only thank God but also pray to Him for revival and ask Him to come upon the Church again, as He has come in ages past, and fan the smouldering embers into a mighty flame of life and power. It is the greatest need of all, and it is only as we understand the teaching of the Scriptures with regard to these blessed matters that we truly enter into these things and become intercessors and pleaders with God to revive His work. May He open our eyes by His Spirit to the truth of the baptism of the Spirit and the infilling of the Holy Spirit.

23

Further Reflections on
the Baptism of the Spirit

We have begun our consideration of certain terms that are used in connection with the work of the Holy Spirit in the Scriptures and with which we have not hitherto dealt. We gave an outline of the biblical teaching with respect to the baptism with the Holy Spirit and then briefly considered the doctrine concerning the filling with the Holy Spirit, and we drew a distinction between the two.

We now come back to the same subject in order to try to give a fuller exposition. Let me preface my remarks by repeating that it is very difficult teaching, and it is because of the difficulties that are inherent in this matter that there are different points of view and different schools of thought. We have already seen this with other doctrines, so it does not surprise us. If these things could be put simply and plainly there would never have been any difficulty about them. In many ways I suppose that this is the most difficult of all the doctrines because it is particularly liable to exaggeration, and people tend to go off at tangents. That was why I put in a little plea earlier that we should try to forget labels and view the statements of the Scripture as dispassionately and with as open a mind as we are capable of commanding.

As we continue, let me repeat that plea. It is essential for this reason: these labels and experiences which we may have had or have encountered in the past tend to drive us to extremes. We are all creatures of extremes. It is most difficult to avoid going either to one extreme or the other. It always seems to be easier to be at an extreme, does it not? It seems clear cut, as people say; you know where you are, you are either here or there! But that is not always right, especially when your extreme has gone beyond the Scripture, or when you have been driven to an extreme in a reaction against another extreme.

Now with regard to this particular doctrine, we all know that there have been excesses. There have been people who have attributed experiences of the baptism of the Spirit to the Spirit, and we have known that what they were claiming as the baptism has sometimes been nothing but animal spirits, and sometimes even evil spirits, because accompanying the great claim there has sometimes been a most unworthy life, in plain contradiction of the Scripture. This doctrine, because it touches with a subject that is experiential, is particularly liable to that kind of excess or violence and that has happened so many times in the history of the Church. The danger then, of course, that at once arises is that in our desire to avoid those excesses and those false claims, we go right over to the other side. We pass the truth, which is somewhere there in the middle, and are again at a non-scriptural extreme. And I feel that this has been happening during this present century. In their fear of the excesses and the riotous emotionalism that have so often been mistaken for a true work of the Spirit, there are many Christian people, it seems to me, who have been guilty of quenching the Spirit.

There is a classic way of putting this whole point: it all happened in the seventeenth century, in connection with Puritanism. Puritanism, which started as one school of thought, divided up into two schools. On the one hand, you had George Fox and the Quakers, and on the other you had some of those great Puritan teachers such as John Owen, and Dr Thomas Goodwin in London. Now looking back, and reading the story in the light of the Scriptures, I have no doubt that both parties were guilty of going a little too far in the right direction. George Fox was most certainly calling attention to something vital but he went too far. He almost went to the point of saying that the Scriptures did not matter, that it was only this 'inner light' and the Spirit within that mattered, and the result of that has been that modern Quakerism – the Society of Friends – is almost entirely non-doctrinal and, indeed, at times almost reaches the point at which you would query whether it is even Christian. It is a vague general benevolence and a good spirit.

But, equally, let us admit that the other school of thought represented by those great men was animated by a fear of the excesses of the Quakers. It was in constant danger of becoming only intellectual and of developing a kind of new Protestant scholasticism which lost the life and the Spirit.

For those who are interested in biographies, the outstanding contribution of the mighty Jonathan Edwards of America was that he combined both schools. He held on to and insisted upon the doctrinal emphasis of the great Puritan leaders, but also was as alive to the work of the Spirit experientially as were the Quakers. He did not go entirely to one or the other extreme, but kept both together, and that seems to me to be the teaching of the Bible itself.

So let us remember that we must not think in terms of slogans or certain things we once knew or certain terms and epithets. Let us be careful lest we go to an excess of riot and of carnality in the name of the Spirit, but let us be equally careful lest we quench the Spirit and rob ourselves of something that God in Christ intends for us.

Bearing that in mind, let us come back and try to make certain definitions. First of all we must emphasise that what we considered in the last lecture is *in addition to everything we have learned previously about the work of the Holy Spirit* – the work of the Holy Spirit in regeneration. This experience, let me repeat, is not regeneration. In Romans 8:9, the apostle Paul says, 'If any man have not the Spirit of Christ, he is none of his.' You cannot be a Christian at all without having the Holy Spirit. So I was not referring to that; I dealt with it in an earlier lecture. As we have seen, the Holy Spirit convicts; it is He who give us this new life, brings us regeneration and unites us to Christ.

Take, again, the 'spiritual man' whom Paul talks about in 1 Corinthians 2 where he contrasts him with the 'natural man'. That man has obviously received the Spirit, otherwise he could not understand these 'things that are freely given us of God' (v. 2); he is a Christian. And then I have emphasised that verse where Paul says that 'By one spirit [or, in one spirit] are we all baptized into one body, whether we be Jews or Gentiles' (1 Cor. 12:13). There is one other piece of evidence which is of tremendous importance, and it is a statement in the Gospel of John. Our Lord is with the disciples in the upper room and, we are told, 'Then said Jesus to them again, Peace be unto you: as my Father hath sent me, even so send I you. And when he had said this, he breathed on them, and saith unto them, Receive ye the Holy Ghost' (John 20:21–22).

Now that, remember, was in the upper room. But going on to Acts 1:4–5, we read, 'And, being assembled together with them, [Jesus] commanded them that they should not depart from Jerusalem, but wait for the promise of the Father, which, saith he, ye have heard of me. For John truly baptized with water; but ye shall be baptized with the Holy Ghost not many days hence.' Now He said that to them after He had breathed upon them and said to them, 'Receive ye the Holy Ghost.' So it is not the receiving of the Holy Ghost we are talking about; it is not regeneration; it is not the *receiving* of the Holy Ghost. Here are men who were regenerate and had received the Holy Spirit as Christ breathed upon them and still He said to them, 'Ye shall be baptized with the Holy Ghost not many days hence.' And it happened ten days later.

So I trust that we are all perfectly clear about this. I am not saying that without this particular experience that I am dealing with now you are not a Christian. You can be a Christian, these disciples were Christians, and others have been Christians, it is not that. Let me make this equally plain also: I am not saying that there must however always be a gap between becoming a Christian and this experience; they may happen together and have often done so, but sometimes they do not. So let us keep them distinct.

Then my second statement is that I am also not dealing with sanctification. We dealt with the doctrine of Sanctification in four lectures and it is vitally important that we should not confuse the two. As I understand the situation, nothing has done greater damage during the last seventy years than the constant confusion between sanctification and this experience of the baptism of the Spirit with which we are dealing. It has been prolific of misunderstanding as people have talked, as we saw, about receiving their sanctification in one experience. To start with, they have regarded sanctification as an experience which seems to me to be entirely wrong, and this has always been due to the fact that they have confused sanctification with this baptism. Sanctification, as we have seen, is a process that begins the moment we are regenerate; it begins, indeed, the moment we are justified. You cannot be justified without the process of sanctification having already started.

We saw that still more plainly when we were studying the doctrine of the union of the believer with Christ. If you are joined to Christ, if you are in Christ, then all the benefits of Christ are yours, and this process of sanctification has begun. I repeat, sanctification is *not* an experience, whereas this baptism to which I am calling attention is essentially an experience, so we must sharply differentiate between them. Experiences help sanctification but they are not an essential part of it. So I am not talking about any so-called 'second blessing' in terms of sanctification or anything like that. Only indirectly has it anything to do with sanctification.

And, in the same way, I must point out again that this experience is not identical and must not be identified with the filling of the Spirit, because, according to the teaching of the apostle Paul, you remember, in Ephesians 5:18, we should *always* be filled with the Spirit: 'Be not drunk with wine, wherein is excess; but be filled with the Spirit' – which means, 'go on being, keep on being, filled with the Spirit'. But what I am trying to describe is not a perpetual condition; it is something much more special than that, something unique. We have also seen that the filling with the Spirit often happens for a special service, for some special task allotted to the children of God.

So, having made those negative statements in order to clear the position, you may well ask me, 'What is this, then, of which you are speaking?' My reply would be that it is precisely what our Lord was speaking about in John 14, and especially in John 14:21: 'He that hath my commandments, and keepeth them, he it is that loveth me: and he that loveth me shall be loved of my Father, and I will love him, and will manifest myself to him.' That seems to me to be the key verse. I am talking about these spiritual manifestations of the Lord Jesus Christ to His own. He does not do it to the world, but to His own. It is something beyond assurance. We have dealt with assurance earlier, so it is not that. I am presupposing assurance, I am suggesting that men and women may be believers and regenerate and have assurance of salvation, and still they have not known this spiritual manifestation of Christ.

Now that is perhaps the simplest and clearest way in which I can put it. But it might also be of some help if I gave you some of the great classic examples of this remarkable experience which the Lord promises in John 14:21. Take, for instance, a Puritan called John Flavel. He was not one of the so-called 'greatest' Puritans. He was rather a quiet man, a man who was used of God in a small sphere, in a very striking way. But this is something that happened to John Flavel: he was alone on a journey, his mind greatly occupied with self-examination and prayer, and thus describes what befell him.

> In all that day's journey he neither met, overtook, nor was overtaken by any. Thus, going on his way, his thoughts began to swell and rise higher

and higher like the waters in Ezekiel's vision, 'til at last they became an overwhelming flood. Such was the intention of his mind, such the ravishing tastes of heavenly joys and such the full assurance of his interest therein, that he utterly lost all sight and sense of this world and all the concerns thereof. And for some hours he knew no more where he was than if he had been in a deep sleep upon his bed.

Arriving in great exhaustion at a certain spring, he sat down and washed, earnestly desiring, if it was God's pleasure, that this might be his parting place from this world. Death had the most amiable face in his eye that ever he beheld, except the face of Jesus Christ which made it so. And he does not remember, though he believed himself dying, that he ever thought of his dear wife or children or any earthly concernment.

On reaching his inn, the influence still continued, banishing sleep, still the joy of the Lord overflowed him and he seemed to be an inhabitant of the other world. But within a few hours he was sensible of the ebbing of the tide and, before night, though there was a heavenly serenity and sweet peace upon his spirit which continued long with him, yet the transports of joy were over and the fine edge of his delight blunted. He, many years after, called that day one of the days of heaven and professed he understood more of the life of heaven by it than by all the books he ever read or discourses he ever entertained about it.

That is it.

But let me give you another example. Let us go from John Flavel to Jonathan Edwards. Now Jonathan Edwards was probably one of the greatest minds – I say it advisedly – that the world has ever known. He is certainly the greatest brain America has ever produced, a brilliant, outstanding philosopher, the last man in the world to be carried away by false emotionalism. Indeed, he wrote a great treatise on the subject, called *The Religious Affections*, to teach people how to differentiate between the work of the Spirit and the carnality that often simulates the work of the Spirit. So Jonathan Edwards was the last man who was likely to go astray at this point. This is what he says:

As I rode out into the woods for my health, in 1737, having alighted from my horse in a retired place, as my manner commonly has been to walk for divine contemplation and prayer, I had a view, that was for me extraordinary, of the glory of the Son of God as mediator between God and man and His wonderful, great, full, pure and sweet grace and love, and meek and gentle condescension. The grace that appeared so calm and sweet appeared also great above the heavens, the person of Christ appeared ineffably excellent and an excellency great enough to swallow up all thoughts and conceptions, which continued, as near as I can judge, about an hour, which kept me a greater part of the time in a flood of tears and weeping aloud. I felt an ardency of soul to be what I know not otherwise how to express, emptied and annihilated, to lie in the dust and be to be full of Christ alone, to love Him with a holy and a pure love, to trust in Him, to live upon Him, to serve Him, and to be perfectly sanctified and made pure with a divine and heavenly purity.

That is Jonathan Edwards.

Then, from Jonathan Edwards we come to a very different man – D. L. Moody, who was not a great brain, not a great philosopher, not a genius in any sense of the term. He always described himself as a very ordinary man, and he was right. But he experienced exactly the same thing. He said:

I can myself go back almost twelve years and remember two holy women who used to come to my meetings. It was delightful to see them there, for when I began to preach, I could tell from the expression on their faces that they were praying for me. At the close of the Sabbath service they would say to me, 'We have been praying for you.' I said, 'Why do you not pray for the people?' They answered, 'You need power.' '*I* need power?' I said to myself, 'I thought I had power.'

I had a large Sabbath school and a large congregation in Chicago. There were some conversions at the time and I was, in a sense, satisfied. But right along the two godly women kept praying for me and their earnest talk about the anointing for special service set me thinking. I asked them to come and talk to me and we got down on our knees. They poured out their hearts that I might receive the anointing of the Holy Ghost and there came a great hunger into my soul, I knew not what it was. I began to cry as never before, the hunger increased. I really felt that I did not want to live any longer if I could not have this power for service. I kept on crying all the time that God would fill me with His Spirit. Well, one day, in the city of New York, oh what a day, I cannot describe it, I seldom refer to it. It is almost too sacred an experience to name. Paul had an experience of which he never spoke to fourteen years. I can only say, God revealed Himself to me and I had such an experience of His love that I had to ask Him to stay His hand. I went out preaching again, the sermons were no different and I did not present any new truths and yet hundreds were converted. I would not be placed back where I was before that blessed experience.

A similar thing happened to the great Baptist preacher, Christmas Evans; it happened to Wesley; it happened to Whitefield.

'Ah, but,' you may say, 'all those men were great preachers and evidently it is something that is intended for men and women who are to perform striking service.' But I have told you that in the case of John Flavel that was not the case, and there are others – large numbers of ordinary people – who can testify to exactly the same thing.

Indeed, we are told specifically in the Scriptures, are we not, that this is something which all Christians should experience. You remember what the apostle Peter said on the Day of Pentecost in Jerusalem? When the people cried out and said, 'What shall we do?', Peter replied and said, 'Repent, and be baptized every one of you in the name of Jesus Christ for the remission of sins, and ye shall receive the gift of the Holy Ghost. For the promise is unto you, and to your children, and to all that are afar off, even as many as the Lord our God shall call' (Acts 2:38–39). That statement means that it is an experience which is meant to be quite universal among Christian people.

So what is it? Well, I cannot, let me repeat, identify this with being filled with the Spirit because these men who looked back to this one great occasion were filled with the Spirit many times afterwards. I would describe it like this: it is the initial experience of the filling or, perhaps, it is an exceptionally outstanding experience of it. It is something they describe as being 'poured forth' – the very terms of Scripture. Finney says that in his case it came wave after wave upon him – a pouring out. It is something unusual, when, say all these people, they seem to be almost lifted up to the heavens. They knew what it was to be filled many times afterwards, but this was something unique and special. It is an occasion in which the reality of divine things becomes plain, in a way that it has never been before and, in a sense, never is again, so that they can look back to it; it stands out in all its glory. And, therefore, this is something which we should seek. But so many, because of their fear of the excesses, have never even sought it and have felt that it is wrong and dangerous to seek it and thereby they have put themselves out of the category that includes these great men of God whose experiences we have just been considering.

Furthermore, this is not something which (according to the current phrase) you 'believe that you have received by faith'. People say, 'You go to the Scripture, you read it, you believe it – yes. Well, ask God for it, then accept it by faith, and you believe that you've had it. Don't worry,' they say, 'about your feelings at all. You take it by faith and believe you've got it.'

But that seems to me to be a complete denial of this teaching. When this baptism happens you do not have to persuade yourself that you have received it, you *know* that you have received it. When God sheds abroad His love in your heart by the Holy Spirit, you do not have to say, 'Yes I've received it by faith.' Love is always love and when you love a person you do not have to persuade yourself that you love, you know that you do, your feelings are engaged. And when God sheds His love abroad in your heart, you feel it and know it, and, like those men, you say, 'God was pouring it into me and I knew it was there and my heart went out in love to Him.'

This has been something which has often been missing from spiritual experience. But if you do love the Lord your God you cannot help knowing it. You say that though you have not seen Him yet you love Him. As Peter writes, 'In whom . . . though now ye see him not, yet believing, ye rejoice with joy unspeakable and full of glory' (1 Pet. 1:8), feeling is engaged. But we have been so afraid of emotionalism that we have cut out emotion. So people today do not seem to know what it is to have a sense of sin and sorrow for sin. There are people today who are Christians, who have never wept because of their sinfulness. They say, 'Of course, I don't believe in emotionalism.'

But there must be emotion! If you have seen the plague of your heart and know what sin is, you will feel it, you will bemoan it and you will weep like a Jonathan Edwards, and like all the saints. And your love for Christ will not be light and glib but your heart will be moved; your feelings will be engaged; a profound emotion will sweep through your being. It happened to the apostle Paul; it happened to these people in the New Testament; it happened to those men whose experiences we have quoted and they are but representative of thousands of others.

Do we know something about this? This is a lecture on biblical doctrine and some people seem to think that that means it is as dry as dust. But it is preaching! I am simply asking you whether you know anything about the reality of Christ and have you felt your heart going out to Him in a love that you cannot understand and that has amazed you? As Christian people, we have no right to stop at anything less than that. If we really knew Him we would love Him like this. Has He manifested Himself to you?

But beware of the counterfeit. Beware lest Satan come in and, as you seek this, try to pass to you something that is not the true experience. How do we recognise that? Here is the final test, always.

Seek not an experience, but seek Him, seek to know Him, seek to realise His presence, seek to love Him. Seek to die to yourself and everything else, that you may live entirely in Him and for Him and give yourself entirely to Him. If He is at the centre, you will be safe. But if you are simply seeking an experience; if you are looking for thrills and excitement, then you are opening the door to the counterfeit – and probably you will receive it.

Let me try to help you at this point by quoting something else. Here is a man who again had this very experience. He writes,

You, entertaining a certain conception of the Spirit, ask for the Spirit. And suppose that His influences will all correspond with the conception that you have formed. You expect Him, for instance, to be to you a Spirit of consolation and compass you about with the ambrosial airs of Paradise. You understand that He is to lift you up into a super mundane ethereal sphere where poetic visions of the islands of the blest shall come flashing upon you, upon the right hand and upon the left. But the Spirit is truth and He must come in His own true character or not at all. You have solicited His ministrations and they are not withheld, but how surprised you are when He takes you by the hand and you prepare for a rapturous ascent into the empyrean to find that He has taken you by the hand for the purpose of conducting you down into some deep dark dungeon-like chambers of imagery. In vain you shudder and draw back; you only discover thereby what an iron grasp He has. He bids you look upon those hideous images and observe how they body-forth the great features of you past life.

One abominable statue is named *selfishness* and its lofty pedestal is completely carved with inscriptions of dates. You look at those dates, your guide constrains you to and you are appalled to find that what you regarded as the most beautiful and consecrated hours of your past life are there, even there.

There is a repulsive image also called *covetousness* and you say boldly, 'I am sure that no date of mine is inscribed there.' Alas, there are many and some that you thought golden, connecting you with heaven. Anger, wrath, malice. See how the odious monsters seem to wink at you from their seats as at a well-known comrade. How the picture of your past life is made ugly on their pedestals.

You look *unbelief* in the face and, frowning, tell him that you know him not. Whatever your faults, you have never been an unbeliever. The Spirit constrains you to observe that unbelief claims, and justly claims, the whole of your past life. A profound humiliation and a piercing sorrow possess your heart.

At least, you say, standing opposite the image of *falsehood*, 'I am no liar. I hate all falsehood with a perfect hatred.' The Spirit of God points you to the fatal evidence. You examine the dates and you see that some of them refer even to your seasons of prayer. At length, altogether humbled, dispirited and conscience stricken, you acknowledge that here in these damp subterranean galleries and in the midst of these abominable images is your true home. You will remember with shame the ideas with which you had greeted the Spirit and you fall at His feet, confessing all your folly. There, in that condition, does He raise you and lead you out into the open air beneath the blessed canopy of heaven and you find a chariot in which you may, unforbidden, take your place beside the Spirit and visit the places of joy that are above the earth.

There it is. The work of the Spirit is always humbling and humiliating. It brings us to the end of self, it reveals sin to us. We want to have the power of the Spirit as we are, and the great experiences, but we shall not have them that way. We must submit entirely to Him and He takes us through those galleries first; and when we feel utterly hopeless, He then, as we are told here, provides this amazing chariot for us which takes us to the very heavens and gives us this glorious experience of the reality of the Son of God, the manifestation of Christ according to His promise, which moves us and grips us to the depths of our being and we are lost in a sense of wonder, love and praise.

24

The Sealing and the Earnest

We come now to something which follows very naturally and logically, and indeed quite inevitably, from all that we have been saying. We come to the next term which is the term concerning the *sealing* of the Spirit. This term is used three times in the Scriptures. First of all in 2 Corinthians 1:21–22: 'Now he which stablisheth us with you in Christ, and hath anointed us, is God; who hath also *sealed* us, and given the earnest of the Spirit in our hearts.'

Then you get it again in Ephesians 1:13: 'In whom' – that is to say, in the Lord Jesus Christ – 'ye also trusted, after that ye heard the word of truth, the gospel of your salvation: in whom also after that ye believed, ye were *sealed* with that holy Spirit of promise.' And indeed, we should go on to verse 14: 'Which is the earnest of our inheritance until the redemption of the purchased possession, unto the praise of his glory.'

And then the third reference is Ephesians 4:30, which is about grieving the Spirit: 'Grieve not the holy Spirit of God, whereby ye are *sealed* unto the day of redemption.' This is clearly a most important bit of teaching.

Each time, the context shows us the extreme practical importance of understanding exactly what is meant by sealing. The best approach, and the way that has been adopted by most teachers considering this doctrine, is to ask the question: What are the normal functions and purposes of a *seal*? What does it signify? Why is it used? And the answer is that a seal has three main functions. The first is to authenticate or to certify something. Very frequently in the past a man would put his own personal seal on a document, and that certified that this document really was his document and said what it purported to say. The word is used like that in the Scriptures. We are told that the person who believes the gospel 'hath set to his seal that God is true' (John 3:33). He is not one who denies it, he does not make out that God is a liar, argues the apostle John. On the contrary, he has set his seal to it. That is his way of authenticating it.

But of course a seal was also used, and still is used, to indicate ownership. You put your seal on a packet and thereby it is known to be your packet. If you deposit something in a bank or a safe deposit, sealing wax is generally put on it and you write your signature across it. This seal shows that it is your property and nobody is to open it but yourself.

And, thirdly, as I have already partly hinted, a seal also makes whatever is sealed secure. It is a form of safeguard. The seal ensures that nobody can interfere with the contents. The seal must not be broken, and when we go to collect our property, the proof that it has not been tampered with is that the seal is still intact.

Now there can be no doubt at all but that the specific teaching of these three portions of Scripture which we are considering is with regard to the Holy Spirit in the believer. First and foremost, therefore, the Holy Spirit Himself is the authentication or the certification of the fact that we are indeed God's people. The Scriptures talk about our being God's own particular possession, translated in the Authorised [King James] Version as 'a peculiar people' (1 Pet. 2:9; Tit. 2:14).

Christians, in other words, are people who have been chosen by God; the claim made for them is that God has set them apart and has granted them all these blessings, that they are a unique people. And the authentication for that is the gift of the Holy Spirit. Now it is very important for us to work that out. Our unique position is surely something that should not only be evident to us but to other people. The seal of the Holy Spirit is God's way of authenticating to others the fact that we are Christians. Now this obviously becomes important from a practical standpoint. I repeat that it is the presence of the Holy Spirit in us, producing the fruit of the Spirit, that certifies to other people that we really are Christians.

It is possible for someone to make a profession of Christianity, it is possible to give a mental or an intellectual assent to the truth and to certain propositions and teachings of Scripture, but merely to do that does not prove that one is of necessity a Christian. But the presence of the Holy Spirit in us is proof, because, when He is present, it means that God, through Christ, has given Him to us. He has been given to us, He is resident within us and working within us, because we are God's people. He is not given to anybody else; He is not given to the world. Our Lord Himself taught the disciples that before His death. He is only given to those who belong to God. So the Holy Spirit as a seal manifests the fact to others, as well as to ourselves, that we are Christian people.

But then, going on to the second meaning of this term, the idea of property speaks very particularly to us as Christians. But it also makes a proclamation to all. In this connection, it is interesting to read Revelation 3:12: the message to the church at Philadelphia: 'I will write upon him my new name.' It is undoubtedly the same thing, put in a slightly different way.

But here, as I said, the message comes especially to *us*. The Holy Spirit is the guarantee to us that we really are God's people and God's property. That is another way of talking about the assurance of salvation and you remember that in chapter 5, where we were dealing with that aspect of the truth, we were at great pains to emphasise that a part of our assurance, and in my opinion the most important part, is the testimony of the Spirit with our spirit that we are the children of God (Rom. 8:16).

How does He do it? Well, one of the ways is to do what we were talking about in the last lecture. You remember how the Puritan John Flavel put it? He said that he learned more of this precious truth in those hours when he was there, not knowing whether he was in the body or out of it, than he had done in all his years of reading and of studying. When the Lord Jesus Christ was made real to him in the astounding way that he described, that was the ultimate authentication. It was the Spirit bearing witness with his spirit. It need not always be as dramatic as that. It is something which, in a sense, cannot be put into words, but we are conscious that the Holy Spirit Himself is witnessing to and with our spirits that we are the children of God.

That, then, is how we know that we are the property of God. And then the third thing is that the sealing of the Spirit makes our salvation secure to us. This is a very wonderful thought – the fact that we know that the Holy Spirit is in us is a perfect guarantee of our ultimate salvation or – to use another scriptural term – of our redemption: 'Who of God is made unto us wisdom, and righteousness, and sanctification, and redemption' (1 Cor. 1:30). Redemption means the ultimate consummation, including glorification itself. 'We,' says the apostle Paul again, in Romans 8:23, are 'waiting for the adoption, to wit, the redemption of our body.' That is something that is yet to come; the redemption is the complete, final salvation when we shall be perfect in body as well as in spirit, the entire, the whole person. Now then, the fact that we are sealed by the Holy Spirit is a guarantee that that is going to happen to us. God has given us this guarantee. He has put the seal of the Spirit – the Spirit as the seal – on us and in us, in order that we may have this blessed certainty that 'neither death, nor life, nor angels, nor principalities, nor powers, nor things present, nor things to come, nor height, nor depth, nor any other creature, shall be able to separate us from the love of God, which is in Christ Jesus our Lord' (Rom. 8:38–39). There is no such thing as falling from grace in that ultimate sense. If we have the Holy Spirit, if we have received the Spirit, He is an absolute guarantee of our final perseverance, our ultimate security, and nothing and no one can pluck us out of the hands of God. The presence of the Holy Spirit within us as a seal is that guarantee to us.

So, in the light of all this, how can the Holy Spirit be a seal if we do not know it experientially? How can it be of value as a seal to us if it is only something that we have to accept and believe by faith, with the experiential aspect entirely absent? The whole point of the seal, according to the teaching of Scripture, is that I may *know* this, that I may enjoy it, that I may have the assurance and this blessed security of my ultimate complete redemption and perfection.

That, then, is something of this teaching concerning the sealing of the Spirit, but with this is coupled another term, which is the *earnest* of the Spirit. There are three references to this in the Bible; the first is in 2 Corinthians 1:22, 'Who hath also sealed us, and given the earnest of the Spirit in our hearts.' The second is Ephesians 1:13–14 – a most important statement – 'In whom ye also trusted, after that ye heard the word of truth, the gospel of your salvation: in whom also after that ye believed, ye were sealed with that holy Spirit of promise, which is the earnest of our inheritance until the redemption of the purchased possession, unto the praise of his glory.'

The third reference is in 2 Corinthians 5:5 which read, 'Now he that hath wrought us for the selfsame thing is God, who also hath given unto us the earnest of the Spirit.' The context of that verse is this: 'For we know that is our earthly house of this tabernacle were dissolved, we have a building of God, an house not made with hands, eternal in the heavens' (v. 1). It is again this blessed assurance that if the whole creation, and our bodies, dissolved and collapsed we would be all right. And how do we know that? 'Now he that hath wrought us for the selfsame thing is God' (v. 5). Well, that is good, but there is still more: '. . . who also hath given unto us the earnest of the Spirit.'

Now what does the Scripture mean by talking about the *earnest* of the Spirit? Well, an earnest is a part of the price that you pay for something. When you make a purchase you put down a deposit – that is the earnest. It means that you are contracting there that you will pay the rest; you are putting it down on account; it is a first instalment, paid as a kind of security. Therefore, an earnest is not only a first instalment, it is also a pledge. It is a pledge that you will follow on what you have already paid with something more.

This is surely one of the most glorious things anywhere in the Scripture, and the teaching is that God, again, has given us the Holy Spirit as an earnest, if you like, as a first instalment. Yes, let us use again the language which the apostle Paul uses in Romans 8:23. He says, 'Ourselves also, which have the firstfruits of the Spirit, even we ourselves groan within ourselves, waiting for the adoption, to wit, the redemption of our body.' It is the same thought. The Holy Spirit, therefore, has been given to us by God in order that we might have some kind of an idea as to what awaits us when we arrive in glory. God has given us the firstfruits. The ancient people used to have a festival in connection with the firstfruits. It was the beginning of the harvest, just something to taste, something to assure them of what was coming, a foretaste. There is something wonderful about all this, and it is the function of the Holy Spirit.

So you see the importance of this further term. The term *earnest* in the first two quotations in the Scriptures we quoted is combined with the word *pledge*. A pledge or seal is not actually used in 2 Corinthians 5:5, but, as I have shown you, the whole context communicates it. It is interesting that these two ideas go together and you see how important it was to emphasise the teaching about the seal of the Spirit. You will notice how Paul puts it in Ephesians 1. We are told 'In whom also after that ye believed, ye were sealed with that holy Spirit of promise, which is the earnest of our inheritance until the redemption of the purchased possession' (Eph. 1:13–14). So our salvation is not complete in one way, but it will be complete, and we are given the Spirit in order that we might not only know that for certain, but that we might even begin to experience it. And all that we experience in this life, in a spiritual sense, is but a firstfruit, or a foretaste, something on account,

a kind of instalment from God in order that we might know what is
coming for us.

Now, obviously, if this is not experiential what is the value of it at
all? What is the point of the Apostle's teaching? Surely the whole purpose is to encourage us and comfort us. He says in effect, 'Look here,
you may find that life is hard and difficult and trying, and you may
say, as the Hebrew Christians were obviously tempted to say, "Well,
what is there in it after all?" And the answer is that what you are
experiencing already as the result of the Spirit is but a foretaste, it is
but a sample, a kind of firstfruits, of the tremendous heritage that
God is preparing for you.' 'Eye hath not seen,' Paul says elsewhere,
'nor ear heard, neither have entered into the heart of man, the things
which God hath prepared for them that love Him. But God hath
revealed them unto us by his Spirit' – we know these things – 'for the
Spirit searcheth all things, yea, the deep things of God' (1 Cor. 2:9–
10). 'We have received,' says the Apostle, 'not the spirit of the world,
but the Spirit which is of God; that we might know the things that are
freely given to us of God' (1 Cor. 2:12). That is the seal, says Paul,
which is, incidentally, also the earnest; the two things go together.

So if I have to accept the seal by faith without any experience, and,
I suppose, I do the same with the earnest, then I have no comfort at
all. How tragic it is that, in our fear of the extravagances and excesses, we should even have to go to the length of denying the plain
teaching of Scripture. So, again, I do not hesitate to put this question:
Do you know that you have received the Spirit? I am not asking you
whether you believe by faith that the Spirit is in you. I am arguing
again on the basis of Scripture that when the Holy Spirit is in us we
cannot help knowing it. His presence will be felt, His presence *is* felt.
And as He works within us, warning us, urging us forward, enlighten-
ing us, we are aware of these things; and as He gives us those seasons
of special blessing, as He moves our heart and gives us glimpses of our
Lord, we know it and we rejoice in it. Our hearts are moved. It is
experiential, and the emotions must be involved, the whole person is
involved, the mind, the heart and the will. It is not some extravagant
ecstasy. No, a true experience of the Holy Spirit leads to conduct and
behaviour and action – the will and the intellect and the heart – and
let us not leave any one of them out. And let us never imagine that we
are being unusually spiritual because we can say, 'I felt nothing, but I
went on in faith.' My friends – you *should* feel.

And I would emphasise again that unless the Holy Spirit has moved you, and unless you know what it is to desire to sing and to praise God, and to burst forth into these hymns with the Apostle, then you should be ashamed of yourself as a Christian. And you should seek that knowledge which will lead you to sing and to praise and with other Christians to make melody in your heart to God for His wonderful salvation. Have you tasted of the heavenly gift? Have you known something of the foretaste of the firstfruits? Do you know already something of the joy that will be yours, unmixed, and without limit when you find yourself in glory? Those, it seems to me, are the inevitable lessons from a consideration of the biblical teaching with regard to the Holy Spirit as a seal and as an earnest.

Let me be still more practical. How are we to enjoy these things? And if there is somebody who says, 'I don't know much of what you're talking about, but I would like to,' then the instruction is perfectly clear. Here are the further terms: there are certain things we must avoid doing. The first is that we must avoid *quenching* the Spirit. In 1 Thessalonians 5:19 you read these words: 'Quench not the Spirit.' This is something that should be interpreted very carefully and taken in its context, which is this: 'Rejoice evermore. Pray without ceasing. In every thing give thanks: for this is the will of God in Christ Jesus concerning you.' – then – 'Quench not the Spirit. Despise not prophesyings. Prove all things; hold fast that which is good' (1 Thess. 5:16–21). Now we know what to 'quench' is. It is to put a damper on, to fight against, to discourage. So quenching the Spirit is something, alas, about which we must all know something in experience. It means tending to argue instead of responding; it means putting up questions and queries. Quenching the Spirit may not only be done in private, but in a gathering, in a church service, in any fellowship of Christian people.

Again, this terrible fear comes in of that which is wrong, and it is right to be fearful of that because here, in the very context, we are told at one and the same time not to quench the Spirit, but also to 'prove all things' and only to 'hold fast that which is good'. There are some people who think that to avoid quenching the Spirit, you must put your intellect out of action, that you must stop thinking, stop examining, that you must let yourself go and be carried away. They think that the more you are carried away, the more certain you are that you have not been quenching the Spirit. But that is unscriptural. While you are not to quench the Spirit, you are also to prove all things, and there certain things that the evil spirits might suggest as being the actions of the Holy Spirit, which are condemned in the Scriptures. So if you find you have an impulse or feel moved to do something which is prohibited in the Bible, you can be certain that it is not the leading of the Holy Spirit. You take the word and the Spirit together.

So you must be very careful not to quench the Spirit, you must not go beyond the teaching of the Scripture in any respect, but while remaining scriptural, you must always be open, and sensitive. You must realise that there are evil spirits and since every spirit is not of God you must test the spirits. There is a spirit of antichrist; there is an evil spirit abroad in the world and we must be careful. He can transform himself into an angel of light. He can be so marvellous as almost to deceive the very elect, says the Son of God Himself (Matt. 24:24).

So there we are as Christians; we must not quench, but at the same time we must not abandon ourselves, without thought, without discrimination and without scrutiny, to those other powers that may be seeking to control us. But with the word and the Spirit this is gloriously possible and, indeed, it is not even difficult.

That, then, is one thing we must avoid – quenching the Spirit. The other thing we must avoid is what is called *grieving the Spirit*. 'Grieve not the holy Spirit of God, whereby ye are sealed unto the day of redemption' (Eph. 4:30). There are many ways in which we can grieve the Spirit: to forget Him and to ignore Him; to neglect His word, in particular; doubt and unbelief concerning Him and His purposes and His desires for us; the assertion of self in every form. He wants to control us and if we want to control ourselves, we grieve Him. Sin, of course, of every kind, any sin, grieves Him. He is holy, He is compared to a dove, and He is sensitive, as the very term 'grieve' suggests. Failure to do His will after He has made it clear, therefore, grieves Him. To be more interested in experiences and power rather than in Him, obviously grieves Him. Nothing is more insulting to a person than to give the impression that you are really not interested in him or her but simply in what you can get out of them. It is very grievous and we tend to do that. We want an experience, or we want power, and we give the impression we do not want Him, and that is grieving. Indeed, I can sum it up by saying that any respect in which the Lord Jesus Christ is not at the centre, and our all and in all, is grievous to the Spirit. He has come to glorify Him and any failure on our part to do that is grievous to the Spirit.

So we must not quench the Spirit and we must not grieve Him; let us be clear about this. We are not told that if we do grieve Him, He will leave us – thank God, we are not told that. The little child who grieves his mother or father does not find that the father or mother abandons him, ceases to have any interest or any concern in him. No, the father or mother is grieved by the action of the child but the relationship is not broken and the parent does not go away and leave the child to fight its own battle and to get on with it as best it can. Thank God that though grieved, the Holy Spirit remains. Then if you go on to the fifth chapter of Ephesians, where, if you remember, we saw that Paul teaches us to be filled with the Spirit, you will find that it is in the context of the most practical exhortations. Paul tells us not to steal and not to be guilty of foolish jesting and talking. He says that no evil communications must come out of our mouths, we must be kind and tender-hearted and gentle and so on – by failing to do all these things we are grieving the Spirit. Read Ephesians 4 and 5 and there you will be told very clearly what you must avoid in order not to grieve or quench the Spirit.

To put this teaching positively, we must be *led by* the Spirit. We must *walk in* the Spirit. And this means that we realise the relationship between us and we must live our lives and walk through this world realising that we are in the presence of the Spirit. We must each realise that our body is the temple of the Holy Spirit (1 Cor. 6:19), in fact, and that He is always within us, and we must be ready to follow His injunctions. We must be ready to listen to Him. We must be ready to do what He prompts and leads us to do. He always wants us to read the Scripture – it is His word and it is the means He uses to build us up that we may grow in grace and in the knowledge of the Lord. And if we refuse to do that, then again, we are not being led by Him and we are grieving Him. But if we listen to Him, we will come to the word and will study it, meditate upon it and pray over it – and He leads us to prayer. He is there prompting us; He is working in us 'both to will and to do' (Phil. 2:13). And as we realise that and respond to it we shall find more and more that we know that we have been sealed by the Spirit and that the Spirit is indeed the earnest of our inheritance.

What an amazing thing it is that God, having purchased us by the precious blood of Christ, as it were, gives us that kind of title deed, that earnest. He says: Here you are; this is a proof of it. You will experience this now, but it is nothing in comparison with what you are going to experience when this purchased possession is finally and fully redeemed.

If we only look at these things in that way, we shall go on our way rejoicing. And not only shall we not quench or grieve the Spirit, we shall enjoy His holy presence, and above all we shall know the Lord more and more, and better and better, and our love for Him will become greater and greater. That is always the ultimate test of the reality of the work of the Spirit and our possession of the Spirit. The final certain test, always, is not what I have felt, not some thrill I have had, but my relationship to the Lord Jesus Christ, my love for Him, especially and my knowledge of Him and the reality of my relationship to Him.

25

The Gifts of the Holy Spirit

In our consideration of the doctrine of the Holy Spirit, we come now to the subject of spiritual gifts. Again, like most aspects of this doctrine, it is a difficult subject which has given rise to much dispute. Many prefer to ignore it altogether, yet it is a definite part of biblical teaching. The classic passage on the subject is 1 Corinthians 12 – and there are certain gifts which are characteristic of the receiving of the Spirit.

Now there are some principles which stand out clearly in the biblical teaching. The first is that the spiritual gifts must be differentiated from natural gifts. We all have natural gifts, but the spiritual gift, which any one of us may possess, is something separate from and entirely different from this. It is a gift that is given directly to us by the Holy Spirit. Let us go further and say that it does not even mean the heightening of a natural gift. Some people have fallen into that error. They have thought that what a spiritual gift really means is that a person's natural gift is taken hold of by the Holy Spirit and heightened or made more vivid so that it therefore becomes a spiritual gift. But that is not what the Scripture would have us believe. A spiritual gift is something new, something different.

Here is a definition given in a well-known Greek lexicon, and up to a point the definition is helpful. Spiritual gifts are described as 'Extraordinary powers distinguishing certain Christians and enabling them to serve the Church of Christ; the reception of which is due to the power of divine grace operating in their souls by the Holy Spirit.' This definition highlights the fact that these gifts are new and special and are given to us directly by the Holy Spirit. They are called the *charismata* and people refer to 'charismatic gifts'.

Then the second principle, and a very important one, is that these gifts are bestowed upon us by the Holy Spirit in a sovereign manner. This is emphasised very clearly in 1 Corinthians 12; notice verse 11, for instance: 'But all these worketh that one and the selfsame Spirit, dividing to every man severally as he will.' As *He* will. It is He who decides and not us. He decides what particular gift to give to a particular person. And I wonder whether we are going too far when we say that the idea of the sovereignty of the Holy Spirit in the dispensing of these gifts carries implicitly not only the *which* and the *to whom* but also the *when*; that it is the prerogative of the Holy Spirit, in His sovereign power as one of the three Persons in the blessed holy Trinity, not only to decide what person and what gift, but also when to give particular gifts, to withhold them if He chooses and to give them if He chooses. He is Lord. It is very important to bear this in mind. As we have seen, His sovereignty is brought out in verse 11, but verse 7 enforces the same point: 'But the manifestation of the Spirit is given to every man to profit withal.' It is a gift, it is given, it is something that comes entirely from the Holy Spirit.

Then we go on to a third principle clearly taught in this chapter, which is that each Christian is given, and has, therefore, some gift: 'But the manifestation of the Spirit is given *to every man* to profit withal' (v. 7). Verse 11 says it again: 'But all these worketh that one and the selfsame Spirit, dividing to *every man severally* as He will.' The clear implication there is that every single Christian is given some particular gift. Indeed, it seems to me that the analogy which the Apostle uses in this chapter concerning the nature of the Church is a perfect analogy of the human frame – the body, of necessity, carries this idea that there is a special function for every member of the Christian Church. You notice that Paul says further on that some are important, some unimportant; some comely, some less comely and so on. But, he says, all these are necessary for the body. Some seem to be more feeble, but they are essential and every single part, however apparently small and insignificant, has its place and position in the body and is enabled to function by the Holy Spirit. So that from this we deduce that every true member of the body of Christ, every true Christian who has been baptised into the body of Christ by this one Spirit, has some particular spiritual gift.

Then the fourth principle taught in 1 Corinthians 12, obviously, is that the gifts differ in value. 'For the body is not one member,' Paul says, 'but many' (v. 14). And still more explicitly in verse 28: 'And

God hath set some in the church, first [you notice] apostles, secondarily prophets, thirdly teachers, after that miracles, then gifts of healings, helps, governments, diversities of tongues.' And, as we have just seen, Paul compares the various parts in these words: 'Nay, much more those members of the body, which we think to be less honourable, upon these we bestow more abundant honour; and our uncomely parts have more abundant comeliness' (vv. 22–23). And Paul goes on to say that 'God hath tempered the body together, having given more abundant honour to that part which lacked' (v. 24).

So there again we have definite teaching that the gifts differ in value, but if you go on to chapter 14 you will find that Paul says it still more explicitly in verse 5: 'I would,' he says, 'that ye all spake with tongues, but rather that ye prophesied: for greater is he that prophesieth than he that speaketh with tongues, except he interpret, that the church may receive edifying.' And, again, in the famous statement in verses 18 and 19 he says, 'I thank my God, I speak with tongues more than ye all: yet in the church I had rather speak five words with my understanding, that by my voice I might teach others also, than ten thousand words in an unknown tongue.' And notice, as I shall emphasise later, the position which he always allots to the gift of tongues in his various lists. Obviously it is done quite intentionally.

The fifth principle is that all or any gifts must always be used in love. That is the great message of the thirteenth chapter: 'Though I speak with the tongues of men and of angels, and have not charity, I am become as sounding brass, or a tinkling cymbal' (1 Cor. 13:1). Paul is most concerned to emphasise that whatever the gift, it must be used in love, which, indeed, entitles us to say that you should never estimate or judge a person's spirituality solely in terms of the gifts that are possessed. These two things do not always run parallel. A man or woman may have a remarkable gift and yet may be failing in certain respects, so you cannot always equate these things.

Now there is teaching in Scripture which says that eventually such people will be deprived of their gift but it is equally clear that for a while their gift may be very much greater than their spiritual condition. Another way of putting this truth is to say that you will often find in the history of the Church, and especially perhaps in the history of revivals, that God has chosen men and women with few natural gifts and has given them some remarkable spiritual gifts. I repeat, on both counts we must never be quick to make deductions about people solely on the basis of the gift that they possess. There are these other factors that have to be brought into consideration. So all the gifts must be used in love. Ultimately they are of no value to us and we shall not profit by them unless we use them in love. The gift may be used, as God could use people like Cyrus and others in the Old Testament, but it does not necessarily tell us anything about the state of the soul.

The last general principle is that there are those who would say that unless we have possessed or manifested a particular gift, we have never been baptised by the Spirit or have never known any fulness of the Spirit. Now I suggest to you that any reading of these three chapters (1 Corinthians 12–14) gives the lie direct to any such teaching. There is not a single gift mentioned here of which we are told that it must be present, rather, the whole suggestion is that one person has one gift and another a different gift, and you never know which gift a person will have. But there is no universal gift which is a *sine qua non*. To teach that is to be utterly unscriptural, indeed it is a denial of the very thing that the Apostle is concerned to say in chapter 12, especially in view of his elaboration of his doctrine in the analogy of the human body.

Those, then, are the general principles about which most people agree, but now there is another problem, which is certainly more controversial, especially, perhaps, at the present time. Are these gifts, and are all these gifts, meant for the Christian Church at all times? What do we have in this chapter? Have we a description here of what was true only of the early Church or is it to be equally true of the Church today? Were these gifts temporary or are they permanent? Can you apply any of these principles to all of the gifts or do you have to subdivide them? Now these are very debatable questions and you will know that there are authorities on both sides, as is invariably the case with these difficult matters, but I suggest to you humbly that in this world we cannot arrive at any finality with regard to these questions. So here, as so often, dogmatism should be avoided and we must approach the Scriptures with as little prejudice as possible as we try to consider what they teach. Again there are certain statements that I should like to put to you for your consideration.

First of all, there are certain scriptural statements which seem to me to throw light on this problem. For instance, in Ephesians 2:20 the apostle Paul talks about the Christian Church being 'built upon the foundation of the apostles and prophets, Jesus Christ himself being the chief corner stone.' The term, you notice, is the *foundation* of the apostles and prophets. Now, surely that term foundation does suggest something that is once and for all. You lay a foundation once, and once only, and then you erect the building on it. By definition, a foundation is something that does not continue. It is laid and there it is, that is the end of the foundation.

The apostles and prophets, then, are the foundation which clearly suggests that they are not to be repeated, but that they were special men at the origin of the Christian Church. Surely it is not difficult to understand this when you come to think of it. These were the men who were there to teach and to preach and to instruct the Christian people before the New Testament canon came into being, before the Gospels and epistles were written. We so often tend to forget that. We do not remember that, putting it at a minimum, there were twenty years when there were Christian people and members of Christian churches without a New Testament. They were dependent upon the oral teaching and instruction of the apostles and prophets who were inspired and authoritative and spoke without error.

But, surely, once the documents had come into being, the necessity for that was no longer there. Having had the testimony and the teaching of the apostles and prophets, which we have in our New Testament documents, we have the foundation and nothing further is required. So there is, in that sense, no further necessity for apostles and prophets. And, as a matter of fact, it is very interesting to observe that the people in the early Church did not claim that they themselves were apostles and prophets; they all pointed back to the original ones. When the Church came to define the New Testament canon, the big test that was always applied, as we saw at the beginning of these lectures, was this test of apostolicity. Could a writing that was put forward be traced to an apostle, or, if not to an apostle, to the direct influence of an apostle?

I always think that Hebrews 2 is interesting at this point. We read in verses 3 and 4, 'How shall we escape, if we neglect so great salvation; which at the first began to be spoken by the Lord, and was confirmed unto us by them that heard him; God also bearing them witness, both with signs and wonders, and with divers miracles, and gifts of the Holy Ghost, according to his own will?' Now surely the suggestion there is this: 'I am calling attention,' says the writer, in effect, 'to this great salvation; and you must not neglect it for certain reasons. It first began to be spoken by the Lord Himself and it was confirmed to us by them that heard it – that is to say the apostles. God bore them

(the apostles) witness, with the signs and wonders . . .' – the suggestion being, surely, that these particular gifts and manifestations were
given to them in order to attest their apostolic authority and, therefore, having had that, and having had their teaching as we have it
here, there is no further need for such gifts.

Now that seems to me to be the argument of Hebrews 2:3–4. There
are some who would even say that this is taught in 1 Corinthians
13:8 where we read, 'Charity never faileth: but whether there be
prophecies, they shall fail; whether there be tongues, they shall cease;
whether there be knowledge, it shall vanish away.' Some authorities
say that in 1 Corinthians 13 Paul was prophesying that these things
would end. But I cannot accept that. I think he is referring to something much beyond this, to the ultimate glory when we shall see face
to face, when love alone will be left, and even faith and hope will be
turned into sight. But there are other scriptural statements that
suggest that these gifts were only temporary for the foundation of the
Church – speaking generally.

Then we come on to a second point which is that it is really important to notice what happened after the days of the apostles – the fact
is that these gifts did disappear. Some would dispute that but you will
find that it really can be established. If you trace the sources right
back, it is clear that these gifts did cease after the days of the apostles.
However, some would say that that was due to the fact that the
Church became less spiritual, and that the trouble today is that the
Church is so unspiritual that the gifts are not given and are not being
manifested. To which, there seems to me to be a very clear and
obvious answer, which is this: the gifts (as I have emphasised) are
bestowed by the Spirit in a sovereign manner, irrespective of us. It is
His prerogative.

But there is a still more powerful argument. If the argument is that
low spirituality means an absence of gifts and high spirituality means
the presence of gifts, then how do you think it ever came to pass that
there were any gifts in the church at Corinth, which is surely one of
the least spiritual of all the New Testament churches? There were
excesses, there were abuses, indeed, the whole church was in a most
pathetic condition and yet the gifts were very much in evidence there.
It seems to me that this one epistle on its own is sufficient to prove
that we must never use such an argument.

Furthermore, there is the argument of history. You will find that
revivals generally came when spiritual life was at a very low ebb.

When some of the saints had almost given up hope, then the power descended. That is why people who think that they can prepare or work up a revival are so unscriptural and unhistorical. It is when everything seems to be going the other way that God visits the Church with revival and reawakening. So that, again, is an important consideration as you try to come to a conclusion about this matter.

Then I would add this further comment, that if we do believe that these gifts (or most of them) were for the apostolic era only, it does not mean for a moment that no miracles have taken place since. It merely means that the gift of miracles is withdrawn. If you say that the gift of healing has been withdrawn that does not mean that you would therefore have to say that no person has ever been healed as the result of the prayers of Christian people. Clearly throughout the history of the Church miracles have taken place.

In other words, we must get this clear in our minds – we are discussing these special gifts that were given to attest the authority of the apostles – these special gifts given at the beginning. But God, being God, can work a miracle whenever He likes and wherever He likes, and He can answer prayer in an unusual manner whenever He chooses to do so. So to say that the gifts were only for that period, is not to deny the possibility of miracles now, nor the possibility of marvellous answers to prayer, and things which clearly belong to the supernatural realm.

So you will see by this that my own tendency is to say that at any rate certain of these gifts were temporary, but I want to go on to suggest that there are other gifts which obviously are permanent. I cannot make a sweeping statement about this – all or none – not at all! I want to try to show you that some gifts were temporary but other gifts have continued ever since, and are in evidence today. So I would suggest this subdivision.

First of all, temporary gifts. What are they? Well, first and foremost – the gift of apostleship. The apostles are not repeated but were once and for all. So the gift necessary to make a man an apostle is no longer present. The same applies to the gift of prophecy. What is this gift of prophecy about which we read in the New Testament? Well, as in the Old Testament, it means two things. It means a *forthtelling*, a conveying of truth from God to people. It means that someone is divinely inspired to become the vehicle and the channel of communicating a revelation or a teaching to people. It also means *foretelling*.

Now it is quite clear that the New Testament prophets exercised their gift in both those respects but, as we have seen, that was obviously necessary before we had our New Testament canon. However, it is no longer necessary and that is why we take our stand upon the position that throughout the centuries there has been no additional revelation.

So if any man has ever claimed at any time, or does today, that he has got some further revelation, we reject that claim. That is why, for instance, we will not accept the authoritative claims of the Roman Catholic Church. That Church claims that she has been receiving revelation exactly as the apostles and prophets did, that she is as inspired as they were, that certain truth has been revealed to her since the end of the canon. That is why the Church has promulgated its doctrine of the immaculate conception and, more recently, the assumption of the Virgin Mary, and so on. It is claimed, you see, that the bishops are the continuation of the apostles and that there is inspiration today as there was then. So you see the importance of having certain clear distinctions in mind – the gift of prophecy, like the gift of apostleship, was temporary and ceased when it was no longer necessary.

I would also put into this same category the gift of healing. Now, again, do not misunderstand me. I am talking about the gift of healing, by which I understand that certain people had been given a gift by the Holy Spirit whereby they themselves could directly heal people. It does not mean that they prayed for them and that as the result of their prayers the patient was healed. It means that they literally, actually, directly and immediately healed the patient. That is what the gift of healing means and I suggest that it was a temporary gift. Now I know that cases are reported in which people today seem to have a healing gift. Yes, you will find some are spiritualists and some do not even claim to be spiritualists or Christians, but say they have some healing power. Now I am not disputing phenomena, but I am asserting that the Holy Spirit's gift of healing is something that ceased with the apostles.

And the same applies to the gift of miracles. I have said, you remember, that miracles have taken place since the time of the apostles, but that is a very different thing from the gift of miracles, which obviously the apostles Peter and Paul possessed. They were given a commission and the ability to exercise the gift of miracles wherever they were. That is a gift which has disappeared. Again, the Roman Catholic Church will tell you that it still has the gift, but we have other explanations for their supposed miracles. Again, I am not disputing the possibility of a miracle, I am merely asserting that the *gift* of miracles ended with the apostles.

And it is the same with the gift of discerning spirits and the gift of tongues. Now this gift of tongues often leads to trouble and to confusion. We are told about this gift of tongues in the second, the tenth and the nineteenth chapters of Acts and then it is dealt with in 1 Corinthians 12, 13 and 14. The great question debated throughout the centuries is this: Do the three chapters in Acts refer to the same thing as the three chapters in 1 Corinthians? Now one school of thought differentiates between Acts and 1 Corinthians. There are those who say that in the book of Acts the apostles and others were literally speaking in other languages, not Greek or Aramaic, but, perhaps, Latin or some of the dialects and languages of the various peoples who were gathered together at Jerusalem on the Day of Pentecost. Whereas it is said that in 1 Corinthians Paul is referring to some sort of ecstatic utterance which is not a language at all but sounds and words uttered without understanding by the person taken up by the Holy Spirit.

But, again speaking for myself, I find it very difficult to accept that view because I find that the terms which are used in Acts and in 1 Corinthians are precisely the same and it seems to me to be unnecessary to postulate two different meanings if one will account for it all. 'But,' someone may say, 'we are told that on the Day of Pentecost, everyone heard the apostles speaking in their own language.' Of course. That seems to me to be a part of the miracle that took place. In other words, I suggest that, by the power of the Holy Spirit, the people who were listening were enabled to hear in their own language though their own language was not being spoken. Now at least fifteen different dialects were spoken by those people at Jerusalem at that time, and it seems to me to be quite incredible that if these fifteen different languages were being spoken at the same time in these conditions, the people who were standing by and listening could each one differentiate not only his own language, but could clearly follow what was being said. It seems impossible. But it is quite possible that the apostles were speaking in some kind of speech and the Holy Spirit, as it were, conveyed that speech to all these people as if it were coming in their own tongue and they understood what was being said. They understood these men telling forth these wonderful works of God.

So I suggest that the difference between the tongues in Acts and

1 Corinthians is simply that it was done in all its perfection and glory on the Day of Pentecost, in the house of Cornelius and in Ephesus. However, in Corinth there was this difference, that sometimes the man speaking did not himself know what he was saying, and the ability to understand it was not conveyed to others except by an occasional interpreter. Of course it was not conveyed to everyone at Jerusalem, because there were some who thought that these men were filled with a new wine, you remember. Not everyone was given the ability to understand, but in Corinth there were these interpreters who were able to explain the meaning.

Another point is that the gift of tongues is not meant for all. The Apostle asks, 'Do all speak with tongues?' (1 Cor. 12:30). And the answer is, of course, 'No, all do not speak in tongues, all do not have the gifts of healing, all do not interpret,' and so on. And you will notice that Paul always puts the gift of tongues last in his list. In chapter 14 he is at great pains to say that everything must be done 'decently and in order', for God is not the author of confusion (vv. 40, 33). So if you meet people who say they speak in tongues, or if you have been at a meeting where this is claimed and if there was disorder and confusion, then you are entitled to say, in terms of the scriptural teaching, that whatever else it may have been, it was not the gift of tongues as described in the church at Corinth. The Apostle always emphasises the order and the control which must be exercised. This is a difficult subject, but if we constantly heed the injunctions and the warnings and the teaching of the Scripture we shall be saved from much trouble.

Now let me suggest to you a list of the permanent gifts in 1 Corinthians 12: the word of wisdom, the word of knowledge, the ability to teach, the gift of ministering and helps, the gift of administrations and governments, the ability that deacons and elders and others have, the gift of evangelism, the gift for the pastorate, the gift of exhortation and the gift mentioned in verse 9 (which is often a cause of confusion) the gift of faith. People have often stumbled at that – what does it mean? The simple answer is that, as we saw earlier, the gift of faith mentioned in 1 Corinthians 12 is obviously the kind of gift that was given to men such as George Müller or Hudson Taylor. Both these men founded a work in which they relied upon God alone to provide the money and their material needs. George Müller founded homes for children in need and Hudson Taylor founded the China Inland Mission – now the Overseas Missionary

Fellowship. It is not the gift of believing in Christ because every Christian has that, whereas every Christian does not have the gift of faith mentioned in 1 Corinthians 12. This special gift of faith enables people to trust God in the way those men and others have done, and God, by that means and through them, manifests His glory and power.

Then as we come to the end of our consideration of the doctrine of the Holy Spirit in the Bible, there is one further question that we must consider. Though not really a part of the doctrine, it is an issue that troubles many friends: it is the great problem of what is called 'the blasphemy against the Holy Spirit'. So for their sake and to help them let me add this. You will find this in Matthew 12:31–32 and in the corresponding places in Mark 3 and Luke 11.

Now I can deal with this subject very, very simply. What is this blasphemy or sin against the Holy Spirit? Christian people are often troubled that they are guilty of it. The answer is this: If you are troubled about it, you can be absolutely certain that you are not guilty of it. Look at it as it is described in those passages. See it in Hebrews 6:4–6 and 10:26. See it also in 1 John 5 where the apostle John says, 'There is a sin unto death: I do not say that he shall pray for it.' These passages mean that a man or woman may deliberately reject Christ and glory in that rejection, perhaps even attributing the powers of Christ to Beelzebub or to a devil as the Pharisees did when they said, 'This fellow doth not cast out devils, but by Beelzebub the prince of devils' (Matt. 12:24). The people, therefore, who are guilty of the sin against the Holy Spirit not only do not believe in Christ, they do not want to believe in Him; they ridicule Him; they treat Him with scorn and derision; they turn their backs upon Him and dismiss Him.

So if you are worried that you have sinned against the Holy Spirit and you want to be right with God and with Christ and feel that you have sinned yourself out of the relationship, if you are groaning because you are out of the relationship and not in it, then not only are you *not* guilty of the sin against the Holy Spirit, you are as far removed from it as a person can ever be. These other people are happy, they are gloating in it; they are glorying in it; they are proud of themselves and of their rejection. You are the exact opposite. It grieves you and troubles you and you would give anything to know Him and to be right with Him. My dear friends, do not listen to the lie of the devil who is trying to depress you and to rob you of your joy.

Turn upon him and say, 'My very desire to know Him and to be right with Him is a proof that I have not committed a blasphemy against the Holy Spirit.'

And if you do so, I can assure you that you will find deliverance. You will find peace, and the joy of the Lord and of salvation will be restored unto you. And then turn to God and thank Him for the gracious work of the Holy Spirit.